BISHOP J. C. RYLE'S AUTOBIOGRAPHY

The Early Years

Edited by
Andrew Atherstone

THE BANNER OF TRUTH TRUST

THE BANNER OF TRUTH TRUST
3 Murrayfield Road, Edinburgh EH12 6EL, UK
P.O. Box 621, Carlisle, PA 17013, USA

•

•

ISBN:
Print: 978 1 84871 686 5
EPUB: 978 1 84871 687 2
Kindle: 978 1 84871 688 9

•

Typeset in 11/15 Adobe Garamond Pro
at the Banner of Truth Trust, Edinburgh

Printed in the USA by
Versa Press, Inc.,
East Peoria, IL

For Alan Munden

CONTENTS

Appendices

LIST OF ILLUSTRATIONS

Most of the family photographs and portraits in this volume are in private collections and have never previously been published. They are reproduced with kind permission of J. C. Ryle's descendants, as detailed below.

Colour Portraits (inset between pp. 152-153)

Thomas Ryle (Rupert Ryle-Hodges)

John Ryle senior (John Prince of Sayn-Wittgenstein-Berleburg / Rupert Ryle-Hodges)

John Ryle junior (John Rowland Ryle)

J. C. Ryle at Eton (William Cavendish / Rupert Ryle-Hodges)

Matilda Plumptre (John Prince of Sayn-Wittgenstein-Berleburg)

Frederic Ryle (Bridget Ryle)

Herbert Ryle (John Prince of Sayn-Wittgenstein-Berleburg / Rupert Ryle-Hodges)

Arthur Ryle (Rupert Ryle-Hodges)

Endpapers

Front: Christ Church, Oxford (Andrew Atherstone)

Back: Helmingham Church (Andrew Atherstone)

ACKNOWLEDGMENTS

ONE of the greatest thrills of historical research is the excitement of discovering important manuscripts, previously unknown or lost to scholarship. J. C. Ryle's autobiography is a prime example – it had only been studied by one historian, shortly after the Second World War, and was last seen half a century ago. Although a poor copy of a copy was published in 1975, the original was presumed lost or destroyed. What a delight it was, therefore, to track down Ryle's manuscript in December 2015 in the private family archive of Their Serene Highnesses, John Prince of Sayn-Wittgenstein-Berleburg and Bettina Princess of Sayn-Wittgenstein-Berleburg. I am grateful for their hospitality and permission to publish this critical edition of Ryle's text, as well as previously unknown photographs from the Ryle family albums and details from the Ryle Family Bible.

Other members of the Ryle family have also been of great assistance in my hunt for Ryle papers. Special thanks to William Cavendish and Rupert Ryle-Hodges, cousins of John Prince of Sayn-Wittgenstein-Berleburg, custodians of other parts of the scattered family archive which has descended from Dean Herbert Ryle (1856-1925). To all three I am grateful for permission to publish family portraits, photographed by the late Eddie Ryle-Hodges (1939-2001). From another branch of the family, descended from Reginald Ryle

(1854-1922), I am grateful to John Ryle for permission to publish the portrait of J. C. Ryle's father; and to Bridget Ryle, widow of the late Michael Ryle (1927-2013), for permission to publish the portrait of J. C. Ryle's brother and family photographs.

Thanks to Alan Munden, author of *Bishop J. C. Ryle: prince of tract writers* (Day One, 2012), for so generously sharing the fruit of his own Ryle research. In several ways his help has been invaluable: by lending Guthrie Clark's 1947 hand-written copy of Ryle's autobiography, to enable comparison with the original; by drawing my attention to Ryle's *A minister's parting words to the inhabitants of Exbury* (1843); and by answering a steady stream of queries. He was the first to solve the long-standing mystery of Jessy Ryle's five confinements, when only four children were known; and to identify the title of Ryle's early anonymous tract, *A word in season about the awful accident at Yarmouth* (1845). Thanks also to Iain Murray for his friendly encouragements to pursue this project from its inception; and to Ben Rogers, author of a recent doctoral study on Ryle, for some helpful references.

For access to archives, I am grateful to the Bodleian Library, Oxford; the British Library; Cheshire Record Office; Cadbury Research Library, Birmingham; Christ Church Archives, Oxford; Eton College Archives; Hampshire Record Office; Lambeth Palace Library; the Latimer Trust; Macclesfield Library; Marylebone Cricket Club Archives; the National Archives; Oxford University Archives; and Suffolk Record Office. Ryle's speeches to the Eton Society in 1833 are published with kind permission of the provost and fellows of Eton College. *A minister's parting words* is published with kind permission of the British Library Board. Thanks also to Michael Dormandy for help with Ryle's Latin, and to Clayton Croy for help with Ryle's Greek. It has been a great pleasure to work with Jonathan Watson, John Rawlinson, and the team at the Banner of

Truth Trust, whose popular edition of *Five English Reformers* was my first introduction to J. C. Ryle almost twenty years ago.

ANDREW ATHERSTONE
Oxford
May 2016

INTRODUCTION

J ohn Charles Ryle (1816-1900) was one of the most influential
evangelical clergymen of the nineteenth century. A popular
platform speaker and prolific tract writer, he spent 36 years as
a minister in rural Suffolk before his surprise appointment by Benjamin Disraeli in 1880 as the first bishop of Liverpool. Whether in
a village parish of 300 people, or the bustling northern metropolis
of 1.1 million, Ryle sought to apply evangelical principles to the
mission of the church. A lover of Reformation and Puritan theology, he exhorted congregations to walk in the 'old paths' when it
came to the gospel message, but to break the shackles of Anglican
institutionalism in their efforts at innovative evangelism. His legacy
for the evangelical movement, especially in the Church of England,
was considerable.[1]

To understand the early decades of Ryle's life and ministry,
his manuscript autobiography is a rich and unparalleled source. It
sheds significant light upon the development of his character, his
upbringing and education, his evangelical conversion and ministry

---

[1] For doctoral studies, see Ian D. Farley, 'J. C. Ryle, episcopal evangelist: a
study in late Victorian evangelicalism' (PhD thesis, University of Durham, 1988),
published as *J. C. Ryle, first bishop of Liverpool: a study in mission amongst the masses*
(Carlisle, 2000); Bennett Wade Rogers, 'John Charles Ryle: an intellectual biography' (PhD thesis, Southern Baptist Theological Seminary, 2015). For popular
studies, see, for example, Alan Munden, *Bishop J. C. Ryle: prince of tract writers*
(Leominster, 2012); Iain H. Murray, *J. C. Ryle: prepared to stand alone* (Edinburgh,
2016).

priorities. Ryle details his pursuit of academic plaudits and sporting prowess, and the impact of the collapse of the family bank upon his ambitions to enter parliament or establish himself as a landed gentleman. He describes his early friendships, his loves and losses, his experiences as a young clergyman in three different parishes, and the deaths of his first two wives. He offers a frank assessment of his joys and struggles, and the reasons behind his crucial life choices. Covering 45 years, from Ryle's birth until his move to a new parish in 1861, his autobiography is essential for a proper appreciation of the man behind the headlines. Written for his children and never intended for publication, Ryle's narrative reveals the shaping of his life and thought in the years before he reached national and international fame.

Biography and Autobiography

The relationship between Ryle's manuscript autobiography and his mid-twentieth-century biographers is a complex saga in need of unravelling.

The manuscript was inherited by Ryle's second son, Herbert Edward Ryle (1856-1925), an influential churchman and scholar, successively president of Queens' College, Cambridge, bishop of Exeter, bishop of Winchester, and dean of Westminster. When called upon in 1916 to preach at Macclesfield at the centenary celebration of J. C. Ryle's birth, Herbert quoted several passages from the autobiography, which he called his father's 'memoirs' – the first known public reference to this private text.[2] It was later amongst the documents lent in 1928 to Maurice Fitzgerald (1877-1963), Herbert's former chaplain, for his memoir of the dean. Fitzgerald sampled

---

[2] 'The dean of Westminster in Macclesfield: centenary commemoration at the parish church', *Macclesfield Courier and Herald*, 21 October 1916, p. 3.

the autobiography, to illustrate the religious atmosphere of the Ryle home, but was at pains to emphasize that Herbert 'outgrew' his father's evangelicalism, which many by the 1920s believed to be 'narrow, inadequate, or even distorted'.[3]

Although J. C. Ryle was largely forgotten during the first half of the twentieth century, there was an unexpected resurgence of interest in his life and teaching in the decades after the Second World War. His pioneer biographer was Marmaduke Guthrie Clark (1908-71), an evangelical clergyman at Ilfracombe in Devon. Clark had initially encountered Ryle as a teenager, in his first term as an undergraduate at Keble College, Oxford in 1927, when he picked up a cheap second-hand copy of *Knots untied* from a bookstall in Holywell Street. Clark was immediately captivated and testified that Ryle 'cast his spell upon me' and strengthened him in evangelical convictions, an author 'to whose writings I owe more than I can say'. When twenty years later, in 1947, he was commissioned by Church Book Room Press to write a brief biography of Ryle for the 'Great Churchmen' series of booklets, he approached it as a 'sacred task'.[4] 'What a tragedy it is today', Clark wrote, 'that we cannot see more men of Ryle's stamp.'[5] He hunted for Ryle manuscripts and, with Fitzgerald's help, traced Herbert Ryle's surviving son, Edward Hewish Ryle (1885-1952), custodian of the family archive, then living at Navan, County Meath, in Ireland.[6] The Ryle

---

[3] Maurice H. Fitzgerald, *A memoir of Herbert Edward Ryle, K.C.V.O., D.D., sometime bishop of Winchester and dean of Westminster* (London, 1928), p. 12. For correspondence about this volume, March 1926 to February 1928, between Edward Hewish Ryle, Maurice Fitzgerald, George A. Macmillan (the publisher) and Archbishop Randall Davidson, see Lambeth Palace Library, Davidson Papers vol. 217, fos 48-88.

[4] M. Guthrie Clark, *John Charles Ryle 1816-1900: first bishop of Liverpool*, 'Great Churchmen' no. 4 (London, 1948), p. 4.

[5] Clark, *John Charles Ryle*, p. 25.

[6] Maurice H. Fitzgerald to M. Guthrie Clark, 26 February 1947 (in possession of Alan Munden).

After his death in 1900, J. C. Ryle's manuscript autobiography passed first to his son, Herbert Edward Ryle (top), and then to his grandson, Edward Hewish Ryle (bottom).

papers were kept in a strongbox at Coutts Bank in London, and Clark was permitted to borrow the manuscript autobiography, of which he made a hand-written copy. He also had sight of some other unique documents, including tracts and letters, but despite this treasure trove he made only the briefest use of them in his biographical sketch, just forty pages. He intended to follow it up with a full-length biography, 'something more fitting and worthy', but it never materialized.[7] Clark's booklet remains a key source because, frustratingly, it includes unreferenced details not found elsewhere.

Clark is the only author – until this present Banner of Truth Trust volume – to have had access to the Ryle family papers. The next men in the field, Marcus Loane (1911-2009) and Geoffrey Hart (1927-2007), published brief studies in 1953 and 1963 respectively, but they were largely derivative.[8] In 1966, the one hundred and fiftieth anniversary of Ryle's birth, Clark picked up his research again and attempted to retrace the family archive. Edward Hewish Ryle had died, but Clark tracked down his daughter, Diana Cavendish, in London who again lent Clark the autobiography.[9] However, the only new fruit of this research was a paper at the 1966 Puritan Studies Conference, seasoned with a few quotations from Ryle's manuscript.[10] Clark described Ryle's life story as 'a Christian romance',

[7] Clark, *John Charles Ryle*, p. 40.

[8] Marcus Loane, *John Charles Ryle 1816-1900: a short biography* (London, 1953); Marcus Loane, *Makers of our heritage: a study of four evangelical leaders* (London, 1967), pp. 19-56; followed by a fuller study, Marcus Loane, *John Charles Ryle 1816-1900* (London, 1983); Geoffrey Hart, 'The writings of Bishop J. C. Ryle', *Christian Graduate* vol. 7 (June 1954), pp. 67-72; Geoffrey Hart, *Bishop J. C. Ryle: man of granite* (London, 1963), a twenty-page 'Falcon booklet' for the Church Pastoral Aid Society; Geoffrey Hart, 'Evangelical bishop', *Expository Times* vol. 93 (June 1982), pp. 270-73.

[9] O. H. J. Foster (Navan, County Meath) to M. Guthrie Clark, 1 March 1966; Diana Cavendish to M. Guthrie Clark, 3 July 1966. These letters are with Ryle's MS autobiography.

[10] M. Guthrie Clark, 'John Charles Ryle', *Evangelical Magazine* no. 46 (June 1967), pp. 19-27, and no. 47 (September 1967), pp. 35-45.

with contemporary lessons 'that will strengthen us in this critical hour', and urged his audience: 'I would encourage young men especially to read Ryle. He will put iron into your blood, heart into your work and joy into your people. Whose faith follow.'[11]

Meanwhile a new generation of Anglican evangelical clergy was investigating Ryle. In 1969 Stuart Casson (born 1932), a vicar in the Carlisle diocese, completed an MPhil thesis on Ryle at the University of Nottingham, under the supervision of Professor Richard Hanson. Casson had no access to the Ryle family and Clark refused to let him borrow his precious 1947 copy of the Ryle text. However, through the mediating offices of J. I. Packer (warden of Latimer House, Oxford, an Anglican evangelical research institute), Clark agreed for a typescript of his copy to be made.[12] One typescript was deposited in the Latimer House library, and another given to Casson who drew on it in his thesis and printed the whole as an appendix – the first publicly accessible copy of Ryle's autobiography.[13]

Casson intended to publish a study of Ryle, and joined forces with Peter Toon (1939-2009), librarian at Latimer House from 1974 to 1976, who re-worked Casson's manuscript.[14] Their plan was a volume entitled *J. C. Ryle: evangelical churchman*, which would contain both Ryle's autobiography and an analysis of his theology.[15]

---

[11] Clark, 'John Charles Ryle', pp. 19-20, 45.

[12] Information from Stuart Casson, January 2016. See also 'Preface', in J. S. Casson, 'John Charles Ryle and the evangelical party in the nineteenth century' (MPhil thesis, University of Nottingham, 1969), p. iii.

[13] 'Appendix: the fragment of autobiography dictated by J. C. Ryle', in Casson, 'John Charles Ryle', pp. 222-80.

[14] 'A report of Peter Toon's current work and a statement of his future intentions' (September 1973), in Oxford Evangelical Research Trust Council Minutes, 2 October 1973, Latimer Trust Archives, London.

[15] For this announcement, see Michael Smout, *Bishop Ryle: ritualism and reaction in Protestant Liverpool*, assisted by Peter Toon (Liverpool, 1973), p. 16 (a stapled booklet; copy at Liverpool University Library).

A wider collaboration was also mooted with two other Anglican evangelical clergy who shared an interest in Ryle, Eric Russell (1919-2005) and Michael Smout (born 1937).[16] However, Casson and Toon did not see eye to eye, and parted company. Toon pushed ahead single-handed and was the first to publish the autobiography (1975), followed by a slim biography (1976), to which Smout also contributed.[17] Russell's study of Ryle did not appear until 2001.[18] Casson's research was never published.

Toon's edition of the autobiography held the field for four decades. It was published in Pennsylvania as *J. C. Ryle: a self-portrait*, and became a standard source for subsequent biographies. However, it leaves a great deal to be desired. In his preface Toon noted, somewhat obscurely, 'Though the original manuscript seems to have been lost, copies of it have been preserved ...'.[19] In fact, Toon's edition is a third-hand version. He had no knowledge of Ryle's manuscript, nor access to Clark's copy, but only to a copy of the copy.[20] Mistakes were thus inevitable. Clark himself often misread

[16] Peter Toon, 'Librarian's report', in Oxford Evangelical Research Trust Council Minutes, 5 June 1974, Latimer Trust Archives, London.

[17] Peter Toon (ed.), *J. C. Ryle: a self-portrait: a partial autobiography*, with biographical postscript by Michael Smout (Swengel, PA, 1975); Peter Toon and Michael Smout, *John Charles Ryle: evangelical bishop* (Swengel, PA, 1976). See also Peter Toon, 'J. C. Ryle and comprehensiveness', *Churchman* vol. 89 (October – December 1975), pp. 276-83; Michael Smout, 'John Charles Ryle: "evangelical champion"' in *A portrait of the first four bishops of Liverpool* (Liverpool, 1985), pp. 6-19.

[18] Eric Russell, *That man of granite with the heart of a child: a new biography of J. C. Ryle* (Fearn, Ross-shire, 2001). See also, Eric Russell, *Not a dead see: some people and episodes in the life of the diocese of Liverpool, 1880-1996* (Southport, 1996); Eric Russell, 'Bishop J. C. Ryle', *Churchman* vol. 113 (1999), pp. 232-46.

[19] Toon, *Self-portrait*, p. vi.

[20] It is not clear what became of Clark's hand-written copy, after his death in 1971. It was rediscovered in 2007 amongst the papers of Geoffrey Hart, who had also harboured an unfulfilled ambition to write a full-length study of Ryle. It passed first to Andrew Atherstone, and then in 2008 into the safe keeping of Alan Munden.

and abbreviated Ryle's text. This was further compounded by the typist of Clark's copy who often misread Clark's handwriting, especially the confusion of names, and sometimes omitted whole lines. All these multiplied errors were transferred into the Toon edition. He added just a handful of footnotes and took the unusual editorial decision to Americanize Ryle's spelling. Although Toon's *Self-portrait* stood unchallenged for a generation, a better version is necessary.

This Banner of Truth Trust edition of Ryle's autobiography is based on a fresh study of Ryle's original text. Half a century after it was last seen by Clark, it was rediscovered in December 2015 amongst the private family archives of John Charles Prince of Sayn-Wittgenstein-Berleburg, grandson of Edward Hewish Ryle and named for his great-great-grandfather, Bishop John Charles Ryle.

Ryle's Text

Maurice Fitzgerald described Ryle's manuscript as a 'fragment of Autobiography'.[21] Guthrie Clark called it a 'Scrap of Autobiography'.[22] However, it is neither a fragment, nor a scrap, but a complete text. None is lost, and no more was probably intended.

The autobiography is written in three exercise books, filling in total 169 pages. It begins with the sentence: 'I dictate this Autobiography of myself at the age of 57, in order that my children may possess some accurate account of my history and life, after I am dead.' The neat hand is not Ryle's own, so perhaps his wife or one of his daughters acted as amanuensis.[23] The method of dictation

---

[21] Maurice, *Herbert Edward Ryle*, pp. vii, 2-3, 10.

[22] Clark, 'John Charles Ryle', pp. 21, 24, 36.

[23] For comparison with Ryle's own hand at the same period, see, for example, J. C. Ryle to John William Burgon, 10 and 14 November 1873, Bodleian Library, Oxford, MS Eng.th.d.16, fos 84-91. One clergyman in Norwich diocese described Ryle's handwriting as 'hieroglyphics'; *A Norfolk diary: passages from the diary of the*

explains why Ryle's style is sometimes repetitious or disordered, and why some names are misspelled – Lyttelton as Littleton, for instance.

The manuscript is undated, but there is strong internal evidence pointing to its composition in mid-1873. For example, Ryle described his Eton contemporary John Wickens as vice-chancellor (of the high court), a role to which he was appointed in April 1871.[24] He declared that his cousin Mary Jane Carill-Worsley was deceased, which occurred in June 1872.[25] He mentioned the 'recent' controversy at Winchester College about 'tunding', which hit the headlines in November and December 1872.[26] Narrating his father's bankruptcy of June 1841, Ryle remembered the events vividly 'at the end of 32 years … as if they were yesterday'.[27] More specifically, if he was aged 57 then 10 May 1873 can be fixed as the *terminus post quem*. The *terminus ante quem* is deduced from the fact that Ryle twice declared that Samuel Wilberforce was 'now Bishop of Winchester'.[28] The bishop was killed on 19 July 1873, aged 67, when he was thrown from his horse and broke his neck. So the manuscript can be dated confidently to a two-month window in the early summer of 1873.

Ryle gives no indication about what prompted him to dictate his life's story. He notes only that it was a memorial for his children, 'after I am dead'. He suffered from several periods of serious illness during the 1870s, so it is possible that a heightened sense of his own mortality was his immediate motivation. For example, in October 1872 Ryle travelled from Suffolk to Leeds to speak at the annual Church Congress, but was taken ill there shortly afterwards.

Rev. Benjamin John Armstrong, edited by Herbert B. J. Armstrong (London, 1949), p. 166: entry for 30 May 1872.
[24] See below, p. 40.
[25] See below, p. 11.
[26] See below, p. 42.
[27] See below, p. 89.
[28] See below, pp. 109, 121.

J. C. Ryle's third wife, Henrietta née Clowes, was probably the amanuensis for his dictated autobiography. The top photograph was taken in May 1860, the year before their wedding.

His third wife, Henrietta, read scriptural passages to him on his sickbed, carefully noted in the back of her Bible, including several penitential psalms, the raising of Lazarus (John 11), and the encouragement that 'whom the Lord loveth he chasteneth' (Hebrews 12).[29] Such experiences likely promoted Ryle to reflect upon his life and legacy, and perhaps also to commit the narrative to paper.

Ryle's autobiography is a personal text, not written for public consumption. Its primary audience, as he made clear in the first sentence, was his five children. This explains the amount of space given to outlining the interwoven network of uncles, aunts and cousins in the first chapter, as well as Ryle's advice concerning how to educate sons and how to choose a wife. It also explains the abrupt ending. Frustratingly, for modern readers, Ryle only narrated his life up to the death of his second wife and the end of his ministry in Helmingham, Suffolk, in 1860-61. Peter Toon suggests this is because he did not want to embarrass Henrietta, whom he married in October 1861, by a description of their years together.[30] Another possibility is that Ryle intended to dictate further chapters on a future occasion – indeed more than half of the third exercise book is blank. More likely, however, he told the story up to 1861 because his children could remember the subsequent years themselves. In June 1873 they were aged 26, 22, 18, 17 and 15, and did not need reminding of their father's life in the previous decade.

This edition maintains the spelling and capitalization of Ryle's original text, which is sometimes idiosyncratic – it often uses older and less common forms such as 'connexion', 'cotemporaries',

[29] This Bible (now in possession of Rupert Ryle-Hodges) was given by J. C. Ryle to Henrietta in February 1871. At the back she noted: 'Portions of Scripture I read to John when he was ill at Leeds, Oct' 15, 1872, chosen by him: Ps 30, 32, 46, 87, 103, 90, 107, 91, 130, Heb. 12, John 11, 2 Tim., Heb. 2.' She also noted passages for his later periods of illness, 13 November – 9 December 1874 at Stradbroke, and 1-4 September 1878 at Scarborough.
[30] Toon, *Self-portrait*, p. vi; Toon and Smout, *John Charles Ryle*, p. 57.

'disagreable', 'independant', 'journies', 'overule'. In a few places the punctuation is silently altered, to aid readability, and most of the occasional abbreviations are expanded – such as 1st, 2^d, 3^d, 2^{ly}, 2dly, 3dly, Col^l (that is, Colonel), Esqre, exams:, $Lieut^t$, Notts, Tinct:, Wed^y, Xtian, and Xtianity. Ampersands (&) are rendered as 'and', but '&c' as 'etc'. There are no chapter titles in Ryle's manuscript, so they are supplied by the editor.

RYLE'S AUTOBIOGRAPHY

CHAPTER 1

FAMILY BACKGROUND

I dictate this Autobiography of myself at the age of 57, in order that my children may possess some accurate account of my history and life, after I am dead.

I was born on the 10th of May 1816 at 4 o'clock in the morning, at Park House near Macclesfield in the County of Cheshire.[1] I was the fourth of six children, and the eldest son. We were born in the following order: 1. Mary Anne – 2. Susan – 3. Emma – 4. John Charles – 5. Caroline Elizabeth – 6. Frederic William.

Of these, Frederic died first, unmarried, about the age of 25, having been curate to Bishop Wilberforce when Rector of Alverstoke, and was buried at Elson near Gosport.[2] Caroline died next, having been married first to the Revd W. Courthope of Malling near Lewes, and secondly to James Innes Esquire of Surbiton.[3] Emma

---

[1] The Ryle Family Bible gives the time of J. C. Ryle's birth as five o'clock in the morning (see Appendix 1).

[2] Frederic William Ryle (1820-46), undergraduate at Christ Church, Oxford 1838-42, fellow of Brasenose College, Oxford 1843-46, curate of Alverstoke, Hampshire 1844-46. The rector of Alverstoke from 1840 to 1845 was Samuel Wilberforce (1805-73), archdeacon of Surrey 1839-45, dean of Westminster 1845, bishop of Oxford 1845-69, of Winchester 1869-73, son of the evangelical abolitionist William Wilberforce.

[3] Caroline Elizabeth Ryle (1818-57), married in 1841 to William Courthope (1816-49), one of J. C. Ryle's friends at Eton, undergraduate at Christ Church, Oxford 1834-38, perpetual curate of South Malling, Sussex 1841-48. She was married again in 1855 to James Innes (1819-1902), wine merchant.

J. C. Ryle's older sisters, Mary Anne Ryle (top, in 1866) and Emma Travers (bottom, in 1868).

married Captain Travers, and is now a widow and lives at Buxton.[4]
Susan married the Revd C. Daniel, vicar of Hope, Derbyshire, and
since his resignation of that living lives with him at Lewes, Sussex.[5]
Mary Anne is unmarried, and lives at Brighton.[6] There is about
twenty months difference in age between each of us.

My father John Ryle was a banker, and the owner of a large
property in land, and houses in and around Macclesfield. He was
worth between 15 and 20,000 a year. He had also a bank at Manchester, which he left in charge of an untrustworthy manager, and
was consequently ruined entirely in the year 1842 [*sic*]. He was the
first member for Macclesfield in the reformed house of Commons,
and sat in Parliament for about 10 years [*sic*];[7] first, as a Liberal
in support of Lord Grey, and secondly as a liberal-conservative, in
support of Lord Derby.[8] He was excessively popular in and around
Macclesfield, and was almost king of the place.

[4] Emma Ryle (1814-82), married on 15 August 1865 to William Steward Travers,
army officer, son of Admiral Sir Eaton Stannard Travers. William Travers died of
kidney disease at Anglesey, Alverstoke, on 6 December 1865, aged 29, less than four
months after their wedding.

[5] Susan Ryle (1813-82), married in 1840 to Charles John Daniel (*c.* 1814-87),
graduate of Trinity College, Dublin, perpetual curate of St Barnabas, Hackney
1846-56, vicar of Hope, Derbyshire 1856-71.

[6] Mary Anne Ryle (1811-82). Bishop Ryle's three surviving sisters all died in 1882,
within six months of each other – Mary Anne in May, Emma in August, and Susan
in November.

[7] John Ryle junior (1783-1862), banker, mayor of Macclesfield 1809-10, MP for
Macclesfield 1832-37, which was created as a new parliamentary constituency by
the Reform Act of 1832. On the collapse of the family bank Daintry, Ryle and Co.
in 1841, see below.

[8] Charles Grey, second Earl Grey (1764-1845) was Whig prime minister 1830-
34. Edward Stanley, fourteenth earl of Derby (1799-1869), resigned from Grey's
government in 1834 at the head of a group of 'Moderate Whigs', nicknamed the
'Derby Dilly'. In a speech to electors, John Ryle proclaimed himself 'independent
of and unconnected with any party ... I care nothing about either Whigs or Tories.
I never knew, nor do I wish to know, any other party save that of my country'
('Election of members for the borough of Macclesfield', *Macclesfield Courier and
Herald*, 15 December 1832).

My grandfather John Ryle died before I was born; he made an immense fortune in the silk trade.[9] I only know he was a very good man, and an eminent Christian, and an intimate friend of the famous John Wesley, who frequently came to stay at his house, and who mentions him in his journals.[10] My grandmother also died before I was born, and I never even knew what her name was, but I think it was Ward. I have heard that she also was a very shrewd sensible Christian woman.[11]

[9] John Ryle senior (*c.* 1744-1808), silk manufacturer, mayor of Macclesfield 1773-74. According to his obituary, 'Every property that constitutes a good, a useful, and a virtuous character, was centred in this man. He acquired an opulent fortune with a character that Calumny itself could not stain; affectionate to his relatives, charitable to the poor, and liberal to all, his best monument is engraven on the hearts of those who had the happiness of knowing him. ... during a long succession of years, in the possession of an ample fortune, which was uninterruptedly accumulating, he still preserved a simplicity of manners, and an unaffected courteousness and humility of disposition' (*Gentleman's Magazine*, August 1808, p. 749). John Ryle welcomed the evangelical revival and contributed liberally to build a Wesleyan Chapel in the town. As bishop of Liverpool, J. C. Ryle had the Wesleyan memorial tablet in honour of his grandfather cleaned and renovated ('Bishop Ryle's visit to Macclesfield', *Macclesfield Courier and Herald*, 29 January 1881). He called him 'a holy old man, whom I believe I shall meet in Heaven' ('The restoration of the parish church: farewell sermon by the bishop of Liverpool', *Macclesfield Courier and Herald*, 7 May 1898, supplement). See further, Benjamin Smith, *Methodism in Macclesfield* (London, 1875); Sarah Jane Griffiths, 'The charitable work of the Macclesfield silk manufacturers, 1750-1900' (PhD thesis, University of Liverpool, 2006).

[10] John Wesley (1703-91) wrote in his journal, Monday, 1 April 1776, 'I went on to Macclesfield. That evening, I preached in the house; but it being far too small, on Tuesday 2, I preached on the Green, near Mr Ryle's door. There are no mockers here, and scarce an inattentive hearer. So mightily has the word of God prevailed!' On a later visit, 16 July 1787, he recorded, 'The house was well filled at five in the morning. At noon, I took a view of Mr Ryle's silk-mill, which keeps two hundred and fifty children in perpetual employment.' See Reginald Ward and Richard Heitzenrater (eds), *Journal and diaries* I-VII, in *The Works of John Wesley*, vols 18-24 (Nashville: Abingdon Press, 1988-2003), vol. 23, p. 7; vol. 24, p. 44.

[11] Mary Ryle née Nixon (*c.* 1750-1814). According to her obituary, 'She closed an existence of great usefulness, benevolence, and piety, with a calm and serene composure, which will be a lasting testimony to those around her of the value and

About my father's family I know little. I have reason to believe that the name was originally Royle, and that they lived at Royle in Lancashire, and came over to this country at the time of the Norman Conquest. Afterwards they removed to the neighbourhood of Marple in Cheshire. The name also appears on monuments in Northenden Church in the Chancel floor, and did appear on an old stained glass window in an old Chancel in Wilmslow Parish Church which used to be called Ryle's Chapel. 'Ormerod's Cheshire' mentions this.[12] So far as I can make out the family belonged to the middle class of independant yeomen, living on small properties of their own. The first of the name of whom I can find a distinct account is Reginald Ryle who married a Miss Bradshaw, of the family of Judge Bradshaw the regicide in the 17th century.[13] From that time down to my grandfather's days, the pedigree is complete, and will be found among my papers.[14] My grandfather was the only Ryle who ever attained great wealth, and my father was the first Ryle who left Cheshire after losing every penny of it. About my grandfather's and grandmother's brothers and sisters I know nothing at all.

---

blessing of a practical faith in the Gospel of Jesus Christ. She was respected and beloved beyond the little circle of her own family and friends; and the tears of her seven children, to whom her loss is irreparable, will not be the only tears that will fall upon her grave' (*Gentleman's Magazine*, September 1814, p. 296).

[12] Latin inscriptions to the Ryle family, dating from the 1520s, from previous stained glass in Wilmslow parish church, near Macclesfield, are recorded in George Ormerod, *The history of the county palatine and city of Chester; compiled from original evidences in public offices, the Harleian and Cottonian MSS, parochial registers, private muniments, unpublished MS collections of successive Cheshire antiquaries, and a personal survey of every township in the county* (3 vols, London, 1819), vol. 3, p. 313.

[13] Reginald Ryle (1584-1658), and his wife Ann Ryle née Bradshaw (*c.* 1585-1657) of Northenden, near Manchester. One of her relatives was John Bradshaw (1602-59), lord president of the high court of justice which sentenced Charles I to death in 1649, and lord president of the council of state during the English Commonwealth. J. C. Ryle gave his eldest son the two Ryle family names Reginald John.

[14] Ryle's original version of the pedigree, drawn up in 1749, is now lost, but a copy of it was made in March 1878 and survives at Cheshire Record Office, CR63/1/179/1.

My father had two brothers: (one) Thomas died about the age of 21 [*sic*], unmarried, from obstruction of the bowels,[15] as did also my brother Frederic. (2) Joshua married someone of inferior rank to himself, went to the south of England, lived and died at Carshalton, Surrey, and I think I never saw him twice in my life.[16] For wise reasons, my father and mother allowed no communications between ourselves, and his family. He had five children. (1) Joshua – dead – having one daughter, Laura, brought up by Miss Liptrap, Southsea, and I do not know whether she is dead, or alive.[17] (2) John who was a short time in the army, after lived at Dinan in France, and I believe is now dead.[18] (3) Thomas, who married a lady in Kent, and now lives at Eastbourne; a very respectable person, addicted to scientific pursuits.[19] (4) Mary, married Thomas George Shaw Esquire, a Scotch gentleman pretty well known in the wine trade, and still alive.[20] (5) Clara who married Mr Parker, a gentleman of good connexion in the neighbourhood of Sheffield. She and her husband are both dead, having one child, Clara, now living at Hampstead, unmarried.[21]

[15] Thomas Ryle (1778-91) was only twelve years old when he died.

[16] Joshua Ryle (1785-1828), and his wife, Janet Ryle (*c.* 1786-1821).

[17] Joshua Ryle junior (1812-32) and his wife, Laura Peyton (*c.* 1812-32), lived briefly at Brighton but died within five months of each other. Their only child, Laura Ryle (1831-87), was brought up at Southsea, Portsmouth, by her great-aunt, Amelia Caroline Liptrap (1799-1857). Laura married twice, in 1856 to Charles Tollit, schoolmaster, and in 1883 to James Sumner, retired royal navy engineer.

[18] John Ryle (born *c.* 1815).

[19] Thomas Ryle (*c.* 1817-88), fellow of the Royal Astronomical Society 1869-83, lived at Ramsgate in Kent and Eastbourne in Sussex. He married twice, in 1853 to Jane Russell (*c.* 1819-78) and in 1880 to Maria Markby (*c.* 1838-1934).

[20] Mary Ryle (1814-74), married in 1835 to Thomas George Shaw (*c.* 1800-80), wine merchant, author of *Wine, in relation to temperance, trade and revenue* (London, 1854) and *Wine, the vine, and the cellar* (London, 1863).

[21] Clara Sophia Ryle (1818–*c.*50) married in 1842 to Samuel Parker (1801-64), whose brother John Parker (1799-1881) was MP for Sheffield 1832-52. Their only daughter Clara Mary Parker (1844-1920) was married in 1878 to Frederick William Orde Ward (1843-1922), clergyman and poet. Samuel and Clara Parker also had a son, John Hugh Parker (1848-64).

My father had also 5 sisters who were all married, and are now dead:

(1) Mrs Daintry – her husband was my father's partner in the bank. They had a large family, all dead excepting George, who now lives at North Rode in Cheshire.[22]

(2) Mrs Charles Wood, whose husband was an eminent cotton manufacturer.[23] He was the cause of my father's ruin by getting him to advance him a hundred thousand pounds to erect large cotton works in Macclesfield, and then persuaded him to set up a bank in Manchester, in order to recover the money. They had no children.

(3) Mrs Samuel Wood, brother to Charles Wood.[24] They had 3 children: John, William and Charlotte. Charlotte married Mr Batt, an Irish gentleman, and is dead.[25] William went into the army, and is dead.[26] John is a clergyman, was tutor to the present Duke of Cambridge, domestic Chaplain to Queen Adelaide, and is now Canon of Worcester. He married first Miss Winnington Ingram, and secondly Miss Childe of Kinlet.[27] N.B. Samuel Wood's children

[22] Elizabeth Ryle (1773-1845), wife of John Smith Daintry (1767-1848), partner in the bank Daintry, Ryle and Co. She was J. C. Ryle's godmother (see Appendix 1). They lived at North Rode, near Macclesfield, and their last surviving child was George Smith Daintry (1810-81).

[23] Mary Ryle (1777-1861), married in 1800 to Charles Wood (*c.* 1775-1867), cotton manufacturer. They retired to Leamington, Warwickshire.

[24] Sarah Ryle (1782-1815), married in 1803 to Samuel Wood (*c.* 1783-1829), cotton manufacturer. Her obituary records: 'The meek patience and resignation with which she was enabled to sustain a painful and lingering illness, had taught her the full value of piety which she had received from her excellent parents, and left her surviving friends. A striking proof of the blessings of that pure and spiritual religion which can thus in either age or youth, teach the Christian how to die' (*Macclesfield Courier*, 13 May 1815).

[25] Charlotte Sarah Wood (*c.* 1815-57) married in 1841 to Robert Batt (1795-1864), of Purdysburn House, County Down, chairman of Belfast Banking Company.

[26] William Jonathan Wood (*c.* 1806-46), captain in the 39th (Dorsetshire) regiment of foot, died at Chinsurah, Bengal.

[27] John Ryle Wood (1806-86), undergraduate at Christ Church, Oxford 1824-28, tutor of Prince George (later duke of Cambridge), domestic chaplain to Queen Adelaide 1834-49, chaplain-in-ordinary to William IV 1837, to Queen Victoria

were brought up by Charles Wood and his wife, as he and his wife died comparatively early.

(4) Mrs Smythe, who married the Revd T. Smythe, first of Brunswick Chapel, Marylebone, and after of St Austle [*sic*], Cornwall. She died early, and he afterwards married Miss Metcalf.[28] Mrs Smythe had 3 children: (1) William, who died suddenly at Brasenose College, Oxford, after distinguishing himself very much.[29] (2) Ryle, who went into orders, and for some time held the parish, where the Agapemone is in Somersetshire, and is now [at] Exeter [?] retired.[30] (3) Mary, who married Mr Morris, a wealthy banker at Swansea.[31]

1837-86, canon of Worcester Cathedral 1841-86, vicar of St John-in-Bedwardine, Worcester 1841-81, master of St Oswald's Hospital, Worcester 1872-86. He was married in November 1843 to Marianne Elizabeth Winnington-Ingram, whose father was also a canon of Worcester Cathedral, but she died of scarlet fever in August 1844, aged 20. John Wood remarried in 1849 to Harriet Childe (1808-81) of Kinlet Hall, Shropshire.

[28] Frances Ryle (1791-1820), married in 1812 to Thomas Scott Smyth (*c.* 1777-1854), fellow of Oriel College, Oxford 1800-13, vicar of St Austell, Cornwall 1815-38, minister of Brunswick Chapel, London 1838-49. He remarried in 1822 to Georgiana Theophila Metcalfe (1792-1864), whose brother Charles Theophilus Metcalfe (1785-1846) was acting governor-general of India 1835-36, governor of Jamaica 1839-42, governor-general of Canada 1843-45.

[29] William Norton Smyth (1814-36), undergraduate at Brasenose College, Oxford 1832-36, won the university prize for Latin verse, published as *Carthago* (Oxford, 1833). On 23 April 1836 he 'was found lifeless in his room at Brazen-nose, his Aristotle on the floor by his side. A blood-vessel had broken – apparently from excess of study, under the excitement of an approaching examination.' See *The tribute: a collection of miscellaneous unpublished poems, by various authors*, edited by Lord Northampton (London, 1837), p. 173.

[30] Thomas Ryle Smyth (1817-90), rector of Charlynch, Somerset 1846-57. The Agapemonites were a heretical sect at Spaxton, near Charlynch, founded in 1846 by Henry James Prince (1811-99), previously curate of Charlynch 1840-42 before his licence was revoked. Prince claimed to be the Holy Spirit incarnate, and taught 'spiritual marriage', though the sexual immorality of the community was notorious.

[31] Mary Elizabeth Smyth (1816-73), married in 1835 to Thomas Charles Morris (1808-86), grandson of David Morris who established the family banking firm, Morris and Sons, in Carmarthen in the 1790s. T. C. Morris was sheriff of Carmarthenshire in 1866 and owned the Bryn Myrddin estate, Abergwili, near Carmarthen.

(5) Lady Darwin who married Sir Francis Darwin of Sydnope near Matlock,[32] and had a large family, of whom I know very little, excepting Mary Jane who married Charles Carill Worsley Esquire, of Platt near Manchester. These are both now dead.[33]

So much for my father's two brothers, and five sisters.

My mother, Susanna Hurt, [was] daughter of Charles Hurt of Wirksworth, a gentleman of independant property, and a younger branch of the Hurts of Alderwasley, who married a younger daughter of the great Sir Richard Arkwright. She was the only sister of the great millionaire Richard Arkwright of Willersley, and had a very large fortune.[34] My mother had two sisters and five brothers:

(1) Frances died unmarried when I was a boy. I remember her well; kind, good natured, and rather like Richard Hurt's daughters.[35]

(2) Marianne, married Peter Arkwright of Rock House, and Willersley, and had 13 children: Frederic, Edward, Henry, Alfred, James, Ferdinand, Augustus, John Thomas, Marianne, Susan, Fanny, Margaret, Caroline.[36]

[32] Jane Harriett Ryle (1794-1866), married in 1815 to Francis Sacheverel Darwin (1786-1859), physician, knighted in 1820, son of the natural philosopher, Erasmus Darwin. They owned Sydnope Hall, near Matlock, and Breadsall Priory, near Derby.

[33] Mary Jane Darwin (1817-72), cousin of Charles Darwin, married in 1840 to Charles Carill Worsley (1800-64) of Platt Hall, Rusholme. The Worsleys were a prominent Manchester family, descended from Major-General Charles Worsley (1622-56), puritan army officer under Oliver Cromwell.

[34] Susanna Ryle (1781-1852) was daughter of Charles Hurt (1758-1834) of Wirksworth Hall, Derbyshire, a lead merchant and iron manufacturer, and Susanna née Arkwright (1761-1835). Her grandfather, Sir Richard Arkwright (1732-92), was a cotton manufacturer and inventor of machines for cotton-spinning. He lived in Derbyshire at Rock House, Cromford, and in his final years built Willersley Castle nearby. It passed to his son, Richard Arkwright (1755-1843), cotton manufacturer, said to be the richest commoner in England. On the Hurt family, see Louis Hurt, *Alderwasley and the Hurts* (Vienna, 1909).

[35] Frances Hurt (1788-1831). On Richard Hurt's daughters, see below.

[36] Mary Anne Hurt (1786-1872), married her cousin, Peter Arkwright (1784-1866), of Rock House, who inherited the Willersley estate from his father in 1843.

*J. C. Ryle's parents, Susanna and John. The photograph of John
was taken in Leamington in 1862, shortly before his sudden death
there from 'apoplexy'.*

My mother's brothers were: [(1)] Charles who lived and died unmarried; a quiet old-fashioned bachelor, very learned, very fond of coins, antiquities etc.[37]

(2) Henry, who went into the navy, and was drowned on the coast of Denmark in the famous storm when the 'St George', 'Hero' and 'Defence' were all lost together.[38]

(3) Richard who went deeply into mining speculations, lived and died at Wirksworth, married Miss Shuttleworth,[39] and was father of Caroline Lady Hatherton,[40] Sophy Lady Martin,[41] Margaret Mrs Hubbersty,[42] Georgiana unmarried,[43] Robert accidently shot at

---

They had sixteen children, thirteen of whom survived childhood: Frederic (1806-74); Edward (1808-50); Henry (1811-89), vicar of Bodenham, Herefordshire 1842-89; Alfred (1812-87), banker; James Charles (1813-96); Ferdinand William (1814-93); Augustus Peter (1821-87), naval officer, MP for North Derbyshire 1868-80; John Thomas (1823-1906); Mary Anne (1807-91); Susan Maria (1816-64), wife of Joseph Cotton Wigram (1798-1867), bishop of Rochester 1860-67; Fanny Jane (1816-94); Margaret Helen (1818-83); Caroline Elizabeth (1825-1907), wife of John Clowes, whose sister Henrietta Clowes became J. C. Ryle's third wife.

[37] Charles Hurt (1782-1852).

[38] Henry Hurt (1786-1811), lieutenant in the royal marines, drowned in the great storm of Christmas Eve 1811 when *HMS St George* and *HMS Defence* were wrecked off the coast of Jutland, and *HMS Hero* was wrecked off the Netherlands. Over 2,000 sailors lost their lives. Ryle has muddled his family tree, as Henry Hurt was his mother's cousin, not her brother.

[39] Richard Hurt (1785-1851) of Wirksworth Hall, married in 1808 to Caroline Shuttleworth (1780-1827).

[40] Caroline Anne Hurt (1810-97), married first to Edward Davies Davenport (1778-1847), MP for Shaftesbury; and second to Edward John Littleton, first Baron Hatherton (1791-1863).

[41] Sophia Elizabeth Hurt (1817-74), second wife of Admiral Sir William Fanshawe Martin (1801-95), baronet.

[42] Margaret Emma Hurt (1813-45), wife of Nathan Hubbersty (1803-81), headmaster of Wirksworth grammar school.

[43] Georgiana Susan Shuttleworth Hurt (1819-1901).

Calvally [*sic*],[44] Stephen accidentally killed at sea,[45] and Phillip [*sic*] who married a French lady and lives at Bayonne.[46]

(4) Edward, who married the only daughter of Joseph Strutt of Derby; read the law for a short time; lived in London afterwards on his wife's large fortune, and had no children and is dead.[47]

(5) John, a clergyman, who took the name of 'Wolley' on his marriage for valuable considerations.[48] His children were: John who died unmarried[49] – George also died unmarried[50] – a daughter married Arthur Arkwright and is dead[51] – Susan married the Revd Mr Ricketts[52] – Charles who took the name of Dod, is a master at Eton and has a large family, married Miss Pelly Parker.[53]

---

[44] Robert Charles Hurt (1815-38), undergraduate at St John's College, Cambridge. In February 1838 he was game-shooting with his brother-in-law, Edward Davies Davenport, at Calveley, Cheshire, when the gun exploded and he was killed on the spot.

[45] Richard Stephen Hurt (1817-34), joined the royal navy as a midshipman, but died in February 1834 when he fell from the maintop of *HMS Snake*, off the coast of Brazil.

[46] Philip Anthony Hurt (1821-1900), farmer, married in 1846 to Maria Louisa Dominica Cabarrus (1821-99). They lived at Bayonne near the French/Spanish border.

[47] Edward Nicholas Hurt (1795-1867) of Dorset Square, London, married in 1823 to Caroline Strutt (1799-1834). Her father, Joseph Strutt (1765-1844), was a cotton manufacturer and social reformer in Derby.

[48] John Francis Thomas Hurt (1796-1877), vicar of Beeston, Nottinghamshire 1822-54. In 1822 he married Mary Wolley (*c.* 1799-1844), and on the death of her father in 1827 he assumed the Wolley surname and coat of arms.

[49] John Wolley (1823-59), ornithologist, studied the dodo and great auk. His large collection of bird eggs was donated to the British Museum.

[50] George Wolley (1824-60), farmer near Durban, Natal.

[51] Emma Wolley (1834-66), wife of Arthur William Arkwright (1831-1903), farmer. They were the parents of Sir Joseph Arthur Arkwright (1864-1944), bacteriologist.

[52] Susan Wolley (1829-1900), wife of Martin Henry Ricketts (1825-1901), vicar of Hatfield, Herefordshire 1862-74, of Knighton, Radnorshire 1878-1901.

[53] Charles Wolley (1826-1904), fellow of King's College, Cambridge from 1847, assistant master at Eton College 1850-78, took the surname Wolley-Dod in 1868. He was married in 1850 to Frances Lucy Parker (1828-1909), daughter of Pelly Parker (1789-1865), rector of Hawton, Nottinghamshire 1849-65, and granddaughter of Thomas Crewe Dod (1754-1827) of Edge Hall, Cheshire.

So much for my mother's family. It will be observed that she was first cousin to all the children of old Richard Arkwright of Willersley, viz., Richard of Ashbourne who married Miss Beresford[54] – Robert of Sutton who married Miss Kemble[55] – Charles of Dunstall, who married Miss Sitwell[56] – Joseph of Mark Hall, who married Miss Wigram[57] – Peter of Rock House who married her sister Marianne – and John of Hampton Court, who married Miss Hoskyns;[58] also to Lady Wigram wife of Sir James Wigram,[59] and to Mrs Hurt wife of Francis Hurt of Alderwasley.[60] She was also first cousin to the same Francis Hurt, and to Major Hurt,[61] and to Mrs Tom Edge, Major Hurt's sister,[62] and to Mrs Gell,[63] and to Mrs Moore of Appleby,[64] and Mrs St John.[65]

---

[54] Richard Arkwright (1781-1832) of Ashbourne Place, Derbyshire, MP for Rye 1813-18 and 1826-30, married to Martha Maria Beresford (1781-1820).

[55] Robert Arkwright (1783-1859) of Sutton Scarsdale Hall, Derbyshire, married to Frances Crawford Kemble (1786-1849), part of the illustrious acting dynasty, on the stage from the age of four until her marriage in 1805.

[56] Charles Arkwright (1786-1850) of Dunstall Hall, Staffordshire, married to Mary Wilmot Sitwell (1786-1858).

[57] Joseph Arkwright (1791-1864) of Mark Hall, Essex, vicar of Latton, Essex 1820-50, married to Anne Wigram (1796-1863), daughter of Sir Robert Wigram, baronet. Her brothers included Bishop Joseph Wigram (see above) and Sir James Wigram (see below).

[58] John Arkwright (1785-1858) of Hampton Court, Herefordshire, married to Sarah Hoskyns (1808-69), daughter of Sir Hungerford Hoskyns, baronet.

[59] Anne Emma Arkwright (1794-1844), married to Sir James Wigram (1793-1866), judge, vice-chancellor of the high court 1841-50.

[60] Elizabeth Arkwright (1780-1838), married Francis Edward Hurt (1781-1854) of Alderwasley Hall. Both were Susanna Ryle's cousins.

[61] James Hurt (1785-1864), army officer.

[62] Ryle appears to mean Major Hurt's wife, Mary Margaret Edge, daughter of Thomas Webb Edge. She was another of Susanna Ryle's cousins.

[63] Anne Emma Hurt (1790-1861), wife of Thomas Gell (1788-1865), army officer.

[64] Elizabeth Hurt (1783-1841), second wife of George Moore (1778-1827) of Appleby Hall, Leicestershire.

[65] Cassandra Hurt (1784-1848), wife of John Fleming St John (1789-1848), vicar of Spondon, Derbyshire 1814-33. They died within four days of each other.

Ryle's aunt and uncle, Mary Anne and Peter Arkwright,
of Willersley Castle in Derbyshire.

CHAPTER 2

CHILDHOOD

I shall now give the statistical facts of my life. I lived at Park House the first 8 years of my life. Of course I can remember very few incidents. I remember generally that we were brought up in the greatest comfort and luxury, and had everything that money could get. My father took little notice of us, and was generally out all day. My mother was excessively anxious about us, and as angrily careful about our health, behaviour, and appearance, as a hen about her chickens. We had plenty of grass, water, and large grounds, extensive walks, and gardens, air and exercise, and liberty to enjoy ourselves.

We never went to London. In the summer we went not unfrequently [*sic*] to Bridlington for sea air, and sea bathing. My father had a yacht, called the Sea-flower. When I was allowed to go with him, I was always tied to the mast by a rope, that I might not fall overboard. We enjoyed Bridlington immensely, and few things are impressed on my memory more deeply than pic-nics to Flambro' Head, and the smell of the turnip fields on the top of the cliffs. We always walked on the pier before breakfast each with a large biscuit in our hands. And one of the earliest events I remember in my life, was a large black Newfoundland dog, as tall as myself coming up to me quietly on the pier and taking the biscuit out of my hand. Our

journies [*sic*] to and from Bridlington were always by posting, and
we always slept at Booth Ferry, which was great fun.[1] One summer
we went to Crosby near Liverpool for the sake of my sister Susan's
health – it was then a very quiet watering place. I remember travelling back from Liverpool to Manchester by the Bridgewater Canal
boat from Runcorn; we were a whole day on the journey.[2] One
winter we went to Hastings on account of my mother's health. We
were at No. 1 Pelham Place. The Crescent was not then built, and
not a single house in St Leonards existed.[3]

At home our greatest outing consisted in going for the day to a
beautiful farm belonging to my father called Upton, near Prestbury,
either riding on asses, or in an ass carriage. On one grand occasion
my father went with us in order that I might plant a Lime tree on

[1] Posting was travel by horse and carriage, sometimes at top speed with the mail,
and by relay from town to town. The journey through Yorkshire included a ferry
across the River Ouse at Booth (now Boothferry).

[2] Speaking in January 1897 at a tea party at St Leonard's, Bootle (near Crosby),
Ryle recalled: 'when I was a boy I had a sister in delicate health, and of all places in
the world to send my sister to my father and mother could hear of nothing better
for her than to take sea bathing at Bootle. And when I was six or seven years of
age I used to go with my sister to Bootle, and she went to bathe in the sea; it was
thought very fine sea-bathing then. I remember those days perfectly well. I can
hardly conceive places so different as Bootle was then from Liverpool. There were
no docks. The furthest dock was the old Prince's Dock filled with American sailing ships – no steamers hardly in those days – sailing ships with great yellow sides.
There was an old windmill by the side of the river among trees and green fields. ...
We went to Cheshire on the old Leeds and Liverpool Canal. Going to Litherland
we got into a boat drawn by a couple of horses, and went to the end of the canal,
where it goes out at the docks now. Then we got into a very old steamer and went
down the Mersey to Runcorn. Then we got into another canal boat and went
to Manchester; got to Manchester at eight o'clock, and got home at ten o'clock
thoroughly tired out. That was the way in which, when I was a boy, folk travelled
about. No railways, no large steamboats, no tramways.' Quoted in W. F. Machray,
The first bishop of Liverpool: John Charles Ryle D.D. (London, 1900), p. 13.

[3] Pelham Place and Pelham Crescent, Hastings, were built 1824-28 as part of
the property development of Sir Thomas Pelham, second earl of Chichester (1756-
1826), to capitalize on the growing popularity of the town as a health resort for the
wealthy. St Leonards-on-Sea, near Hastings, was laid out as a new town from 1826.

the top of a hill, which stands there now, and may be seen from the railway. In returning, he led me back riding on the donkey late in the evening, and as we went through the outskirts of Macclesfield I fell off, and was stunned, and my father being in an absent frame of mind led the donkey on for several yards, without being aware that I had fallen off. I was then about 4 years old.

The first public event I remember was the coronation of George 4th.[4] The first piece of property I ever possessed was a Lyme mastiff puppy given by Mr Legh of Adlington, which afterwards grew to be a huge dog, and I have his brass collar now.[5] I hope it will always be kept in my family. I remember going to Church for the first time at Christ Church, Macclesfield, and thinking that the preacher was the King. I also remember my mother giving me a Pontefract cake in order to keep me quiet.[6] I dropped it on the flour [*sic*], and was told to pick it up. I scrambled about under the seats of a large square pew and could not find it, and then shouted out to my mother's dismay, 'I cannot find it anywhere.' I used to wear in those days a blue jacket, nankeen trowsers [*sic*] buttoned over it,[7] low shoes, white stockings, and a frill over my collar – and was a very broad, stumpy, awkward, plain boy.

My education was begun by Isaac Eaton, clerk of St Michael's Church, Macclesfield.[8] He used to come up every morning for an hour and a half, and taught me to read, write, and cipher. He was a most respectable old man, lived to a great age, and came to hear me preach in Gawsworth Church, about the year 1867.[9] He used a

---

[4] George IV was crowned at Westminster Abbey on 19 July 1821.

[5] Adlington Hall, Cheshire, seat of the Legh family, inherited in 1806 by Richard Crosse (1754-1822), who changed his surname to Legh.

[6] Pontefract cakes are liquorice sweets.

[7] Nankeen is a pale yellow cloth.

[8] Isaac Eaton (*c*. 1784-1872), clerk of St Michael's, Macclesfield, actuary of Macclesfield Savings Bank, registrar for births and deaths.

[9] Gawsworth, near Macclesfield, where the rector from 1827 to 1872 was Henry William Stanhope (1790-1872), son of the third earl of Harrington.

Porcupine quill to point out the letters, and occasionally scratched his head, and ears with it. I also received some instruction in the rudiments of Latin from my sisters' first governess, Miss Holland. She was a connection of Sir Henry Holland's,[10] a very respectable person, but a most severe teacher, and boxed my ears most unmercifully, though I dare say I deserved it. Her family were most of them Unitarians, and I have no reason to believe that she was not one, but such points were not thought much of in those days.

I was thrown most with my sister Emma in those days, and I believe we were both excessively troublesome children. Perhaps the best point about me was that I was always extremely fond of reading. I could read well at four years old, and could at any time be kept quiet with a book. On one occasion when a large dinner party were assembled, I was in the drawing room with the other children before the company went to dinner; someone observed me standing against the window looking out very seriously, and asked me what I was thinking of. I excited great merriment by replying gravely, 'I am meditating about an Elephant.' Travels, Natural History, Battles and Shipwrecks, were the subjects I cared most to read about.

The only other event I can remember at this time of my life, occurred at Colonel Parker's at Astle.[11] He used once a year in the summer to gather together immense children's parties, consisting of 50 or 60 children from all the principal families in the east of Cheshire together with their friends. I was there when about seven years old, and after an excellent dinner at 2 o'clock I suddenly astonished Colonel Parker, my mother, sisters, and all the company, by standing up on my chair and exclaiming at the top of my voice, 'Well, Colonel Parker, I have had a good dinner.' This was the first public speech I ever made – it was quite extemporaneous and

---

[10] Henry Holland (1788-1873), from Knutsford, a fashionable physician in London, created baronet in 1853.

[11] Thomas Parker (c. 1766-1840), army officer, of Astle Hall, near Macclesfield.

unpremeditated. I believe poor old Colonel Parker always said it was the greatest compliment he ever was paid by his young friends.

I cannot remember anything else worth mentioning in the first 8 years of my life. They were happy, and pretty harmless years, although destitute of any real religion. We had few cares, no sickness, no death, no moves, no anxieties, and wanted for nothing. We might have been better done for, and we might have been worse. We were not particularly disagreable children, and if we were not very amiable at any rate we did not quarrel. We had no metal baths in those days but we were all well washed and soaped in a huge wooden tub every Saturday night, over and above our regular daily ablutions – and that night too we endured the most painful thing in the week, having our heads combed with a small tooth-comb. This was torture indeed.

Christmas Eve was always kept with immense festivities. A yule log, a yule cheese, posset,[12] an enormous apple pie always appeared that night. We danced country dances with the servants in the kitchen to the music of a dulcimer. The men servants sang songs in the servants' Hall, with all the labourers, gardeners, and farm servants; 'John Barleycorn', and 'The Cheshire Cheese' being two of the favourite songs – and we did not go to bed till the clock had struck 12, and the 'waits' had come to the Hall door, and sung 'Christians awake'.[13] I hear them sing it at this moment though it is 52 years at least since I first heard it.

[12] Posset was a drink made of hot milk, curdled with ale or wine, flavoured with sugar, herbs and spices.

[13] 'Christians, awake, salute the happy morn', a Christmas hymn by John Byrom (1692-1763). Waits were carol singers and musicians.

CHAPTER 3

EARLY EDUCATION

I began my school life in the year 1824, when I was only 8 years
old, too early in age in my opinion by at least 2 years. I went
to a private propriet[ar]y school kept by the Revd J. Jackson,
first at Bowden [*sic*] where he was curate, and afterwards at Over
near Nantwich where he was Vicar.[1] I remember going to school for
the first time on the 8ᵗʰ of August 1824.[2] My father took no part or
interest in such matters, and I was taken there by my mother and
her old friend Miss Watson – a great friend of our family, who got
up the match between my father and mother.[3]

Mr Jackson's was a good school for learning but a very rough
one so far as the comfort of the boys was concerned, to judge by the
standards of the present day. There were 16 boys there, and we all
slept in two rooms. We were not allowed to wash in our bedrooms,
but went down stairs when dressed and washed in a stone sink where
there were two iron basins, at which we each had our turn; of course

---

[1] John Jackson (*c.* 1790-1863), undergraduate at Brasenose College, Oxford 1811-
14, curate of Bowdon, near Altrincham 1818-26, vicar of Over 1821-63.

[2] The Ryle family archive includes a sketch book embossed on the cover 'John
Charles Ryle 1824', containing pencil sketches, mostly of ships (in possession of
William Cavendish).

[3] Miss Watson was godmother of John and Susanna Ryle's first child (see
Appendix 1).

at this rate, we could not be very clean. Yet at this school there were boys from all the leading families in Cheshire. I remember the following: Three Brooks [*sic*] of Norton,[4] Tatton of Withenshaw [*sic*],[5] Harper of Davenham,[6] Aston of Aston,[7] Townshend of Wincham,[8] two Swettenhams, Kaye, Entwistle of Foxholes,[9] besides several other Lancashire boys, Ratcliffe, Milne, Calrow etc. – most of them now dead.

I was not very happy there, and there was a great deal of petty bullying, and tyranny, to an extent which I suspect is often to be found in a private school, far more than at a public one. One of my first disasters was being tossed in a blanket for not getting up in the morning by the other boys, with the master's permission; this, as I was a little boy was easy enough to execute, but it was rather hard considering that I was not strong, and required a great deal of sleep, and have done all my life through. The boys managed to let the blanket go at one corner after tossing me to the ceiling. I fell on the floor on my head, had concussion of the brain, and was very ill for some time. Of course it was hushed up, and my family was never told of it, and it is my firm belief that it has affected my bodily health ever since.[10]

Our schoolmaster being a clergyman, we were necessarily left some days very much to ourselves, and often ran wild over the

[4] Sir Richard Brooke, baronet (1785-1865) of Norton Priory had a large family, including Richard Brooke (1814-88), Thomas Brooke (1816-80), Foster Brooke (1817-40), and Arthur Brooke (1819-1903).

[5] Thomas William Tatton (1816-85) of Wythenshawe Hall.

[6] William Hosken-Harper (1814-72) of Davenham Hall.

[7] Arthur Wellington Hervey-Aston (1815-39) of Aston Hall.

[8] Henry Townshend (1813-96) of Wincham Hall.

[9] John Smith Entwistle (1815-68) of Foxholes, near Rochdale.

[10] Rowland Williams (1817-70), Anglican theologian and contributor to *Essays and reviews* (1860), was almost killed in 1828 in a similar 'blanket-tossing' incident at Eton, during an initiation ceremony, when he hit his head on the corner of an iron-bound oak bedstead. See *The life and letters of Rowland Williams*, edited by Ellen Williams (2 vols, London, 1874), vol. 1, pp. 6-7.

whole country, and ate more green apples than any imagination can conceive possible. As to book learning, I was well grounded in Latin and Greek. The first Greek that I ever had was the gospel of St John. We were also taught writing very badly, arithmetic, history, geography, French, and dancing. Out of doors I was always great in cricket, and throwing stones. I don't think I was an ill-natured bad-tempered boy, but I was sturdy, very independant, and combative. I had a very strong opinion of my own, and never cared a bit for being in a minority, and was ready to fight anybody however big if necessary. I don't think I was at all happy at school. I liked the holidays, and thoroughly hated going back to school.

At home, in the holidays, which were very short, I can remember little, except that I used to amuse myself as much as I could. I was out of doors from morning till night and was always either fishing, making rigging or sailing little boats, working in the carpenter's shop, constructing water-wheels, shooting with bow and arrow, jumping with a leaping-pole, and constructing all sorts of carts and sleighs. I was also very fond, in my sisters' play hours of driving them four in hand with string reins, as they were all very good runners. On rainy days I used to dig up celery in the garden for them, and get 'Washington' apples out of the apple chamber. Provided with these we used to go to a huge straw loft over the cattle yard, eat far too much, and read amusing books. In the evening after dark, I would read all night long till I went to bed – travels, adventures, shipwrecks, naval and military memoirs were my chief literature.

My general impression is that I was a very disagreable boy, not at all particular about my dress, disliked visitors and company, made a great grievance of being called in to see strangers, particularly disliked being taken to call, or be shown off anywhere, had my pockets stuffed with large knives, and quantities of string, and was a general nuisance to the house throughout the holidays.

Such was my life for three years and a half. I dare say it was a good breaking in, but I have a general impression that if I had been to a different kind of school, where the master had not a parish to attend to and had given more individual attention to the boys, it would have been much better for me. As it is, I am quite certain that I learnt more moral evil in a private school, than I ever did in my whole life afterwards, and most decidedly got no moral good. I record it as my firm conviction, which I beg every one of my children to remember, that the first school a boy goes to when he leaves home, is the most important thing in his life; and that nothing is so important for a boy as to choose a good preparatory school. I regard parents who think the first preparatory school of little moment so long as the boy goes to a good public school afterwards as being nothing better than short sighted, foolish, unintelligent, senseless geese. I hope my children will never forget this. A boy's first school is a turning point in his life. People should choose a small school; a school where there are no ushers,[11] and a school where a master gives his whole time and attention to the boys, and has no parish or other business to look after.

I left Mr Jackson's school in December 1827, tolerably well grounded in Latin, and Greek, but having learnt a vast amount of moral evil, and got no moral good.

So much for my private school life.

---

[11] That is, assistant masters.

CHAPTER 4

ETON COLLEGE

I went to Eton in January 1828, and was there for six years and three quarters.[1] My father had no connexion with Eton himself, and none of his family ever went there. Professor Smythe of Cambridge, brother of my Uncle Mr Smythe, who occasionally stayed with us, strongly urged it;[2] moreover, my first cousins, the Arkwrights, nearly all went there.

I went to Hawtrey's house, the same Hawtrey who was afterwards head master.[3] It was then the largest, and best house in the school. The building is the same now occupied by the present head master, Dr Hornby.[4] I did not like going at all. I did not know a single boy of the 600 in the school, and was awkward, shy, and young for my age. Moreover I had been brought up entirely in the north of England, and felt somewhat out of my element in going

[1] According to the headmaster's register, Ryle entered Eton College on 7 February 1828, aged 11; Keate's Entrance Book, Eton College Archives, SCH/HM/1/3. In 1873, Ryle's two youngest sons (intended readers of this autobiography) were themselves pupils at the school, which may explain the length of this chapter.

[2] William Smyth (1765-1849), regius professor of modern history at Cambridge University 1807-49, elder brother of Thomas Scott Smyth.

[3] Edward Craven Hawtrey (1789-1862), master at Eton College 1814-34, headmaster 1834-52, provost 1852-62.

[4] James John Hornby (1826-1909), headmaster of Eton College 1868-84, provost 1884-1909.

to the south – in short I was thoroughly miserable for the first half year, and if my father had let me have my own way, I would gladly have been taken away. This however he wisely would not consent to, though I believe I caused him a good deal of anxiety.

I don't know that I had more to contend with than most little boys who go to a large public school, but I certainly was very slow in getting acclimatized to Eton. Fagging went on to an extent which public schools know nothing of now,[5] and occasional acts of petty tyranny about trifles made a small low boy's position sometimes very uncomfortable, but I have no doubt it was very good for me.

Hawtrey's house was full of boys of noble family, or highly connected. When I went there, the present Bishop of Tuam (Barnard) [sic],[6] Lord Congleton (Mr Parnell),[7] Mr Craven,[8] Mr Villiers,[9] Mr Cowper,[10] Mr Cadogan,[11] Mark Wood,[12] Colonel Robert Wood,[13]

[5] Fagging was the performance of menial chores by junior boys for their seniors.

[6] Charles Brodrick Bernard (1811-90), bishop of Tuam, Killala and Achonry 1867-90, son of the second earl of Bandon.

[7] John Henry Parnell (1811-59), deputy lieutenant and high sheriff for County Wicklow, was father of Charles Stewart Parnell (1846-91), Irish nationalist. J. H. Parnell was not Baron Congleton, but his cousin.

[8] Frederick Keppel Craven (1812-64), son of the first earl of Craven.

[9] Frederick William Child Villiers (1815-71), MP for Weymouth 1847-52, or Francis John Robert Child Villiers (1819-62), MP for Rochester 1852-55. These brothers, sons of the fifth earl of Jersey, both overlapped with Ryle in Hawtrey's house.

[10] Charles Spencer Cowper (1816-79), British diplomat, son of the fifth Earl Cowper, nephew of Lord Melbourne (prime minister) and step-son of Lord Palmerston (prime minister). In 1843 he inherited the Sandringham estate, in Norfolk, which he sold to the royal family. His older brother, William Francis Cowper (1811-88), later Baron Mount-Temple, also overlapped with Ryle in Hawtrey's house. The Cowper sisters married the evangelical politicians, Lord Shaftesbury (1801-85) and Viscount Jocelyn (1816-54).

[11] George Cadogan (1814-80), army officer.

[12] William Mark Lockwood (1817-83), army officer, changed his surname to Wood in 1838 on inheriting the property of his uncle Sir Mark Wood (1794-1837), baronet.

[13] Robert Blucher Wood (1814-71), army officer.

J. G. Smyth afterwards M.P. for Yorkshire,[14] Mr Talbot (Lord Shrewsbury's brother, since a pervert, and now Lord Chamberlain to the Pope),[15] his brother Patrick Talbot, who married Lord Derby's sister,[16] Mr Brodrick (Lord Middleton's [*sic*] family),[17] Arthur Kinnaird,[18] the present Lord Howe and his brother Dick Curzon,[19] Lord Cremorne,[20] Sir Thomas Munroe [*sic*],[21] Lord Hatherton (then Mr Littleton),[22] Sir Robert Brownrigge [*sic*],[23] besides others were my cotemporaries. It may well be imagined how awkwardly a raw Cheshire boy like myself would fit in, amongst such a set. However I gradually fell into my place, and I have no doubt it was an excellent thing for my character, and taught me to bear, and forbear, and put up with much, and mortify my self-will, and accommodate myself to the various characters and temperaments of others. In fact

[14] John George Smyth (1815-69), MP for York 1847-65.

[15] Gilbert Chetwynd-Talbot (1816-96), undergraduate with Ryle at Christ Church, Oxford 1834-37, fellow of All Souls College from 1838, convert (Ryle has 'pervert') to Roman Catholicism in 1843, ordained as a Roman priest, appointed as papal chamberlain in 1850 by Pope Pius IX. He was younger brother of Henry John Chetwynd-Talbot, eighteenth earl of Shrewsbury (1803-68).

[16] Wellington Patrick Manvers Chetwynd-Talbot (1817-98), army officer, serjeant-at-arms in the House of Lords, married in 1860 to Emma Charlotte Stanley (1835-1928), sister of Edward Henry Stanley, fifteenth earl of Derby (1826-93), foreign secretary 1866-68 and 1874-78.

[17] John Robert Brodrick (1815-48), grandson of George Brodrick, third Viscount Midleton (1730-65).

[18] Arthur Fitzgerald Kinnaird, second Baron Kinnaird of Rossie (1814-87), banker, MP for Perth 1837-39 and 1852-78, evangelical philanthropist.

[19] George Augustus Frederick Louis Curzon, second Earl Howe (1821-76), MP for South Leicestershire 1857-70, and Richard William Penn Curzon, third Earl Howe (1822-1900), army officer.

[20] Richard Dawson, third Baron Cremorne (1817-97), created earl of Dartrey in 1866.

[21] Thomas Munro, baronet (1819-1901), army officer.

[22] Edward Richard Littleton (1815-88), MP for Walsall 1847-52, for South Staffordshire 1853-57, second Baron Hatherton from 1863.

[23] Robert William Colebrooke Brownrigg, baronet (1817-82). His grandfather, Sir Robert Brownrigg (1759-1833), was governor of Ceylon 1812-20.

I believe that a public school is about the best discipline that a boy can be put through, and the want of it is a great detriment to a boy all his life through.[24]

In point of temporal comfort, Hawtrey's house was everything that could be desired. We were well fed, well cared for, and wanted for nothing. In the evening after dark, we were certainly left too much to ourselves, and though each boy had his own room, invasions, alarums, and excursions, made it often difficult for a little boy to be quiet even if he wished it at night.[25] There was no positive cruelty, but there was a good deal of teazing [sic], and especially towards boys who showed any temper.

As to intimates, I began by messing with Mr Talbot (now Lord Chamberlain to the Pope), but he was a bullying, disagreable boy and this soon came to an end. I complained to other boys of his bullying and teazing me, and they advised me to settle it by fighting him; this I had no objection to. We picked a quarrel that night after tea, a small party of other boys rushed in who were lying in wait behind the door, and we proceeded to settle matters at once in the usual manner, with our fists, before a small company of delighted spectators. After two or three rounds I knocked him down, and his head fell on the hearthstone, and though he was not much hurt, he said he had had enough, and so the combat ceased. This was my

---

[24] Elsewhere Ryle wrote: 'Unquestionably there are many evils in "public schools", however carefully conducted. It must needs be so. We must expect it. But it is no less true that there are great dangers in private education [that is, at home with a private tutor], and dangers in their kind quite as formidable as any which beset a boy at public school. Of course no universal rule can be laid down. Regard must be had to individual character and temperament. But to suppose, as some seem to do, that boys educated at public schools must turn out ill, and boys educated at home must turn out well, is surely not wise. It is forgetting our Lord's doctrine, that the heart is the principal source of evil. Without a change of heart a boy may be kept at home, and yet learn all manner of sin.' J. C. Ryle, *Expository thoughts on the gospels: for family and private use: St Mark* (Ipswich, 1857), p. 143.

[25] 'Alarums and excursions' are commotion and uproar.

first, and only fight the whole time I was at Eton. It is fair to say that matters were soon made up between me and Talbot; we bore each other no malice. My principal friends in those early days were, Cowper, Littleton, Brodrick.

As to learning and school work, I went on steadily, though not brilliantly; but it is fair to say my tutor Hawtrey was often very unwell and all his pupils suffered much in consequence. I have often thought since those days that if I had had a tutor who had given more attention continuously I should have done far better. I was placed in middle remove, fourth form, took a great number of places when I was moved into the remove and took a great many more, and rose to the top of my class when I passed into the 5th form.[26]

I was also 'sent up' frequently, and became a very tolerable verse maker.[27] It is literally and simply a fact that in those days nothing was taught in Eton of necessity, excepting Latin and Greek, and a boy might pass through the school, without receiving any instruction except in those two dead languages. Some tutors, of whom Hawtrey was one, used privately to encourage their most promising pupils to read Roman and Greek history, and English books of an improving character. To this private system I owe a great deal.[28] Beside this, I

[26] At Eton the fourth form was subdivided into 'lower remove', 'middle remove' and 'upper remove', based on academic ability – not to be confused with 'the remove', which was a separate form between fourth and fifth.

[27] That is, sent to the headmaster for outstanding work, especially for distinction in the composition of classical poetry. Several examples of Ryle's Latin and Greek verse survive in the Eton College Archives (uncatalogued miscellaneous bundles).

[28] Ryle later wrote (2 January 1890): 'I have none but the most favourable recollections of Hawtrey. His house was extremely well managed, and, in the matter of food and attendance to all our wants, I could not find a fault. As a tutor, I shall always be grateful for Hawtrey. He took great pains with any boy that was disposed to read, gave excellent advice, encouraged private reading, and helped me immensely in preparation for Oxford. In fact, under his guidance, I read privately nearly all the books in which I was finally examined at Oxford ... I always found Hawtrey very good-tempered and good-natured, and though rather a prim old

Nov: 21. 1833.

Ryle.

πόθεν ἐκεῖνος θανάτου μνημονεύσειεν ἂν
ἐν ἀκμῇ τοσαύτῃ.

Αἲ, αἲ, Μναμοσύνας, θρηνήματος ἄρχετε, κῶραι,
Δάφνις ὁ πανδάκρυτος ἀπώλετο, καὶ νεολαίας
Πρᾶτος ἐὼν στυγεροῖο πύλας εἴσηνθ' Ἀίδαο·
Ὑμεῖς δ' οἵ ῥα νομῆος ἐπὶ χθονὶ δερκομένοιο
Ἐνὶ νάπαις ἄρθμοιο μετέσχετε καὶ φιλότητος,
Δάκρυα τεθνειῶτι δότ' αἴσιμα, καὶ τιν' ὀδυρμὸν
Δάφνιδι τῷ τριποθάτῳ, ὃν ἀιδκίας ἐρατεινᾶς
Ἄνθεσι τερπόμενον λάχεν ὄξεος ἲς θανάτοιο·
Οὔρεα γὰρ μετὰ βουσὶ πάις, διὰ δ' ἄγκεα βήσσων
Χαῖτος ἔβα, ἠδ' οὐκ οἶδε νοσῶν, τὸν δ' ἄδε μὲν ἰαὺς
Νέκρον ἴδεν, ταχέως δὲ χύτη κατὰ γαῖα καλύψει.
Ἁδὺ δὲ κοιμᾶται θανάτῳ μέλος· ὄμμα δὲ τηνον,

*Part of one of Ryle's 'sent up' papers at Eton College,
from November 1833, a Greek poem lamenting the death of Daphnis.*

χαιρ' Ἰθάκη.

Salve Ithaca, collesque mihi salvete paterni;
    Jam tandem pedibus littora nota premo.
Post tempestates, et diri pericula belli;
    Nunc redeo faustis ad mea tecta Deis.
Laeta mente dies quis non reminiscitur actos?
    Cui patria nullo pectus amore tumet?
Me quamvis rabie commota saeva Charybdis
    Terruit, et crebris per mare Scylla minis.
Carmine me frustra conata est flectere Siren,
    Praeterii victor cuncta pericla maris.
Frustra conata est Circe mutare figuram,
    Nam magici cantus nil nocuere dolis.
Et mihi nequicquam promisit regna Calypso,
    Qua possem aeterna conditione frui.
Quamvis non faveat nobis hic copia frugum,
    Rideat et nullis messibus alma Ceres;
Munera si campis nostris Pomona recuset,
    Nullaque graminea floreat herba solo;
Nec decoret tumidis Bacchus vineta racemis,
    Haec patria est tellus, hanc ego semper amo.
"Care pater, salve longa confecte senecta,
    Si videt malas aspera juga tuas,
En adsum, ut relevem curas, spes una, senectae,
    Mortua qui claudam lumina, amicus ero."

Another of Ryle's 'sent up' papers, a Latin poem in the voice of Odysseus, returning home to Ithaca after the Trojan War.

had extra instruction in French and took lessons in fencing, and occasionally attended lectures on natural science, given by a lecturer from London – but these were very few, though very useful. Not one word of Arithmetic, Algebra or Mathematics did I learn the whole seven years I was at Eton. The Newcastle scholarship, it will be remembered had not been established at this time; and did not begin till the last two years I was at Eton. Until it was established, there really was no stimulus to any boy to take much pains.[29]

No one in fact in the present day can have the smallest idea of the difference between Eton as it was then, and Eton as it is now, as a place of training and education. Few masters took the slightest interest in the boys in private. So long as the public school work was done, a boy was left to his own devices. There was a high gentlemanly tone unquestionably, throughout the school but religion was at a very low ebb, and most boys knew far more about the heathen gods and goddesses, than about Jesus Christ.

There were too many holidays, and too little work. Fighting in the playing fields before two or three hundred boys was the approved mode of settling all disputes. The foundation was wretchedly managed. Fifty of the 70 boys slept in one long room, 240 feet long, and 20 in another. There was no competition for getting on the foundation and the boys as a rule, were of very inferior rank, and description, and were rather looked down upon by the Oppidans, and not without reason.[30] On Sunday there was nothing whatever

bachelor in his ways, ready to give attention to any boy who would take pains.'
See Francis St John Thackeray, *Memoir of Edward Craven Hawtrey* (London, 1896), pp. 51-52.

[29] Three prestigious Newcastle scholarships, each worth £50 a year and tenable for three years, were founded at Eton in 1829 by Henry Pelham-Clinton (1785-1851), fourth duke of Newcastle-under-Lyme. The scholarship was awarded each year to the best student in classics.

[30] There were seventy pupils on the foundation at Eton, known as 'Collegers', who boarded together within the college itself. Their rivals, the 'Oppidans', were Eton pupils who boarded in the town, often wealthier and in better accommodation.

to do us any good, the preaching of the 'fellows' was beneath contempt.[31] There was nominally very little liberty, practically a great deal. There were bounds but nobody kept within them, and rules about not going to certain Inns, etc., which no one ever attended to. No one was ever spoken to about his soul, except in the most careless formal manner, at the time of Confirmation. And the tone of morality on some points was decidedly not high. Montem, which took place every three years was a perfect Saturnalia, and a custom only worthy of the dark ages.[32]

The first five years of my Eton life I shall pass over with little remark. They were years in which my character was forming and during which my mind was silently watching, thinking, planning, considering, calculating, measuring, and taking note of men, books and things. I did not come forward much in any way; I did not distinguish myself much in any game. One whole summer I did not play at cricket, and spent most of my time in boating. All this time I read a good deal of every book on which I could lay hands, and kept myself up to the place in school which I had attained. I think my schoolfellows did not understand me, and had little idea what I was thinking of.

At the end of this five years, I suddenly came forward as a leading boy in the school, and kept my position as such till I left. I competed for the Newcastle scholarship, and surprised everyone by the position which I took. I came forward as a cricketer, and was at

[31] The Eton governing body consisted of a provost and ten fellows, who appointed the headmaster and the other masters.

[32] 'Montem' was a rowdy Eton College festival, triennially on Whit-Tuesday, attracting large crowds, when pupils in fancy dress processed to Salt Hill, an ancient burial mound near Slough. Ryle experienced the festivities twice, in 1829 and 1832, the second attended by William IV, Queen Adelaide and other members of the royal household. The montem of 1844 was the last, after which it was abolished by the college authorities.

35

once put into the eleven.[33] I joined the Debating Society, and took a prominent part in the proceedings.[34] In the last three quarters of the year I was at Eton I was captain of the eleven, very high in the 6th form, and one of the most prominent boys in the school – so much so, that nothing was done in which I did not take a leading part one way or another. This last year and three quarters was decidedly my happiest time at Eton. I was ambitious, and fond of influence and power, attained power, and was conscious of it. Eton at that time so far as the boys were concerned, was a perfect republic. Rank and title, and name, and riches went for nothing at all, and a boy was valued according to his cleverness, or boating powers, or cricketing skill, or bodily strength, or good nature, or general agreableness, and pleasantness, and for nothing else at all. This exactly suited me, and I have certainly never seen anything like it since I left Eton. I had always an instinctive dislike to the custom of honouring people because of their rank or position, if they had no intrinsic merit. Nothing used to annoy me so much, as being invited to Windsor Castle, by my cousin John Ryle Wood, in order to be playfellow to Prince George of Cambridge, of whom I did not form a very high opinion.

Nothing did I enjoy so much as cricket, when I was in the eleven, and as long as I live I think I shall say, that the happiest days I ever spent in a simple earthly way, were the days when I was captain of the eleven in Eton playing fields and absurd as some may think it, I believe it gave me a power of commanding, managing,

---

[33] For the Eton College Cricket Club Book (1834), with detailed scores from Ryle's early matches, see Eton College Archives, SCH/SP/CR/1/1. Ryle played for Eton against Harrow School and Winchester College, at Lord's cricket ground, in 1833-34; and for the Old Etonians against the Old Harrovians, at Lord's, in 1835-36 and 1838. See MCC scorebooks, 1791-1835 and 1836-47, Marylebone Cricket Club Archives, MCC/CRI/4/10.

[34] The Eton Society, a debating society and social club, was founded in 1811. For Ryle's involvement, see Appendix 2.

The Captain of the Eton Eleven presents his compliments to the Captain of the Harrow Eleven, and requests the pleasure of a meeting between the Two Elevens, to play a match at cricket on Lord's ground, on Thursday the 31st of July.

J. C. Ryle.

Rec'd E. C. Hartley,
Har. May 6th

Broughton Esq're
Rec'd Mr Emery's
Harrow.

Ryle's earliest surviving letter, from May 1834, as captain of the Eton cricket team, challenging Robert Broughton (1816–1911), captain of the Harrow cricket team, to a match at Lord's cricket ground in Marylebone.

organizing, and directing, seeing through men's capacities, and using every man in the post to which he is best suited, bearing, forbearing, and keeping men around me in good temper, which I have found of infinite use on hundreds of occasions in life, though in very different matters.

The friends I was most intimate with this year and three quarters, were the three Cootes, sons of Sir Charles Coote;[35] William Courthope who afterwards married my sister; Charlton of Chilwell, Nottingham;[36] Ady, now Archdeacon Ady;[37] Carter, now fellow of Eton;[38] Vance, son of Dr Vance the Physician;[39] Frank Villiers, son of Lord Jersey, now dead; Littleton, now Lord Littleton [sic];[40] Garland now Rector of Brixton;[41] and some others. Cricket certainly diminished the amount of my reading, and this together with my tutor's frequent illnesses, prevented my ever doing so well for the Newcastle scholarship, as I think I might have done, so that I only came in fourth the last time I ever tried for it. I often think that what I lost in some ways I gained in others, especially in the general formation of my mind and character.

[35] Sir Charles Henry Coote (1792-1864), ninth baronet, of Castle Cuffe, Queens County, Ireland, had three sons at Eton: Charles Henry Coote (1815-95), tenth baronet; John Chidley Coote (1816-79), army officer; and Algernon Coote (1817-99), rector of Marsh Gibbon, Buckinghamshire 1844-56, vicar of Nonington, Kent 1856-71, eleventh baronet.

[36] Thomas Broughton Charlton (1815-86) of Chilwell Hall, near Nottingham.

[37] William Brice Ady (1816-82), rector of Little Baddow, Essex 1842-82, archdeacon of Colchester 1864-82.

[38] William Adolphus Carter (1815-1901), fellow of King's College, Cambridge 1837-45, master at Eton College 1839-64, fellow 1864-1901.

[39] John Epworth Vance (1816-71), undergraduate at Christ Church, Oxford 1834-38, barrister. His father, Dr George Vance (1769-1837), died of a head injury after being accidentally knocked down the stairs by a mentally-ill patient he was attending.

[40] George William Lyttelton (1817-76), fourth Baron Lyttelton from 1837, educationist.

[41] Nathaniel Arthur Garland (1816-1911), undergraduate at Christ Church, Oxford 1834-38, vicar of Sibertswold, Kent 1851-53, rector of Deal, Kent 1853-56, vicar of St Matthew's, Brixton 1856-97.

I take occasion here to remark that cricketing, and boating were far more mingled together in those days, than they seem to have been of late years. It was no uncommon thing in those days for a boy to be in the school eight as a good oar, and at the same time in the school eleven as a good cricketer. Nevertheless, as a rule the followers of the two amusements formed two very distinct parties, and there was sometimes a good deal of ill-feeling between the two. I certainly think that in general the boating set was less refined, and more given to coarse habits than the cricketing set; but they were more numerous, and more popular. Between Collegers and Oppidans there was a much wider gulf than there is now, and no wonder; boys got into College without any competition, lived in a very rough way, and were often less refined and gentlemanlike than the Oppidans. In learning and scholarship they certainly were not distinguished, and were as unlike the present order of Collegers in that respect as darkness is unlike light. In games however they were far superior to the present order of Collegers, and it was a very rare thing for the school eleven not to have several Collegers in it. In football, they generally beat the Oppidans. They kept themselves much more to themselves than they have done of late years, and it was a very rare thing to see any intimacy between the Collegers and Oppidans. I believe I was one of the first to break down this state of things. Football in my time was certainly not a popular game; in this respect there seems to be a great change, not, I think, for the better. Hockey, on the contrary, was very popular, and played as it was with large sticks expressly made for the purpose at Eton Wick at no small expense,[42] was really a very fine game, affording splendid exercise, and giving scope for great skill. I was always extremely successful at it, and I regard the extinction of it at the present day, as a great loss.

[42] Eton Wick was a small village near Eton.

The debating society held at the Reading room, at Hatton's shop,[43] next door to the present Mr Wolley Dod's house every Saturday afternoon, was a really useful institution, and I have heard much good boys' speaking there. I used to take much part in it myself. Vice-Chancellor Wickens[44] and Lord Littleton [*sic*] were two of my principle [*sic*] cotemporaries and fellow speakers in it. Our speeches were all taken down, and the old Chronicles of the Society must be at the present day very interesting documents.[45] Speeches of Mr Gladstone's and the late Lord Derby may be found there as well as my own.[46]

It is difficult to conceive a greater change than has taken place at Eton in every respect since the days that I was there. Dr Keat [*sic*] the head master was a good disciplinarian, a good scholar, and kept good order.[47] He was a thorough Tory of the old school, and of the worst sort, and set his face steadfastly against any sort of reform, or any effort to meet the times. The Provost Goodall[48] and the Fellows were men of the same sort, and like old fossils were utterly unable to see the necessity of changes. The tutors as a rule, took very little interest in their pupils individually. Hawtrey, Chapman,[49]

[43] From 1811 to 1846, the Eton Society met in a room above the shop of Mrs Hatton, a pastry-cook and confectioner. The society's nickname, 'Pop', probably derives from *popina* (cook shop).

[44] Sir John Wickens (1815-73), barrister and judge, vice-chancellor of the high court 1871-73.

[45] For Ryle's speeches at the Eton Society, see Appendix 2.

[46] Early members of the Eton Society included Edward Stanley, fourteenth earl of Derby (1799-1869), at Eton 1811-17, and William Ewart Gladstone (1809-98), at Eton 1821-27. Both served as prime minister – Derby three times (1852, 1858-59, 1866-68) and Gladstone four times (1868-74, 1880-85, 1886, 1892-94).

[47] John Keate (1773-1852), headmaster of Eton College 1809-34. Ryle was twice flogged by Keate (see Appendix 3).

[48] Joseph Goodall (1760-1840), provost of Eton College 1809-40.

[49] James Chapman (1799-1879), fellow of King's College, Cambridge 1822-35, master at Eton College 1822-34, rector of Dunton Wayletts, Essex 1834-45, first bishop of Colombo 1845-61, rector of Wootton Courtenay, Somerset 1863-79.

Wilder,[50] and Coleridge[51] were to a certain extent exceptions. But no boy ever dreamed of looking up to his tutor as a friend or adviser, and Arnold's plan of taking by hand, fostering, helping, encouraging, watering, pruning, training, picking out, and pressing on the cleverest, and most promising intellects, was utterly unknown at Eton in my time.[52] The consequence was that when we went up to Oxford and Cambridge to compete for University honours, and degrees with boys fresh from the Rugby hotbed, trained and crammed to the uttermost, we Eton boys were placed at an enormous disadvantage. My own generation felt this deeply. Littleton [*sic*] went to Cambridge at the same time with Dr Vaughan,[53] and I went to Oxford at the same time with Dean Stanley,[54] and were competitors all through our University career; but I always felt, and still feel that we competed at a great disadvantage with these two distinguished Rugby men. However I am not sure, that in the long run the Eton system did not produce a greater number of men able to take their position, and fit it well in any place of life. We were all thrown upon ourselves, and obliged to think for ourselves with very little help of any kind and I think the system made us more

[50] John Wilder (1801-92), fellow of King's College, Cambridge 1823-31, master at Eton College 1824-40, fellow 1840-85, vice-provost 1885-92.

[51] Edward Coleridge (*c.* 1801-83), fellow of Exeter College, Oxford 1823-26, master at Eton College 1824-57, rector of Mapledurham, Berkshire 1862-83.

[52] Thomas Arnold (1795-1842), headmaster of Rugby School 1828-42.

[53] Charles John Vaughan (1816-97), pupil at Rugby School 1829-34, undergraduate of Trinity College, Cambridge 1834-38, fellow 1839-42, headmaster of Harrow School 1844-59, vicar of Doncaster 1860-69, master of the Temple 1869-94, dean of Llandaff 1879-97. G. W. Lyttelton was also an undergraduate at Trinity College 1835-38, and competed with Vaughan for the top university prizes – they were bracketed together in 1838 as top classicists and as winners of the chancellor's gold medal for poetry.

[54] Arthur Penrhyn Stanley (1815-81), pupil at Rugby School 1829-33, undergraduate at Balliol College, Oxford 1833-37, fellow of University College 1838-51, regius professor of ecclesiastical history 1856-64, dean of Westminster 1864-81. While at Oxford, Stanley carried off many of the top prizes.

independant and able to do our duty anywhere, than the Rugby system did.

Fagging, in my time was certainly much more severe in my time [*sic*] than it is now. Public fagging in play hours, such as towing a couple of big boys in a boat up the river to Surley; or fagging out at cricket to throw up the ball for two big fellows hitting about, or being sent up [to] Windsor for some trumpery errand, or carrying a master's chair, tea-things, milk, butter and bread, up to Poet's Walk in summer, were not pleasant things. Private fagging in the houses, was systematic, and the harshness of it depended much on the character of the biggest boys in the houses. The last half year I was at Eton, I had eight fags of my own in my tutor's house – four of them to wait on me in the morning at breakfast, and four in the evening at tea. But the work they did was a mere trifle only taking up a few minutes, and did them no harm. On the contrary as half of them generally were young noblemen, it probably did them good, and brought them to their proper level. On the whole, my experience is, that cases of oppressive tyranny and violent beating under the fagging system were thoroughly exceptions. No one was formally sanctioned to administer corporal punishment except the head master. Anything like 'tunding' such as we have recently heard of at Winchester, was a thing utterly unknown at Eton, and the Head Master would not have tolerated it for a moment.[55] My opinion is distinct and decided, that a certain quantity of fagging in large public schools does no harm at all. On the contrary, I think that it often does good to young boys who have been petted and spoilt, and indulged at home, and taught to think that their own will is

[55] In November and December 1872, Winchester College hit the national headlines because of allegations of brutality in which younger boys were 'tunded' (caned across the shoulders) by school prefects. See further, Peter Gwyn, 'The "tunding row": George Ridding and the belief in "boy-government"', in Roger Custance (ed.), *Winchester College: sixth-centenary essays* (Oxford, 1982), pp. 431-77.

law. It obliges them to submit to the will of others, and teaches the great lesson which we all have to learn in life, that we cannot always have our own way. I should not like to send a boy to any public school, where there was no fagging at all, or corporal punishment. I cordially dislike schools where boys are incessantly watched and superintended by tutors, and ushers, even at play, and not allowed to form their own laws and act and think for themselves. I regard such schools with contempt, and think them unlikely to fit boys for the great battle of life. As for those parents who think their dear boys' sacred persons must never be touched, and their dear boys' wills must never be crossed, and their dear little boys must never be made to do anything they don't like by other boys, I regard them with unmixed pity, and I marvel at their ignorance. Fagging, as it now exists at Eton I believe to be a thoroughly good system.

In a material point of view Eton in my time was wonderfully unlike what it is now. Where the New Buildings for the Collegers now stands, the Provost's stables formerly stood.[56] At the end of Poet's Walk the road to Slough was carried over a bridge of fifteen arches, very narrow and inconvenient; it was pulled down in my time and replaced by the present one.[57] Where Eton Street begins at Barne's Pool Bridge there was a stagnant muddy branch of the river which flowed down to the Thames like an open drain in front of four Dame's Houses,[58] and I wonder those houses were ever free from fever. It is now arched over and turned into a garden. Just beyond Williams the bookseller's shop[59] there was a large Hotel

[56] The New Buildings, improved accommodation for the Collegers, were erected in 1844-46. Prince Albert laid the foundation stone.

[57] Although the new bridge, erected in 1833, had only three arches it was still called Fifteen-Arch Bridge.

[58] Dame's houses were boarding houses for Eton pupils, run by matrons.

[59] Edward Williams (*c.* 1775-1838), Eton bookseller and publisher. His son, George Williams (1814-78), was a prominent ecumenist, working for reunion between the Anglican and Eastern Orthodox churches.

called Christophers[60] where parents used to stay when they came down to see their boys, and where boys fond of eating and drinking often spent a deal of money. Where the new Class rooms now stand, opposite Wolley Dod's house, was a large old Tutor's house occupied by Knapp.[61] Beyond Sheep's bridge on the right hand side, there was a large coal wharf, and dwelling house, occupied by Major Brine.[62] This is completely cleared away, and there is nothing between the Upper fields and the river. Between the Upper cricket fields, and the Slough road, were the remains of a large old gravel pit, which is now filled up. The Chapel itself was fitted up in the most incongruous style, with classical Inigo Jones oak fittings, entirely out of character with the Architecture. These fittings are all gone and replaced in a suitable manner.[63]

Windsor itself is totally altered. In my time there were low shops and houses on the left hand side all the way from the hundred steps up the hill to the Castle gates. A public road went from the south side of Windsor across the head of the long walk to Datchet; this has been stopped and a new road made on the north side of the Castle across the Home Park.[64] Of course there were no railways in

---

[60] The Christopher Inn, on Eton High Street, named after the patron saint of travellers.

[61] Henry Hartopp Knapp (1782-1846), fellow of King's College, Cambridge 1804-21, master at Eton College 1808-34, rector of Ampthill, Bedfordshire 1820-46.

[62] James Brine (1784-1859), army officer, who served in the Peninsular War 1809-14 and in North America 1814-15.

[63] Inigo Jones (1573-1652), classical architect, surveyor of the king's works 1615-42, designed many royal and prestigious buildings, including the Banqueting House at Whitehall, the Queen's House at Greenwich, and Covent Garden. Eton College chapel had been built in the 1440s, in gothic style, so the seventeenth-century neo-classical fittings were removed in the 1840s and replaced by neo-gothic ones, more in keeping with the original.

[64] The 'long walk', the avenue of trees leading from Windsor Castle across Windsor Great Park, was laid out by Charles II and William III in the late seventeenth century. The public roads around the castle were considerably altered by the Windsor Improvement Act of 1848, partly to provide greater privacy for the royal family.

my time, and the Windsor coaches ran through Eton up the Slough road to London.[65] When we broke up for the holidays however, it was a common thing for three boys to club together, and go up to London in a Post Chaise.[66] There was no Church at Slough or at Chalvey, and none for the inhabitants of Eton; those few who went anywhere were expected to come to Eton College Chapel.[67] There were many other little points of difference that I cannot now remember.

I left Eton with unfeigned regret. The last year and three quarters that I was there were perhaps in a natural point of view one of the happiest periods of my life and did most for the formation of my natural character. But I believe it was high time I should leave, and I should have got no good by staying there any longer. I was master of as much Latin and Greek as I ever knew in my life, and was fit to compete for anything in Classics at either Oxford or Cambridge. If I had stayed longer at Eton I think it would have been bad for me, and would have developed perhaps much that was evil in my character.

I have not mentioned during the last 3 years I was at Eton, my brother was there, and boarded in the same house.[68] There was just that difference between our ages that we could not be

[65] The first section of the Great Western Railway, between Paddington and Maidenhead, opened in June 1838, but the Great Western Railway Act (1835) prevented the building of a station within three miles of Eton College without permission of the provost and fellows. This restriction was soon repealed, and a station was opened at Slough in 1840, and a branch line to Eton and Windsor in 1849, despite strong opposition from the college authorities.

[66] That is, a horse-drawn carriage.

[67] When Eton College was founded in the fifteenth century, the medieval parish church was requisitioned and replaced by a new college chapel which continued its parish functions. During the nineteenth century, new Anglican churches were consecrated for Slough (1837), Eton (1854), Chalvey (1861), and Eton Wick (1869).

[68] Frederic Ryle arrived at Eton in April 1833, aged 12, so overlapped with his older brother for just four terms; see Keate's Entrance Book, Eton College Archives, SCH/HM/1/3.

companions to one another, and we were very little together. His natural character moreover was very different to my own. He was an exceedingly gentle, quiet, undemonstrative person, and never acted or spoke strongly about anybody, or anything, and was a most blameless amiable fellow. But he never distinguished himself in any way, either in cricket, boating, or reading, and both at Eton, and ever after, to the end of his life, we seemed to move in different orbits; but I shall always say, that I never knew anyone who had fewer positive faults, or seemed to have fewer strong passions. I must honestly confess, that in all these respects I was exceedingly unlike him, and though there never was a disagreement between us, there never was much congeniality. He walked steadily on in his own way, and I rushed on impetuously in my own. And this was the case till he died.

About my holidays during the six years and three quarters that I was at Eton I can say little, except that I was always glad to get home, and always sorry to go back to school.[69] I don't think they were well spent, I certainly never did anything to prepare for school. They were almost always spent at home, excepting once or twice when we went to Hastings. I very rarely visited anywhere, except at Wirksworth, or Rock House. I saw little of my father during the day, when he was generally out, and left me very much to myself. My days were chiefly spent in fishing, boating, carpentering, shooting, occasionally riding, cutting down trees, or some violent exercise

[69] Ryle exhorted his Helmingham parishioners to spiritual alertness, by recalling the delight of returning home to Macclesfield for the school holidays: 'I remember when I was a school-boy I could wake up, however tired with a long journey, when I begun to draw near home. Soon as I saw the old hills, and trees, and chimnies [sic], the sense of weariness was gone, and I was alive. The prospect of soon seeing much-loved faces – the joy of thinking of a family gathering, all this was able to drive sleep away. Surely it ought to be the same with us in the matter of our souls.' J. C. Ryle, *What time is it? Being thoughts on Rom. xiii. 12* (Ipswich, 1855), p. 28.

– unless someone was staying with us, generally alone. There was little or no society for us in and about Macclesfield, and unless friends came to stay with us, I was thrown very much on myself. I think this was decidedly bad for me. The Hurts and Arkwrights frequently stayed with us for many weeks together. Edward Arkwright who lived for some time in Macclesfield, having a farm in the neighbourhood; Henry, Alfred, James, Ferdinand used all to stay with us, and at times I was very intimate with every one of them. Caroline Hurt (now Lady Hatherton) used to stay with us for months, and her sisters Sophy, and Margaret for shorter times. Marianne Arkwright, and Mary Moore were also frequent visitors, and occasionally Sophy and Teresa Holden and Clara too.[70]

In the evenings, we almost always played at cards or danced, and occasionally had dancing parties by gathering together all the young people in the neighbourhood. I was always passionately fond of dancing from the time I was 15 – and especially fond of waltzing, reels, country dances, Sir Roger de Coverley,[71] and anything that had steam, and life, and go in it. It was a passion that I kept up until I found out that I had got a soul; and I think it nearly led me to some scrapes, which might have ruined my happiness for life. When kept indoors by weather during the day, or when there was nothing going on at night, I was always reading, but without aim, end, or purpose; and in one way or another scrambled through an enormous quantity of miscellaneous literature, in my father's large library. Bad and thoughtless as I was at any rate I was never idle,

---

[70] Sophia Elizabeth Rosamond Holden (1797-1867), Teresa Amelia Holden (1800-62), and Isabel Clara Holden (1810-67), were daughters of Charles Holden (1749-1821) of Aston Hall, Derbyshire. In 1839 Clara became the second wife of George Moore junior (1811-71) of Appleby Hall. Another sister was Antonia Henrietta Holden (1798-1849) who married William Legh Clowes (1781-1862) of Broughton Hall, Lancashire – the parents of Ryle's third wife, Henrietta Clowes.

[71] Sir Roger de Coverley is the name of a country dance.

and never spent my time with my hands in my pockets, whistling and doing nothing. My brain was never still, nor my hands, and it is a pity they were not better employed. But it really must be remembered in fairness, that I had no guide, director, or counsellor, and was sadly too much left to myself. It is only a special mercy that I had no taste for low company, or for the coarse vices and habits into which many young men run. For these things I had no natural inclination, my taste revolted against them, though I really do not think I had a bit of principle to keep me right. My general impression is that my holidays during the time I was at Eton were very badly spent, and form a miserably unprofitable portion of my life. Perhaps the chief taste I developed was for dogs, and I was incessantly accompanied by two huge Lyme mastiffs, such as are not to be seen in these degenerate days.

The holidays after I left Eton I went over to Ireland, and spent a month with the Cootes at Ballyfin. I was very intimate with all the three brothers at Eton, through the connecting link of cricket. I think it was a very unprofitable visit, we were all restless and thoughtless, and behaved like people who have no souls. The principal events in the visit, were my playing in cricket matches on the side of Queen's County against Kilkenny and Carlow, and Maryborough Heath and against Ballinasloe in Lord Clancarty's park at Ballinasloe.[72] I also took John Coote to Cork to join the 43ᵈ Regiment, and dined at the Barracks with the mess,[73] and went to sleep at the Cathedral on Sunday under a miserable sermon. Altogether I returned to

[72] Richard Le Poer Trench, second earl of Clancarty (1767-1837), British ambassador to the Netherlands 1814-23. Both he and his younger brother, Power Le Poer Trench (1770-1839), archbishop of Tuam 1819-39, were supporters of evangelicalism.

[73] The 43ʳᵈ infantry regiment was quartered in Ireland 1832-35, before it sailed to New Brunswick where it played an active part in quelling the Canadian rebellions of 1837-38. John Coote was promoted to the rank of captain in 1842.

England with a very unfavourable impression of Ireland. But this was a bad period of my life, my judgement about anybody, or anything at that time is worth very little.

CHAPTER 5

OXFORD

I n October 1834, I entered Christ Church, Oxford, and remained
there exactly 3 years. It will be observed that I went straight
from Eton to Oxford, without the intermediate stage of going
to a private tutor. This was a wise arrangement; a public school
which is not fit to prepare a boy for a University, is a miserable
concern; and a parent who thinks as a matter of course that his boy
must go to a private tutor between school and college, is a very foolish and ignorant goose.

My tutors at Christ Church were first Augustus Short, now
Bishop of Adelaide, Australia,[1] and second, Henry Liddell, now
Dean of Christ Church, better known as one of the Authors of
Liddell and Scott's Greek Lexicon.[2] Short as a tutor was perfectly
useless, and I never learned anything from him. Liddell was a very

---

[1] Augustus Short (1802-83), student (fellow) of Christ Church, Oxford 1820-36,
vicar of Ravensthorpe, Northants 1835-47, first bishop of Adelaide 1847-82.

[2] Henry George Liddell (1811-98), student (fellow) of Christ Church, Oxford
1830-46, headmaster of Westminster School 1846-55, dean of Christ Church 1855-
91. The first edition of Liddell's *Greek-English lexicon*, jointly edited with Robert
Scott, was published in 1843. Liddell became a tutor in January 1836 and described
his thirteen pupils (including Ryle) as 'a *very good* set who will keep all my wits at
work'; Henry L. Thompson, *Henry George Liddell, D.D., dean of Christ Church,
Oxford: a memoir* (London, 1899), pp. 27-28.

good tutor and I heartily wish I had been under him during the whole time I was at Oxford.

At the end of the first year I was at Oxford I got one of the Fell Exhibitions at Christ Church.[3] At the end of the second year, I got the Craven University Scholarship,[4] and I wound up at the end of the third year by getting a very brilliant first class in classics, side by side with Dean Stanley. This was in October 1837. I was in the University Eleven all the 3 years I was at Oxford, and was Captain of the Eleven the second and third years, beating Cambridge the first time the match was played.[5]

I thoroughly disliked Oxford on many accounts. Of course the place, the buildings and colleges are things matchless in the world, and to talk of comparing Oxford and Cambridge is simply ridiculous. But I thoroughly disliked the tone of society at Oxford among the undergraduates, and the more so, from its complete unlikeness to what I had been used to at Eton. Nothing disgusted me so much as the universal idolatry of money, rank, and aristocratic connexion. I never saw such an amount of toadying,

[3] John Fell (1625-86), dean of Christ Church, Oxford 1660-86 (after the expulsion of John Owen), bishop of Oxford 1676-86, established ten exhibitions for undergraduates at Christ Church.

[4] John Craven, Baron Craven of Ryton (c. 1610-48), a royalist during the English Civil War, established four scholarships, two at Oxford and two at Cambridge, worth £25 a year. In 1819 the trust was augmented to five Craven scholarships in each university, worth £50 a year, tenable for up to seven years each. In November 1836 twenty-five candidates were examined for two vacancies, to which Ryle and William Linwood (1817-78) were elected. Ryle held his scholarship for three years. See the Register of Craven Exhibitioners 1776-1858 (15 November 1836, 15 November 1839), Oxford University Archives, WPgamma 26/7.

[5] The first Varsity cricket match was in fact in 1827, repeated in 1829, but it was revived in 1836 and from 1838 became an annual event. Ryle took ten wickets in the match on 23-24 June 1836, played at Lord's, when Oxford beat Cambridge by 121 runs. He also played in the Varsity match on 6-7 July 1838, after his graduation; and for Oxford University against the MCC in 1835-36 and 1838. See MCC scorebooks, 1791-1835 and 1836-47, Marylebone Cricket Club Archives, MCC/CRI/4/10.

flattering, and fawning upon wealth, and title, as I saw amongst the undergraduates at Oxford. It thoroughly revolted me, and almost made me a republican. There was also a coldness, and a distance, a want of sociability and sympathy amongst undergraduates, which to a boy fresh from Eton was extremely offensive. Add to this, tutors and College authorities seemed to me to give reading men no help, counsel, or advice, and really seemed not to care what became of you, so long as you did not give them trouble. Balliol was perhaps an exception to other Colleges to a certain extent, and there the Rugby men, such as Stanley, Jowett etc.[6] congregated, like plants in a hotbed; and the Arnold system of picking out and fostering prime specimens was thoroughly worked out. As to men like myself in Christ Church and other Colleges, I have a distinct recollection that we got no help, or advice, or assistance or encouragement, and the College authorities really did not seem to care whether we took a College degree, or took honours. I always have thought and always shall think, that if any kind and sympathising tutor had taken me by the hand when I first went to Oxford, directed my reading, stimulated me by encouragement and stirred me up to try what I could do, I could have done ten times as much, and carried off ten times as many honours as I did. As it was, I never should have tried for the Craven University scholarship if Liddell had not suggested it, and put it in my head, yet I was just as fit to compete for it the first year I entered Oxford as I was the third. The neglect of undergraduates was simply pitiable and deplorable. My first two years at Oxford were practically thrown away. I read desultorily, and spasmodically, kept up few friendships, kept myself to myself

---

[6] Benjamin Jowett (1817-93), undergraduate at Balliol College, Oxford 1835-39, fellow 1838-70, master 1870-93, regius professor of Greek 1855-93, vice-chancellor 1882-86. Jowett attended St Paul's School, London, not Rugby School, but he was a close friend of Arthur Stanley and they helped to establish Balliol's reputation for academic excellence.

very much, and contracted rather a soured misanthropical view of human nature, keenly observing men and things around me and thoroughly convinced that the whole system needed a complete reform. I left Oxford with a brilliant reputation for the honours which I had taken, but with very little love for the University, and very glad to get away from it.

The vacations of the three years I spent at Oxford, were passed very much like the vacations at Eton, and I do not know that there is anything very particular to remark about them. The last summer vacation before I took my degree was spent reading at Malvern. The others I think were chiefly at home. That my 3 months at Malvern were not very well spent will be pretty evident when I mention that I spent a great deal of time in going to balls at Worcester and Malvern, and dancing with two handsome Miss Leycesters, who waltzed very well.[7] In fact it made so much talk, that at last I left Malvern and went home, and never saw them again. Singularly enough I first met them at the house of Colonel Parker who then lived at Malvern, the same Colonel Parker at whose house I made my first speech about my good dinner.[8] I have very little faith in vacation parties for reading. Between dancing with the Miss Leycesters in the evenings, dining at the ordinary at the Hotel,[9] playing at billiards, and reading Byron's works,[10] my recollection is, that I wasted a great deal of time.

The circumstances of my taking my degree at Oxford, when I got a first class are perhaps worth mentioning. I read a great deal the year before I took my degree, excepting in summer time when I was always playing at cricket. I was in lodgings at that time, according

[7] The two Miss Leycesters were perhaps relatives of the Leycesters of Toft Hall, Cheshire (see below, p. 75).

[8] Thomas Parker had sold Astle Hall in 1833 and moved to Malvern.

[9] That is, a regular fixed-price meal.

[10] George Gordon Byron, sixth Baron Byron (1788-1824), poet.

to the custom of Christ Church under which undergraduates go into lodgings for their two last terms, and lodged at Jubbers in High Street, opposite St Mary's Church.[11] A great deal of my reading was done at night, chiefly because of the extreme quietness of that time. I don't defend the practice, as I have no doubt it tells upon the health in the long run, but I always must maintain that to those who value quietness and silence, there is no time for reading like that between 10 and 1. Beside Liddell my College tutor, I had a private tutor, or coach, named Cox, vice-principal of St Mary's Hall.[12] He had a great reputation as a coach, but I never thought much of him, and I am sure he quite misunderstood me. At any rate he predicted that I should hardly get a second class, and very likely a third. I cared little for what he said, read on steadily and doggedly and learned more in private from my own reading, than I ever did from any tutor. In fact I must honestly confess I never could read with anyone, as some men did, but got on best alone.

A first class of honours in those days was a very serious affair. Moderations were not known, but only two examinations, Littlego, and Greatgo.[13] The consequence was that a candidate for first class honours, had to take up a very large quantity of books, and to be prepared in so many things, that not many men could stand it. The present system of three examinations may produce a greater

[11] Jubbers was a confectionary shop at No. 96 High Street, Oxford, founded by George Henry Jubber (1770-1837), and continued by his son, Henry Jubber (1808-70), later a London hotelier. The property was demolished in 1909 to make way for Oriel College's Rhodes Building.

[12] William Hayward Cox (*c*. 1804-71), fellow of Queen's College, Oxford 1828-33, vice-principal of St Mary's Hall 1836-48, rector of St Martin's (Carfax), Oxford 1839-52, of Tenby, Pembrokeshire 1852-54, of Eaton Bishop, Herefordshire 1854-71.

[13] Towards the end of their first year of study, all Oxford undergraduates took an elementary examination, Responsions (nicknamed 'Little-go'), followed in the third or fourth year by a final public examination (nicknamed 'Great-go'). In 1850 Moderations was introduced, an intermediate examination, taken at the end of the second year.

number of first class men, but I doubt whether it produces as many brilliant men as the old first class did. In my time a candidate for a first class had to present for examination sixteen of the best Latin and Greek authors, eight of each, and to be prepared for examination in any one of them. He had also to take up Logic, ethics, and rhetoric (Aristotle's)[14] and moral Philosophy, either Paley,[15] or Bishop Butler;[16] and to answer general critical papers, and do original Latin and Greek composition. He had also to go through one whole day of viva voce examination and specially in the 39 Articles, the Bible, Prayer book, and Church History. In all he had five days of paper work, and one of viva voce examination. All this was pretty stiff work, and one cannot wonder that many men could not stand it, and would not face it.

As to myself, I took it very coolly, and was not at all nervous. The viva voce part of the matter was the most trying because it was carried on in front of a large number of witnesses. College tutors, friends, enemies, and about 50 or 60 undergraduates. The unfortunate candidates were taken five a day, placed in a large room on one side of a table, with three examiners on the other side, and then called up one by one, and examined in anything the examiners thought fit to ask, especially in Divinity. To answer off-hand orally anything that was asked before so many witnesses, was a very trying thing, and to men who were physically nervous, I am not sure that it was quite a fair system. It favoured impudent men, and depressed humble men far too much. For my own part, I remember being horrified by the questions which were asked of

[14] The philosophical writings of Aristotle (384-322 BC) included the *Organon* (six treatises on logic), *Nicomachean Ethics*, and *Ars Rhetorica*.

[15] William Paley (1743-1805), moral theologian, author of *Natural theology: or, evidences of the existence and attributes of the deity* (London, 1802).

[16] Joseph Butler (1692-1752), moral theologian, bishop of Bristol 1738-50, of Durham 1750-52, author of *The analogy of religion, natural and revealed, to the constitution and course of nature* (London, 1736).

men who were examined before me, and kept wondering what I should have said. When my own turn came, I came off with flying colours, and answered every question put to me with perfect ease, because as luck would have it, they did not ask me anything I did not perfectly know. In fact I received the public thanks of the examiners for my brilliant answers in Moral Philosophy and Divinity which was always esteemed a very great honour.

Singularly enough I was examined in Divinity by Oakley [*sic*], since a pervert, and now a Roman Catholic Priest.[17] Curiously enough I remember to this day how many questions he asked me, about Tradition, the Fathers, the Creeds, Augustine, Pelagius,[18] and other kindred subjects, all showing the direction in which his mind was going at the time. In short my examination made a good deal of stir at the time in the University, and it was commonly thought that Stanley, Highton, and myself were rather ill-used in not being made a small first class by ourselves, as we were so far superior to the rest. But as it was, the examiners made a large first class of eleven, whose names appear according to the Oxford system alphabetically, and the respective merits of men no doubt after a few years were clean forgotten. Some of these eleven are dead, and none of them has

[17] There were four examiners for 'Greats' in November 1837, on divergent theological trajectories:

(i) Thomas Tyssen Bazely (1808-94), fellow of Brasenose College 1831-39, father of the Oxford evangelist, Henry C. B. Bazely (1842-83), who often preached in the open-air at the Martyrs' Memorial;

(ii) Frederick Oakeley (1802-80), fellow of Balliol College 1827-45, a prominent Tractarian who followed John Henry Newman into the Church of Rome and became a missionary priest in Islington;

(iii) William Palmer (1811-79), fellow of Magdalen College 1832-55, pioneer of ecumenism with Eastern Orthodoxy, another Tractarian convert to Rome;

(iv) Henry Bristow Wilson (1803-88), fellow of St John's College 1825-50, a prominent 'broad churchman', later prosecuted for his contribution to *Essays and reviews* (1860).

[18] Augustine of Hippo (354-430), patristic theologian and opponent of the heretic Pelagius.

made much mark in the world, except Dean Stanley, and I suppose I must add, myself.[19]

After the names of the first class came out, I was of course much fêted and congratulated. Nothing succeeds like success. I believe I might have had a studentship at Christ Church,[20] or a Fellowship at Balliol, or Brazenose [sic] at once if I had liked; but I declined every offer to be a candidate for such positions. In my foolishness I thought that I had a very different line of life before me, and left Oxford as soon as I could, never to return.[21] Doubtless, if I had had the least notion of what was going to happen to me within the next four years, I should have accepted a Fellowship, thrown myself into Oxford life, and might very likely have been head of a College at this day.[22] So little do we know what is before us, and so hastily do we choose and decide.

[19] There were actually twelve students placed in the first class, though Ryle and Stanley were listed last, in alphabetical order. The others included Arthur West Haddan (1816-73), ecclesiastical historian, curate to John Henry Newman 1841-42, and contributor to the Library of Anglo-Catholic Theology; Henry Highton (1816-74), master at Rugby School 1841-59, principal of Cheltenham College 1859-62; James Gylby Lonsdale (1816-92), fellow of Balliol College, Oxford 1838-64, professor of classical literature at King's College, London 1863-70; and William Henry Ridley (1816-82), author of many theological tracts.

[20] 'Students' at Christ Church were similar to 'fellows' at other Oxford colleges, although they were not members of the governing body (which comprised the dean and cathedral chapter) until the 1860s.

[21] Ryle did eventually return to Oxford in 1865 as a visiting preacher (see Appendix 4) and regularly thereafter. Although entitled to his MA degree from 1841, he did not take it until 1871, and therefore played no part in the famous controversies of the University Convocation between the 1840s and 1860s when Oxford MAs from across the country frequently returned to the Sheldonian Theatre to cast their votes against Tractarianism and other theological innovations.

[22] Elsewhere Ryle wrote of the spiritual dangers of university life: 'No earthly condition appears to be so deadening to a man's soul as the position of a resident Fellow of a college, and the society of a Common room at Oxford or Cambridge. … How hardly shall resident Fellows of colleges enter the kingdom of God!' J. C. Ryle, 'John Berridge and his ministry; or, England a hundred years ago', *The Family Treasury of Sunday Reading* (March 1867), p. 153; republished in *Christian leaders of the last century* (London, 1869).

As to my Oxford life, I may remark generally, that I came forward very little except at cricket. During the summer time I played incessantly, from 12 o'clock in the morning till dark, every day in the week. During the other terms I did very little beyond taking long walks and playing at billiards, and had very few friends and associates. At nights I idled a great deal of my time away in the rooms of my friends, excepting during the last year before I took my degree. On the whole I can only repeat the opinion I have already expressed, that I suffered a great deal at Oxford for want of some wise friend, or adviser, and that I might have done a great deal better than I did if I had had one. The advice I give to all young men who go to the University is, to be begin [*sic*] from the very first the habit of regular reading, and to beware of dawdling away time in objectless, purposeless, mischievous way[s]. Without hunting, shooting, or driving, or any other expensive amusement, it is astonishing how much time an undergraduate may waste if he does not take care. If I had not come up from Eton with such a thorough knowledge of Latin and Greek, as I picked up there, I should never have done much at Oxford; and if I had only had such a wise and kind tutor as Liddell was, all the time I was there, I believe I might have carried off three times as many honours as I did.

So much for Oxford.

Chapter 6

About the end of the year 1837, my character underwent a thorough & entire change, in consequence of a complete alteration in my views of religion, both as to my belief & practice. This change was so extremely great, & has had such a sweeping influence over the whole of my life ever since, that I think it right that my children should know something about it.

—— Up to the time that I was about 21 years old, I think I had really no true religion at all. I do not mean to say that I did not go to Church, & was not a professed Christian, I had no Infidel or Roman Catholic opinions, but I think I was perfectly careless, thoughtless, ignorant, & indifferent about my soul, & a world to come. I certainly never said my prayers, or read a word of my Bible, from the time I was seven, to the time I was 21. I do not

A page from Ryle's manuscript autobiography.

CHAPTER 6

CONVERSION

About the end of the year 1837, my character underwent a thorough and entire change, in consequence of a complete alteration in my views of religion, both as to my belief and practise [*sic*]. This change was so extremely great, and has had such a sweeping influence over the whole of my life ever since, that I think it right that my children should know something about it.

Up to the time that I was about 21 years old, I think I had really no true religion at all. I do not mean to say that I did not go to Church, and was not a professed Christian. I had no Infidel or Roman Catholic opinions, but I think I was perfectly careless, thoughtless, ignorant, and indifferent about my soul, and a world to come. I certainly never said my prayers, or read a word of my Bible, from the time I was seven, to the time I was 21. I do not say I never had any qualms of conscience on spasmodic occasions, and I quite remember being startled and annoyed, and making a stubborn resistance when I first went to Eton, on being ordered by my fag-master to go and buy things at a shop upon Sunday. But I certainly had no settled religious principles at all, the whole time I was at a private school, at Eton, and the greater part of the time I was at Oxford. In short if I had died before I was 21, if there is such a thing as being lost for ever in hell, which I do not doubt, I certainly should have been lost for ever. I never plunged into the immoralities that many young men do, because I had no natural taste for them.[1] I was never led into drunkenness, gambling, theatre-going, race-going, betting, or other things into which young men run. I really had no taste for them. But I really was altogether without God in the world,[2] and though many thought me a very proper, moral, respectable young man, I was totally unfit to die.

In explanation of this, though not as an excuse, a few things ought to be mentioned. I really had no opportunities or means of grace, so to speak, when I was young. My father's house was respectable, and well-conducted, but there really was not a bit of religion in it. We had no family prayers at all, excepting on Sunday nights and that only occasionally. My father and mother went to Church, and took us on Sundays, but I never could see that the service, or the sermons, were regarded as anything but a mere form. Conversation on Sunday went on much as on a weekday. Letters were read and written, and newspapers read just the same as on weekdays. We dined early and had plum pudding, which was always a joyful thing, and we also had an extremely good hot supper, and sometimes oysters and hot ale. The elder members of the family on Sunday evenings in winter used to read sermons to themselves in separate corners of the room. But they all used to look so unutterably grave and miserable over them, that I privately made up my mind that sermons must be very dull things, and religion must be a very disagreable business.

The plain truth is, that for the first 16 or 17 years of my life, there was no ministry of the gospel at the Churches we attended.

---

[1] Arthur Downer (1847-1943), as an undergraduate at Brasenose College in the late 1860s, joined the Oxford University Tract Distribution Society. On his delivery rounds in New Hinksey, near Oxford, he met Ryle's old college scout (servant) who told him that Ryle 'was full of mischief, as an undergraduate, but not guilty of anything to be ashamed of'. See A. C. Downer, *A century of evangelical religion in Oxford* (London, 1938), pp. 99-100.

[2] Ephesians 2:12.

Macclesfield with only 35,000 people had only two Churches, and
in neither of them was the gospel preached. The clergymen were
wretched high and dry sticks of the old school, and their preaching was not calculated to do good to anybody. I can truly say that
I passed through childhood and boyhood without ever hearing a
single sermon likely to do good to my soul.[3] We had no real religious
friends or relatives and no real Christian ever visited our house. We
never had any really religious books or tracts given us – The only
2 books I can ever remember to have rather affected me when I
was a child, were Bunyan's Pilgrim's Progress, and Mrs Sherwood's
Conversations on the Church Catechism. Each of these books in
some places made me cry[4] – and the utmost teaching our mother
ever gave us, was occasionally hearing us [say] our Catechism,

[3] Later Ryle declared: 'I remember the time when there were only two churches
in Macclesfield. You might have slept as comfortably in those churches under the
sermons of their ministers as you might in your own armchairs, with nothing
to wake you up'; *Abstract of report and speeches at the forty-fifth annual meeting
of the Church Pastoral-Aid Society* (6 May 1880), p. 8 (copy at Cadbury Research
Library, Birmingham). The two churches in question were the 'old' parish church
(St Michael's) and a 'new' Georgian church (Christ Church), built in 1775 by
evangelical industrialist, Charles Roe. The first minister at Christ Church was
David Simpson (1745-99), a prominent evangelical and close friend of John Wesley
and Rowland Hill, but Anglican evangelical ministry in the town ended with his
death. During Ryle's youth, the local clergymen were Lawrence Heapy (c. 1765-
1828), perpetual curate of St Michael's 1800-28; William Cruttenden Cruttenden
(1776-1863), perpetual curate of Christ Church 1811-28 and of St Michael's 1828-47;
and John Steele (c. 1795-1876), perpetual curate of Christ Church 1828-76. Charles
Simeon bought the advowson of St Michael's in 1836, to secure an evangelical
ministry for the burgeoning population, but his patronage trust had to bide their
time until Cruttenden's departure before making an evangelical appointment. By
1880 Ryle was celebrating: 'at this moment in Macclesfield, where fifty years ago
no Gospel was preached, there are seven churches, seven schools, seven Evangelical
incumbents' (*Abstract of report and speeches*, p. 9).
[4] John Bunyan, *The pilgrim's progress from this world, to that which is to come*
(London, 1678); Mary Martha Sherwood, *Conversations on the shorter catechism,
with scripture proofs, for the use of children* (London, 1824). Ryle inserted this paren-
thesis as an afterthought.

which she did in a very grave and rather gloomy manner. As to my
father, the utmost he did was sometimes to show us pictures out of
an old Bible when he was not sleepy on Sunday night. One picture
I specially remember used to be shown us as a great favour, that was
the devil dancing over the ruins of Job's house.[5] And then he used to
tell us this was what we should come to, if we were not good. Poor
dear man! He ought to have known better. My grandfather was a
really good man, but my grandfather died unfortunately when he
was young, and he came into his fortune unfortunately too soon, left
the Wesleyans, and got thrown into the company of men who did
him no good. But I always think that he secretly remembered what
he used to hear when he was a boy, and knew more about religion
than he cared to confess or practise. The plain truth is that neither
in my own family, nor among the Hurts or Arkwrights with whom
I was most mixed up when young can I remember that there was a
whit of what may be called real spiritual religion. There was literally
nothing to make us young people thorough Christians. We never
heard the gospel preached upon Sunday, and vital Christianity was
never brought before us by anybody from the beginning of the year
to the end on a weekday. In my own family, the first governess we
had was a Socinian,[6] and no subsequent governess had any real spirituality about them. We sometimes heard rumours when we were
children, of certain strange clergymen who were called Evangelical,
but we never came across any of them; and were sedulously brought
up to regard them as well-meaning, extravagant, fanatical enthusi-
asts, who carried things a great deal too far in religion. But I always
remembered among these, the names of Harry Grey of Knutsford,[7]

[5] See the engraving from the Ryle Family Bible, p. 65 opposite.

[6] That is, Miss Holland (see above, p. 20, where Ryle calls her a Unitarian).
Socinianism was an anti-Trinitarian heresy, named after the Italian theologian
Faustus Socinus (1539-1604).

[7] Harry Grey (1783-1860), vicar of Knutsford 1809-24; see *The autobiography*

An engraving of the devil dancing over the ruins of Job's house,
from the Ryle Family Bible.

and Phillip [*sic*] Gell of Matlock (at that time),[8] and secretly wondering in my own mind what kind of men they could have been.

As to the religion at private school there was literally none at all, and I really think we were nothing better than little devils. I can find no other words to express my recollection of our utter ungodliness, and boyish immorality. As for Eton, there was nothing to do me any good there. The Sunday sermons preached by the old Fellows in the College Chapel were a perfect farce and a disgrace to the Church of England. While Arnold was stirring young minds at Rugby by his very imperfect teachings of Christianity, we Eton boys were entirely left alone, as to our consciences and souls. I was prepared for Confirmation at Eton by my tutor, afterwards Dr Hawtrey, and confirmed by Kaye, Bishop of Lincoln.[9] But anything more ludicrously deficient than my tutor's preparation and instruction on this solemn occasion, I cannot conceive. At Oxford things were very little better. In College no one cared for our souls any more than if we had been a pack of heathen. The University Sermons which Undergraduates are expected to attend, were at that time so exceedingly dry, and lifeless, that very few of us attended them. Dr Pusey at Christ Church was drawing around him a few

---

of the Rev. Harry Grey, with a short account of his last illness and death, to which is added a selection from his latest letters, and a few of his remarks on Scripture subjects (London, 1861).

[8] Philip Gell (1783-1870), perpetual curate of Matlock 1806-29, of St John's, Derby 1829-46, founder in 1816 of the Matlock Bath Clerical Society of which Ryle was later a member. His son, John Philip Gell (1816-98), was announced in 1853 as the first bishop of Christ Church, New Zealand, but the see was not created until 1856 by which time the appointment had lapsed. Another son, Frederick Gell (1820-1902), was bishop of Madras 1861-99.

[9] John Kaye (1783-1853), master of Christ's College, Cambridge 1814-30, regius professor of divinity at Cambridge 1816-27, bishop of Bristol 1820-27, of Lincoln 1827-53. The bishop of Lincoln was *ex officio* visitor of Eton College. Although confirmed at Eton, Ryle first attended holy communion at St Michael's, Macclesfield; see 'The restoration of the parish church: farewell sermon by the bishop of Liverpool', *Macclesfield Courier and Herald*, 7 May 1898 (supplement).

young men who were seriously disposed, and I really hope did good to some, but as God would have it, I never came under his influence.[10] The only preaching I ever heard at Oxford that ever did me any good, was on Sunday evenings at St Peter's from Denison and Hamilton, who were afterwards successively Bishops of Salisbury.[11] They were much more Evangelical men then, than they afterwards were when they became Bishops, and though their preaching was very defective, I think it did me a little good. To sum up all, I wish my children to remember that for about the first 18 years of my life, neither at home, nor school, nor college, nor among my relatives or friends, had I anything to do good to my soul, or to teach me anything about Jesus Christ. I repeat that I do not mention these things at all as an excuse for my very irreligious condition to the time I was 21. But they do perhaps supply some explanation of it.

The circumstances which led to a complete change in my character were very many and very various, and I think it right to mention them. It was not a sudden immediate change but very gradual. I cannot trace it to any one person, or any one event or thing, but to a singular variety of persons and things. In all of them

[10] Edward Bouverie Pusey (1800-82), regius professor of Hebrew at Oxford University 1828-82, canon of Christ Church, a figurehead of the Tractarian movement which rose to prominence in the mid-1830s. Ryle recalled a private conversation in 1837 with the evangelical leaders, J. B. Sumner (bishop of Chester) and Henry Raikes (chancellor of Chester), in which one of his Oxford undergraduate friends warned of the emerging threat of Tractarianism. But the senior men smiled, 'evidently thinking us young, short-sighted alarmists ... I thought, then, that they did not rightly estimate the extent of the danger. I suspect they both lived to change their minds.' See J. C. Ryle, 'Archbishop Laud and his times', in *Church Association lectures 1869, delivered at St James's Hall, London* (London, 1869), pp. 167-68, reprinted in J. C. Ryle, *Light from old times; or, Protestant facts and men* (London, 1890).

[11] Edward Denison (1801-54), fellow of Merton College, Oxford 1826-37, vicar of St Peter-in-the-East, Oxford 1826-37, bishop of Salisbury 1837-54; Walter Kerr Hamilton (1808-69), fellow of Merton College 1832-42, Denison's curate at St Peter's from 1834, vicar 1837-41, bishop of Salisbury 1854-69.

I believe now the Holy Ghost was working though I did not know it at the time. Some account of these circumstances will not be without interest.

Perhaps one of the first things that ever made me think seriously, and begin to consider the sinfulness of sin, was rebuke for swearing which I had from my friend A. Coote, about a year after I left Eton when I was 19. I do not for a moment mean to say that it did more than startle me and make me think, but certainly it was one of the first things that I can ever remember that made a kind of religious impression upon my soul.[12]

About the same time in my life also, a new Church was opened in Macclesfield, and the gospel was really preached in it first by Mr Wales and afterwards by Mr Burnet.[13] I hardly ever heard either of them at that time, but I certainly remember that the opening of this new Church introduced a new kind of religion into the Church of England, in that part of Cheshire, and was a kind of era. It certainly set many people thinking who never thought before about religion, even though they were not converted, and of these I was one. There was a kind of stir among dry bones, and a great outcry, and kind of persecution was raised, against the attendants of this new Church.[14] This also worked for my good. My natural independance,

[12] For an alternative account of this incident, linked to Algernon Coote's father, see Appendix 4.

[13] The Congregational Chapel at Sutton, in Macclesfield, built in 1822-23, was acquired by the Church of England in 1828 and renamed St George's Church, consecrated by Bishop Sumner of Chester in 1834. The first two incumbents were William Wales (1804-89), perpetual curate of St George's, Macclesfield 1828-32, vicar of All Saints, Northampton 1832-59, rector of Uppingham, Rutland 1859-79; and John Burnet (1800-70), perpetual curate of St George's, Macclesfield 1832-46, vicar of St Peter's, Bradford 1847-70.

[14] Elsewhere Ryle recalled that the arrival of 'a true preacher of the Gospel' at St George's, Macclesfield, led to 'a stirring among the dry bones. Large congregations gathered together, and people were set talking and thinking about the Gospel of Jesus Christ' (*Abstract of report and speeches* (1880), p. 9).

combativeness and love of minorities, and hearty dislike to swimming with the stream, combined to make me think that these new Evangelical preachers who were so sneered at and disliked, were probably right. About the same time too, I was a good deal struck by the great change that took place in the character and opinions of Henry Arkwright, with whom I had been very intimate, and who was reading for orders at that time with Mr Burnet.[15] About the same time too, my sister Susan took up Mr Burnet's opinions, and began to be regarded as one of his adherents. And Evangelical religion in one way or another began to be talked of, and too often ridiculed and abused in our family.[16]

I do not however pretend to say, there was anything like a real change in me at this time. I was not comfortable inwardly, and was rather perplexed by things that I saw and heard, but there was no change in my habits or outward behaviour and I still neither read my Bible, or said my prayers. I continued in this state of mind till I was 21 – for two years – then about Midsummer, a severe illness which I had at Oxford, of inflammation of the chest confined me to bed for some days and brought me very low for some time.[17] That was the time I remember distinctly when I first began to read my Bible, or began to pray. It was at a very curious crisis in my life – it was just about the time that I was taking my degree, and I have a

[15] Ryle's cousin, Henry Arkwright, was five years his senior. After Eton, Arkwright was an undergraduate at Trinity College, Cambridge 1831-35, and was ordained by the bishop of Lichfield and Coventry in October 1835. Within the Church of England there was no formal training for ordination, beyond theological lectures at university, so ordinands often read privately with a clergyman.

[16] Ryle hints that John Burnet's evangelicalism was disapproved of in his family, but his father, John Ryle, gave generously to St George's Church, including donation of a spacious plot of land for a burial ground; see *The British Magazine* (November 1833), p. 585.

[17] The Christ Church Collections Book, with a brief report of Ryle's reading at the end of each term, records for Trinity Term 1837 '*aeger*' (that is, sick); Christ Church Archives, Oxford.

strong recollection that my new views of religion helped me very greatly to go through all my examinations very coolly and quietly. In short, from about Midsummer 1837, till Christmas in the same year, was a turning point in my life.[18] I had many struggles and inward fights, and I am sure I was guilty of many gross inconsistencies.[19] But by the beginning of 1838, I think I was fairly launched as a Christian, and started in a road which I think I have never entirely left from that time to this.

Few can imagine what difficulties I had to contend with. I had no advisers or helpers, and had to fight out everything for myself. I did not even know what books to read to assist me, and made sad blunders for want of someone to tell me what books in religion were good. I remember however that the books which helped me most, if any, were Wilberforce's Practical View of Christianity,[20] Angel [sic] James' Christian Professor,[21] Scott's reply to Bishop Tomline,[22]

---

[18] For analysis of the circumstances and dating of Ryle's conversion, see Appendix 4.

[19] Preaching to undergraduates at New College, Oxford, in May 1880, Ryle declared: 'I can remember the days when I tried hard to be an unbeliever, because religion crossed my path, and I did not like its holy requirements. I was delivered from that pit, I believe, by the grace of God leading me to a book which, of late years, has undeservedly fallen out of sight, I mean "Faber's Difficulties of Infidelity". I read that book, and felt it could not be answered. But the remembrance of the struggle I went through in those days is still fresh in my mind, and I always have a deep feeling of sympathy, when I hear of the mental conflicts of young men.' See J. C. Ryle, *Unbelief a marvel: a thought for the times* (London, 1880), p. 17. George Stanley Faber, *The difficulties of infidelity* (London, 1824; second edition 1833), argued that there were many more intellectual difficulties with philosophical deism than with Christianity.

[20] William Wilberforce, *A practical view of the prevailing religious system of professed Christians, in the higher and middle classes in this country, contrasted with real Christianity* (London, 1797).

[21] John Angell James, *The Christian professor addressed: in a series of counsels and cautions to the members of dissenting churches* (London, 1837).

[22] Thomas Scott, *Remarks on the refutation of Calvinism by George Tomline, D.D., F.R.S., lord bishop of Lincoln, and dean of St Paul's, London* (2 vols, London, 1811).

Newton's Cardiphonia,[23] Milner's Church History,[24] and Bicker-steth's Christian Student.[25] I always feel respect for these books, for I really believe they were useful to me. As to doctrinal system, I never had much trouble. Diligent study of the 39 Articles when I was reading for the Newcastle at Eton, and for my degree at Oxford, undoubtedly did me a great deal of good, and insensibly prepared my mind to receive Evangelical principles, when my heart began first to turn to think of religion.[26] I shall always feel thankful for the Articles and I think it an immense pity that young people are not taught them more systematically than they are. In my own case they enabled me to regard the arguments with which I was often plied by the adversaries of Evangelical religion among my relatives, and especially by my cousin Canon Wood who was horrified at my change, with perfect indifference. I found that whatever they might say they could not prove that my views were not those of the 39 Articles, and therefore of the Church of England – and the whole result was that the more they argued, the more I was convinced that they were wrong and I was right, and the more tightly I clung to my new principles.

[23] John Newton, *Cardiphonia: or, the utterance of the heart: in the course of a real correspondence* (2 vols, London, 1781).

[24] Joseph Milner, with Isaac Milner, *The history of the church of Christ* (5 vols, York, 1794-1809).

[25] Edward Bickersteth, *The Christian student: designed to assist Christians in general in acquiring religious knowledge. With lists of books, adapted to the various classes of society* (London, 1829).

[26] In 1872 Ryle wrote: 'It is a burning shame that the Articles are not made an essential part of the system of every school connected with the Church of England, whether for high or low, for rich or poor. It is a simple fact, that the beginning of any clear doctrinal views I have ever attained myself, was reading up the Articles at Eton, for the Newcastle Scholarship, and attending a lecture at Christ Church, Oxford, on the Articles, by a college tutor. I shall always thank God for what I learned then. Before that time I really knew nothing systematically of Christianity.' J. C. Ryle, *Who is the true churchman? Or, the thirty-nine articles examined* (London, 1872), p. 38, republished in *Knots untied: being plain statements on disputed points in religion, from the standpoint of an evangelical churchman* (London, 1874).

Nothing I believe so firmly roots principles in people's minds, as having to fight for them and defend them. Argument, controversy, and combat are of course very disagreable things and especially about religion. But God overrules them I believe entirely for our good. They help to make us know what we believe, and to develope [*sic*] more distinctly our religious system. What is won dearly, is prized highly, and clung to firmly. I have often observed that young Christians who are brought up in the midst of ease and freedom from controversy hold their opinions very weakly, and hardly know what they believe, or why they believe it. My experience therefore is, that however painful it may be, it is useful for us to have our religious opinions rudely assailed.

It may interest my children to know what were the points in religion by which my opinions at this period of my life became strongly marked, developed, and decided, and what were the principles which came out into strong, clear and distinct relief when this great change came over me. I will try and state them. The leading things which seemed to flash out before my mind as clearly and sharply as the picture on a Photographic plate when the developing liquid is poured over it, were such as these – The extreme sinfulness of sin, and my own personal sinfulness, helplessness, and spiritual need – The entire suitableness of our Lord Jesus Christ, by His sacrifice, substitution and intercession to be the Saviour of a sinner's soul – The overwhelming nature of the soul, as compared to anything else – The absolute necessity of anybody who would be saved being born again, or converted by the Holy Ghost – The indispensable necessity of holiness of life, being the only evidence of a true Christian – The absolute need of coming out from the world and being separate from its vain customs, recreations, and standard of what is right, as well as from its sins – The supremacy of the Bible as the only rule, of what is true in faith, or right in practice, and the need of regularly studying and reading it – The absolute necessity of daily private prayer and communion with God if anyone intends to lead the life of a true Christian – The enormous value of what are called Protestant principles as compared to Romanism – The unspeakable excellence and beauty of the doctrine of the second advent of our Lord and Saviour Jesus Christ – The unutterable folly of supposing that Baptism is Regeneration, or formal going to Church Christianity, or taking the Sacrament a means of wiping away sins, or clergymen to know more of the Bible than other people or to be mediators between God and man, by virtue of their office.

I say that all these principles seemed to grow upon my mind about the winter after I was 21. I am quite certain I knew nothing of them at all before, and I am as certain as I am of my own existence that they rose up within my mind in a distinct though mysterious manner, without the instrumentality of any particular person. Nothing I remember to this day, appeared to me so clear and distinct, as my own sinfulness, Christ's preciousness, the value of the Bible, the absolute necessity of coming out from the world, the need of being born again, and the enormous folly of the whole doctrine of Baptismal Regeneration. All these things, I repeat, seemed to flash upon me like a sunbeam in the winter of 1837, and have stuck in my mind from that time down to this. People may account for such a change as they like, my own belief is, that no rational explanation can be given of it, but that of the Bible; it was what the Bible calls 'conversion', and 'regeneration'. Before that time I was dead in sins, and on the high road to hell, and from that time, I became alive, and had a hope of heaven.[27] And nothing to my mind can account for it, but the free sovereign grace of God. It was the greatest event and change in my life, and has had an influence over the whole of my subsequent character and history.

[27] Ephesians 2:5.

The consequences of this change were very great indeed, and it brought with it many losses as well as gains. As to losses, it caused great uncomfortableness in my own family, and made my position very unpleasant indeed. In fact no one can tell what I had to go through, in hundreds of petty ways. Nor was this all – it made a complete breach between all the friends and all the relatives I ever had before. I mean by this, that it made a kind of gulf between us, and there was a kind of tacit understanding that my tastes, and likings, and habits, had undergone a complete change. All this was extremely disagreable, and few people have an idea [of] the incessant pain and suffering which it occasioned me. It made an awkwardness, and uncomfortableness, and an insensible kind of estrangement which no one can comprehend but those who have gone through it. For a period of time, between three and four years, I had a daily amount of discomfort, and painful feeling that my friends thought me wrong, and I thought them wrong. That they were annoyed at me, yet could not alter me; that I was sorry for them, and could not alter them. It was a miserable state of things. I do not think that people who are brought up in religious families have the smallest idea, of the priviledges [*sic*] they enjoy. Such were my losses.

On the other hand, I must freely admit that the change in my religious character brought me many friends, by a kind of immediate free-masonry, and made me acquainted with many kind-hearted excellent Christians. Among these I may name the following – John Thornycroft,[28] and his two sisters, afterwards Mrs Henry Arkwright,[29] and Mrs Massey[30] – The two Miss Leycesters

[28] Thornycroft Hall, near Macclesfield, was inherited in 1831 by Charles Mytton (1770-1840), rector of Eccleston, who changed his surname by royal licence to Thornycroft. His son, John Thornycroft (1809-84), undergraduate at Brasenose College, Oxford 1827-31, ordained as a clergyman 1833, inherited the estate in 1840.

[29] Henrietta Thornycroft (1804-44), known as Harriet, married in 1838 to Henry Arkwright, died in childbirth.

[30] Sophia Thornycroft (1805-72), married in 1845 to Edward Massie (1805-

of Toft[31] – Mrs Tollemache, then at Tilston;[32] Admiral Harcourt, and his wife;[33] Captain Hope, afterwards Admiral Sir Henry Hope;[34] beside others. All these I gratefully record were great helps to me in one way or another; strengthened me in my principles, encouraged me in my practice, solved many of my difficulties, assisted me by their advice, counselled me in many of my perplexities, and cheered me generally by showing me that I was not quite alone in the world. For the acquaintance I formed at that period of my life with these excellent people, I shall always thank God, for I am sure they did me a great deal of good, and mightily helped my soul. Most of them are now dead, and gone to heaven, and it is a comfortable thought that I hope to see them all again, and to thank them again for what they did for me.

Once more I repeat that the three years and a half following the winter of 1837, and the change which then took place in my

---

93), chaplain of Wadham College, Oxford 1840-45, fellow of University College, Durham 1841-49, curate of Gawsworth, Cheshire 1857-60.

[31] The Leycesters of Toft Hall, near Knutsford, were a prominent Cheshire family. Ralph Leycester (1763-1835), MP for Shaftesbury 1821-30, was survived by three of his children – Ralph Gerard Leycester (1817-51), Ryle's contemporary at Eton, who inherited the Toft estate, and two evangelical daughters, Charlotte Leycester (1799-1893) and Emma Theodosia Leycester (1809-65). They were not the same Miss Leycesters with whom Ryle waltzed at Malvern (see above, p. 54).

[32] Georgina Louisa Tollemache née Best (1809-46) was wife of John Tollemache (1805-90), MP for South Cheshire 1841-68, for West Cheshire 1868-72, created Baron Tollemache in 1876. Tollemache was the largest landowner in Cheshire, including Peckforton Castle (built between 1844 and 1850), and resided for a time at Tilston Lodge. He also owned Helmingham Hall, Suffolk, where he nominated Ryle as rector in 1844 (see below).

[33] Frederick Edward Vernon Harcourt (1790-1883), naval officer, one of the founders of the British Reformation Society, son of Edward Harcourt (1757-1847), archbishop of York. His wife Marcia née Tollemache (1804-68) was John Tollemache's sister.

[34] Henry Hope (1787-1863), naval officer, a British hero for capturing an American frigate in 1815 during the war against the United States of America, naval aide-de-camp to the monarch 1831-41, knighted 1855, promoted to admiral 1858. He was a generous supporter of evangelical missions.

character were a season of very great trial to me, and I trust that no one of my children will ever have to go through the same; but I have no doubt it was all for good. I believe it gave a decision and a thoroughness to my Christianity with all its defects, for which I shall always have reason to thank God.

I think it well to remark by the way, that the Christians whom I recollect in those days strike me as having been much more decided and thorough-going than the Christians I have met of late years. The line of demarcation between religion and irreligion, was much more distinct than it appears to be now. If a Christian was a Christian there was no mistake about it. In fact, it made it more difficult to be a Christian; if once you were one, in some respects it was more easy.

CHAPTER 7

HENBURY HALL

The facts in my life from 1837, to 1841, will form a chapter of themselves. They were many and various, and form a peculiar epoch in my existence.

To begin with, in the year 18[41]37,[1] my father bought the estate of Henbury, about 3 miles to the west of Macclesfield, and we all migrated there from Park House, the place where we were born, to return no more. Hence when I left Oxford Henbury became my home. The change was in all respects a very pleasant one. Park House though an agreable place in itself, was far too near a growing manufacturing town; and we really had no society of what could be called real gentlemen and ladies. Henbury on the contrary was thoroughly in the country, was in itself a very pleasant place, and was surrounded by the residences of gentlemen. Standing out-side the door at Henbury on any fine evening, we could hear the dinner bell ring at Mr Hibbert's of Birtles,[2] at Mr Thornycroft's of

---

[1] The manuscript originally has 1841, rewritten as 1837. Both are incorrect: the Henbury estate was bought in 1835 (see below).

[2] Birtles Hall was built in the 1790s by Robert Hibbert (1750-1835), part of a wealthy mercantile family with slave-estates in Jamaica, and passed to his son, Thomas Hibbert (1788-1879).

Thornycroft,[3] at Mr Davenport's of Capesthorne.[4] Harehill,[5] Alderley Park,[6] Astle,[7] and Joddrell Hall [sic][8] were also all within an easy distance. Hence there was as much society as we liked.

The estate of Henbury was bought by my father of the Joddrells [sic], who bought it formerly of Sir William Meredith, many years ago.[9] The acreage itself was not large, not exceeding 1000 acres, but the house, woods, and water were out of all proportion to the size of the estate, and made it a very desirable residence. No one who sees the place now can have the least idea of what it was, because the best trees have been cut down, and one third of the house taken down. When we lived there, there was much that was extremely beautiful about it both in the grounds, and the distant views from them, and I soon became exceedingly attached to it.

Within a year after I left Oxford, I went to London to read the law, with Mr Christie a conveyancer in Lincoln's Inn.[10] I lodged in

[3] On the Thornycrofts of Thornycroft Hall, see above p. 74.

[4] Capesthorne Hall, inherited in 1837 by Edward Davies Davenport, who had married Ryle's cousin, Caroline Hurt.

[5] Hare Hill Hall, home of William Hibbert (1759-1844), younger brother of Robert Hibbert of Birtles.

[6] Alderley Park, home of Sir John Stanley, baronet (1766-1850), raised to the peerage in 1839 as Baron Stanley of Alderley. His brother, Edward Stanley (1779-1849), bishop of Norwich 1837-49, was Ryle's diocesan bishop in Suffolk.

[7] Astle Hall was sold by Thomas Parker in 1833 to his nephew Henry Dixon (1794-1838), army officer, and then passed to Dixon's younger brother, John Dixon (1799-1873), army officer.

[8] Jodrell Hall, home of Egerton Leigh (1779-1865), whose son Egerton Leigh (1815-76) was MP for Cheshire 1873-76 and an antiquarian of Cheshire dialects, ballads and folklore.

[9] Sir William Meredith (c. 1724-90), baronet, MP for Wigan 1754-61, for Liverpool 1761-80, lord of the admiralty 1765-66, campaigned for the abolition of clerical subscription to the Thirty-Nine Articles of Religion. An extravagant lifestyle and mounting debts forced him to sell the family estate of Henbury to John Bower Jodrell in 1779 for £24,000. John Ryle bought the estate from John William Jodrell in 1835 for £54,000 (for deeds of conveyance, see Cheshire Record Office, Henbury Hall papers, D5678/25 and D6568/13).

[10] Jonathan Henry Christie (1793-1876), killed the radical journalist John Scott in a pistol duel in February 1821, barrister at Lincoln's Inn from 1824.

Pall Mall, and lived chiefly at the Oxford and Cambridge Club.[11] I did not read the law more than half a year, and left it because I was not well. London did not suit me, and the plain truth is that I really had not recovered the exertion of taking my degree in Oxford, when I went to settle there. I have reason to believe that I did pretty well in law, and it is curious to think what I might have come to, if I had been able to continue in it. But God ordered it differently, and would not allow me to be a lawyer. While I was in London, I was a regular attendant at Baptist Noel's Chapel, in Bedford Row, and became a regular communicant there.[12] I saw very few people in London during the six months, made no friends, felt very much isolated, and did not like it at all; in fact I got off the rails with my old worldly companions, and had not yet got their place supplied by others of a better kind.[13]

When I gave up the law, and returned to Cheshire, I went into my father's bank at Macclesfield, and continued in it until we left

[11] The Oxford and Cambridge Club (founded 1830), a gentlemen's club for members of Oxford and Cambridge Universities, opened its clubhouse on Pall Mall in 1838.

[12] Baptist Wriothesley Noel (1799-1873), Anglican minister of St John's Chapel, Bedford Row, Holborn (an evangelical proprietary chapel) 1827-48, seceded from the Church of England because of its connection with the state, and became minister of John Street Baptist Chapel, Holborn 1849-69.

[13] When speaking in the 1880s on the experience of Daniel in Babylon, Ryle recalled: 'When I had finished my college education I was launched in London by myself, and went there to read law. It was only a comparatively small circumstance which prevented me from following the law altogether; however, when I was there I remember that I thought that it was impossible for a man to serve Christ and be a true Christian when living in a great wicked and corrupt city such as London, the metropolis of the world, is sure to be. The thought came across my mind – How can a man serve and follow Christ and be able to resist the world, the flesh, and the devil, when he does not know any one, and there is no one to help him or encourage him? How can it be done? Is it possible? The doubt came across my mind again and again, and it was only by the great mercy of God that I was able to resist it.' J. C. Ryle, 'Daniel the prophet', in *The rule of life and conduct: discourses delivered before the members of the Liverpool Young Men's Christian Association* (Liverpool, 1889), p. 8.

Cheshire in 1841. I was never a member of the firm, and knew nothing of its inward affairs. My only business was to sign notes, use my eyes, and learn as much as I could generally of banking business. Happily I never got any further.

Beside this I became a County Magistrate and attended regularly every week the Sessions in Macclesfield, where there was always plenty of Magisterial business going on. Beside this I became Captain of the Macclesfield troop of the Cheshire Yeomanry, a regiment comprising 10 troops and 600 men, and containing amongst its officers all the leading men in Cheshire.[14] Of course this brought me forward very much in the County, and made me acquainted with almost everybody in it. The principal business it entailed, was the going to Liverpool every year for 10 days for exercise and inspection. Beside this however, to keep up the troop in a state of efficiency caused a world of trouble and vexation. Beside this too in this four years I began to come forward frequently on public occasions as a speaker. At religious meetings from my recognized character as a religious man, and at political meetings from my position as my father's eldest son, and from my supposed ability as a speaker.

During these four years, it may easily be supposed that as a young man who had taken his degree, and as eldest son and heir to a large fortune, I was often asked out in my own county, for two or three nights at a time to many different houses in Cheshire. My father and mother liked my going, but to myself I must confess it was a very great bore. In summer I used occasionally to go to Derbyshire for cricket matches. Sometimes to Frank Hurt at Yeldersley,[15]

[14] Ryle was commissioned as a captain in the King's Regiment of Cheshire Yeomanry Cavalry (Macclesfield Troop) on 15 September 1836, while still an Oxford undergraduate, and resigned in October 1841 (see *London Gazette*, 27 September 1836, p. 1676; 29 October 1841, p. 2653).

[15] Ryle's second cousin, Francis Hurt junior (1803-61), son of Francis and Elizabeth Hurt of Alderwasley Hall. He lived in the 1830s with his wife and children at Yeldersley near Ashbourne, and inherited the Alderwasley estate in 1854.

sometimes to Henry Wilmot's at Chaddesden,[16] and sometimes to my friend Charlton at Morley,[17] and afterwards at Chilwell, and took part in all sorts of gentlemen's matches in Derbyshire, Staffordshire, Nottinghamshire, and Leicestershire. Cricket in fact was the one amusement which I never gave up after I became a Christian, so long as I was a layman, and I do not think I ever got any harm from it. Cricket however was wonderfully little thought of in those days, compared to what it is now.

My whole life during these four years was a somewhat singular one. I had the constant uncomfortable feeling that on account of my religious opinions I was only a tolerated person in my own family and somewhat alienated and estranged from all my old friendships among my relatives. However none of these things moved me, and I held on my way supported by the conviction that however disagreable my position might be, I was right.

One summer of these four years, I went to Beaumaris with the whole of our family, and saw a good deal of North Wales. Another summer during the same period I went to Scotland with Thornycroft and saw a great deal of that country. Another summer I went to London for about six weeks, and saw a good deal of the Hurts of Alderwasley, as old Mr Hurt was then Member for Derbyshire, and was then residing in Town.[18] I distinctly remember old Lady Keats being exceedingly cross, because I would not go with her and the girls to Drury Lane Theatre.[19]

During this period of four years two men who both became my brothers-[in]-law afterwards, both came to reside at Macclesfield

[16] Sir Henry Sacheverell Wilmot (1801-72) of Chaddesden Hall, near Derby.

[17] Morley, near Derby, where Thomas Charlton's brother-in-law, Samuel Fox (1801-70), was curate and rector.

[18] Francis Hurt senior, of Alderwasley Hall, was MP for Derbyshire South 1837-41.

[19] Francis Hurt's sister, Mary Keats (1779-1855), was widow of Admiral Sir Richard Goodwin Keats (1757-1834), governor of Newfoundland 1813-16. The 'girls' were the Hurts' unmarried daughters.

in order to read for orders with John Burnet, the only Evangelical clergyman in Macclesfield, after[wards] Vicar of Bradford. It was some help to me having them near me but of course it was only an alleviation of my position.[20]

I used to read a great deal in those times, and my reading took the line of such subjects, as would prepare me for going into Parliament, which I saw clearly was a thing likely to come before many years. I believe I might have come in even then for the borough of Macclesfield, but I declined to come forward, from a deep sense of my own inexperience, and from a natural backwardness which has clung to me all the days of my life.[21] As it was, it was just as well that I did not come forward, but my reading was not thrown away.

It may seem strange at first sight that I did not marry at this period of my life, between 21 and 25. I have reason to think my father and mother would have made no objection, and would have been rather glad if I had, but somehow I felt no disposition to it. I was desperately afraid of women, and did not understand them, and I did not feel that I could make a wife happy. Moreover I had a singularly exalted opinion of women, and a very strong feeling I was not good enough for them. Above all I saw extremely few women that I fancied at all, although there were some that I liked better than others, but I could not fancy for a moment that anyone would marry me if I had asked them. Not least, there were several women whom my father and mother would have liked me to marry,

[20] Two of Ryle's old Eton friends later became his brothers-in-law – William Courthope graduated from Christ Church, Oxford, in January 1838 and was ordained at Chester in February 1839; Algernon Coote graduated from Brasenose College, Oxford, in June 1840 and was ordained at Chester in February 1841.

[21] Ryle's father announced in May 1837 his intention not to stand again for election as MP for Macclesfield (see 'To the parliamentary electors of the borough of Macclesfield', *Macclesfield Courier and Herald*, 20 May 1837). The subsequent general election in July / August 1837 (triggered by the death of William IV) took place while Ryle was still at Oxford. The next general election was in June / July 1841.

I know, but unfortunately, I did not feel the smallest inclination to marry them. The plain truth is that I was very ignorant about women's characters in those days. I had not studied the subject. If I had known them then as well as I do now, I have not the least doubt I should have been married between 21 and 25. However I have no doubt it was all overruled by God for good that I should remain single and it certainly would have probably given an entirely different direction to the whole of my life, if I had married at that time. My father was ready to give me 800£ a year and a house, and I have reason to think now there was more than one person who would have said 'yes' if I had asked them. But I did nothing about it, and did not feel disposed to stir.

On a calm retrospect of this period of my life, I can see clearly that it was a period in which God was fitting me for after work in a way which I did not know. I was training much and learning much, in passing through a school of experience which afterwards was very useful to me. I often think now, that my chief fault in those days was, that I was too much wrapped in my own daily spiritual conflict, and my own daily difficulties. I did not sufficiently aim at works of active usefulness to the souls of others. At the same time it is but fair to say that it would be hard to point out what work there was that I could have done. Teaching, preaching, visitation, evangelization, and such like works were out of the question. As long as I lived under my father's roof they would have been strongly objected to, and would have given great offence. The utmost that I could ever do, was to read family prayers in the housekeeper's room before breakfast every morning to my sisters, the housekeeper and all the maids, but not to the men-servants. My father and mother tolerated this but never attended it. This, and an occasional visit to a sick person, or a dying person was all the work that I could do. And I have sometimes thought since that I ought to have done more, but

I really do not know how it could have been done. It seems to me as if God intended that period of my life to be one for patient learning, and not for active doing. Looking back at the period, I often think it was a strange thing, that I did not go into Parliament, or marry, as doubtless I might have done. In either case I should have become comparatively independant, and might have done many things which I could not do while living under my father's roof, but as I have already said, my natural caution and diffidence and fear of not doing justice to what I undertook, kept me back from going into Parliament, while on the other hand my extreme fear of women and thorough misunderstanding of women's character made me shrink from the idea of marrying. Both these things I have no doubt were overruled by wiser hands than my own.

I have omitted to mention that during this period of my life, I first heard McNeile, and formed an opinion of him which I never altered from that time.[22] I heard him when I used to visit Henry Arkwright when he was curate at Everton shortly after he married Harriet Thornycroft.[23]

[22] Hugh McNeile (1795-1879), a prominent evangelical preacher and controversialist, perpetual curate of St Jude's, Liverpool 1834-48, of St Paul's, Princes Park, Liverpool 1848-67, canon of Chester 1860-68, dean of Ripon 1868-75.

[23] That is, 1838-39.

CHAPTER 8

BANKRUPTCY

I n the month of June 1841, I had to pass through the greatest change in a temporal point of view, that I ever went through in my life. The change to which I refer was my father's complete ruin by bankruptcy and the consequent alteration of all my position and prospects in life. It would be difficult to convey any adequate idea of the entire alteration which this entailed on my whole existence. Much has been said in late years about the consequence of Overend and Gurney's bankruptcy,[1] but no change which took place in consequence of that bankruptcy could possibly exceed the change that took place in the circumstances of my father's family, and especially in myself.

The facts of the bankruptcy are as simple as possible.[2] The London bankers with whom my father's bank corresponded stopped payment. My father's two banks at Manchester and Macclesfield immediately stopped payment also, and every single acre and penny my father possessed had to be given up to meet the demands of the

---

[1] Overend, Gurney and Co., a prominent London bank, collapsed in 1866.

[2] For the bankruptcy proceedings against Daintry, Ryle and Co., see *Macclesfield Courier and Herald*, 7 August, 4 September, 2 and 16 October, 13 November, 4 December 1841. For a narrative summary, see 'Rise and fall of Daintry, Ryle, and Co.', in Leo H. Grindon, *Manchester banks and bankers: historical, biographical, and anecdotal* (Manchester, 1877), pp. 111-17.

Five pound note from Macclesfield and Cheshire Bank (Daintry, Ryle and Co.), signed by J. C. Ryle. It dates from 18 February 1841, shortly before the bank collapsed.

creditors. My father had never had the forethought to entail any portion of his property, and the consequence was that everything was swept clean away,[3] except my mother's settlement property of 30,000£ settled upon her entirely at her marriage which of course could not be touched.

The original cause[s] of the Bankruptcy are soon explained. My father when he was quite a young man advanced nearly 200,000£ to his brothers-in-law the Woods to enable them to start a cotton manufacturing business in Macclesfield. This business never answered, and the Woods persuaded him to open a bank in Manchester in addition to the one he already had in Macclesfield, in order to retrieve his fortunes. This was an enormous mistake. His Manchester bank might have answered, if it had been properly conducted. Indeed when it started his credit was said to be as high in Manchester as that of Jones, Lloyd [*sic*],[4] and it might have been a source of immense wealth if it had been properly managed. But it never was properly managed. My father and his partner Mr Daintry never went near it hardly, and left its affairs in the hands of a manager. The funds of the bank were squandered away by hundreds of thousands, by loans and advances to people who ought never to have had a penny, and the result was my father's ruin. The Macclesfield bank on the contrary always prospered, and even when it was dragged down with the Manchester bank, the Macclesfield bank paid 13/6 in the pound.[5] The plain truth is my father was never fit to be a banker. He was too easy, too good natured, and too careless about details. The three great principles which a banker should never forget are these: first, He must be able to say 'No'; secondly, He must never change his mind; thirdly, He must never waste good

---

[3] By entailment the succession of an estate is permanently fixed.

[4] Jones, Loyd and Co., a prominent Manchester bank.

[5] That is, of 20 shillings in the pound, Macclesfield creditors were paid 13 shillings and 6 pence.

money in trying to recover bad debts – or to speak briefly, he must never send good money after bad. In all these points, my father was totally and entirely deficient, and never ought to have been a banker at all. The whole result was, that he lost everything that his father had left him, including property which had probably doubled since his father's death. His income at the time of the bankruptcy must have been I think at least 15,000 a year and the property swallowed up must have been between half a million and 600,000£.

I myself had no part whatever in the matter, and knew nothing whatever of the internal affairs of the bank. I suspected my father was uncomfortable for two or three years before the crash came, but he never told me anything about it. I certainly cannot say I was surprised as much as some, and simply because I was a Christian I had long been vexed with the Sabbath-breaking which took place in connexion with the bank, visits to partners, and consultations about worldly business, and the like, and I had a strong presentiment that such a complete departure from my Grandfather's godly ways, would sooner or later be severely chastised.[6]

It would perhaps be impossible to give any correct idea of the stunning violence of the blow, which the ruin inflicted upon us all. We got up one summer's morning, with all the world before us as usual, and went to bed that same evening completely and entirely ruined. The immediate consequences were bitter and painful in the extreme, and humiliating to the utmost degree. The creditors

---

[6] Elsewhere Ryle warned against 'private Sabbath desecration': 'I mean that reckless, thoughtless, secular way of spending Sunday, which every one who looks round him must know is common. How many make the Lord's Day a day for visiting their friends and giving dinner parties – a day for looking over their accounts and making up their books – a day for going journies [sic] and quietly transacting worldly business – a day for reading newspapers or new novels – a day for writing letters or talking politics and idle gossip – a day in short for anything rather than the things of God. Now all this sort of thing is wrong, decidedly wrong.' J. C. Ryle, *Keep it holy! A tract on the Sabbath day* (Ipswich, 1856), p. 21, republished in *Knots untied* (1874).

naturally, rightly and justly, seized everything and we children were left with nothing but our own personal property and our clothes. I luckily had two horses to sell, which I sold, and my yeomanry uniform, sword, saddlery, accoutrements, and so on which old Colonel Egerton kindly bought for 100£ as a matter of charity.[7] And the proceeds of these horses, uniform etc., about 250£, were all with which I had to start in the world. This for a young man of 25, about to go into Parliament, a County magistrate, and commonly reckoned to be a son and heir with 1,5,00 [*sic*][8] a year was rather a fall.

The whole circumstances of that time were just about as painful as could be conceived, and at the end of 32 years, are as vividly before my mind as if they were yesterday. Our household of course was immediately broken up; men-servants, butler, under butler, footman, coachman, groom, housekeeper, housemaids, in fact a whole staff, one of whom had been with us 30 years, another 25, two more 20, etc., etc., were all at once dismissed, and paid off, and dispersed to the four winds. Henbury was sold over our heads with every single thing in it.[9] My mother went to my Uncle Edward Hurt's in London. My sister Susan had already been married a year to Mr Daniel. My sister Caroline was married about that very time to Mr Courthope. My sister Emma went to Colonel Thornhill's in the New Forest.[10] My brother Frederic was on the Continent

[7] Wilbraham Egerton (1781-1856) of Tatton Park, near Knutsford, MP for Cheshire 1812-31, lieutenant-colonel from 1831 in the Cheshire Yeomanry Cavalry.

[8] The two commas suggest some confusion about whether 1,500 or 15,000 is meant – presumably the latter.

[9] The assignees permitted only a few personal items to escape the sale: 'There were at Henbury a few family portraits which were of little comparative value except to the parties, and a few little ornaments, which properly belonged to Mr Ryle's daughters, and Mrs Ryle.' See 'Daintry and Ryle's bankruptcy', *Macclesfield Courier and Herald*, 13 November 1841. Thomas Marsland (1776-1854), MP for Stockport 1831-41, bought the Henbury estate (for deeds of conveyance, see Cheshire Record Office, Henbury Hall papers, D5678/26 and D6568/14).

[10] William Thornhill (*c.* 1786-1850), army officer, deputy-surveyor of the New Forest 1837-50, lived at New Park, Lyndhurst, with his sister Mary Bache Thornhill.

reading for his degree. My father had to stay at Henbury in order
to assist the assignees in the winding up his affairs. My sister Mary
Anne and I remained with him, to put together the few things that
belonged to us, and my sisters and brother, and to be some company to my father. This occupied about six weeks, I think perhaps
about the most trying and miserable six weeks I ever passed in my
life. The place was in full beauty in Midsummer but everything
seemed as deserted and silent as a tomb. Morning, noon, and night,
the crushing feeling was upon me, that we were about to leave the
place never to come back again. Worst of all, I had the constant
recollection that all the plans of my life were broken up at the age
of 25 and that I was going to leave my father's house without the
least idea what was going to happen, where I was going to live,
or what I was going to do. No one, in fact, but God has the least
idea what I suffered in those times. From sun-rise to sun-set everything one saw and touched gave one pain, and to this day no one
has the least conception how much I went through, and what a
serious effect it had upon my constitution. The plain fact was there
[was] no one of the family whom it touched more than it did me.
My father and mother were no longer young, and in the down hill
of life. My sisters and brother of course never expected to live at
Henbury, and naturally never thought of it as their home after a
certain time.[11] I on the contrary as an eldest son, 25, with all the
world before me, lost everything, and saw the whole future of my
life turned upside down, and thrown into confusion. In short if I
had not been a Christian at this time, I do not know if I should not
have committed suicide. As it was everybody said, how beautifully
I behaved, how resigned I was, what an example of contentment I
was. Never was there a more complete mistake. God alone knows

---

Colonel Thornhill was Frederic Ryle's godfather (see Appendix 1).

[11] As the eldest son, Ryle expected to inherit Henbury Hall.

how the iron entered into my soul, and how my whole frame, body, mind, and spirit reeled, and was shaken to the foundation, under the blow of my father's ruin. Of course I know it was all right, but I am quite certain that it inflicted a wound both on my body and mind of which I feel the effects most heavily at this day, and shall feel if I live to a hundred. To suppose that people don't feel things because they do not scream, and yell and fill the air with their cries, is simple nonsense.

My children and those who read these lines, may perhaps be surprised at the strength of this language. But the plain truth is that it is a very unthinking world, and I do not believe I ever met with any person who appears to realize or understand what I went through in 1841. To be suddenly turned out of a place which on many accounts I liked extremely, and where I had hoped to live and die; to be sent away from a county in which I was born, and had attained some position; to have the whole of my plans and prospects in life in a moment smashed, broken up, and shivered to pieces; to be compelled in a moment to give up all my intentions, and to choose some entirely new line of life; to be reduced from thorough independance in money matters, to such thorough poverty, that I have often hardly known how to get on; to be obliged at the age of 25 to descend from the terms of equality in which I had lived with scores of people, and feel I was no longer able to live on terms of equality with them, and was in fact not much better off than their butlers and footmen; and have the deep abiding conviction the best thing I could do was to get away from every one I had ever seen, and never see them any more; to bury myself in some distant part of England, and try to form new acquaintances and new friendships and drop the old ones; all this was a very bitter cup to drink. Unthinking people I repeat did not see much in it, and fancied it was no trial to me at all. For myself I can only say, that the wound it inflicted in me both in body and mind was nearly mortal, and I do not think there has been a single day in my life for 32 years, that I have not remembered the pain and humiliation of having to leave Henbury. During that 32 years I have lived in many houses, been in many homes, and been in many positions. I have always tried to make the best of them and to be cheerful in every circumstance, but nothing has ever made me forget my sudden violent expulsion from Cheshire in 1841.

Taking a moral and spiritual view of it, I have not the least doubt it was all for the best. If my father's affairs had prospered, and I had never been ruined, my life of course would have been a very different one. I should probably have gone into Parliament very soon, and it is impossible to say what the effect of this might have been upon my soul. I should have formed different connexions, and moved in an entirely different circle. I should never have been a clergyman, never have preached a sermon, written a tract, or a book. Perhaps I might not have been as useful and might have made shipwreck in spiritual things. So I do not mean to say at all, that I wish it to have been different to what it was. All I mean to say is, that I was deeply wounded by my reverses, suffered deeply under them, and I do not think I have ever recovered in body or mind from the effect of them. Trees are too old to transplant at 25, and I was too old ever to take root again in any other part of the world. And ever since I left Cheshire, I have never felt at home, but a sojourner, and a dweller in a lodging, and I never expect to feel anything else as long as I live.

I and my eldest sister finally left Henbury, in August 1841, never to return to the house any more. Nothing I think touched me that morning so much as the face of my old Lyme mastiff 'Caesar', who was excessively fond of me. I remember he looked at me as if he did not understand it, and could not see why he might not go with me too. Poor dog, for a whole month afterwards he made his way into the house every morning as soon as the doors were opened, and went up to my room; there he lay at the door from morning till night, and nothing would induce him to stir. When the sun went down in the evening, and it became dusk, he used to get up, smell at the bottom of the door, whine piteously and walk down stairs. This he repeated every day for a month. At last it affected the few people who were left in the house so much that they could stand it no longer, and he was given to my friend Thornycroft. There he was not understood, was treated as a dog, and not as a friend, became soured in temper, was always chained up, and did not live very long. I never saw him again.

I went for a few days to my Uncle Edward Hurt's in London, and then went to Colonel Thornhill's in the New Forest, Hampshire. He was Deputy Ranger [*sic*] of the New Forest, and lived there with his sister Miss Thornhill. There [*sic*] were old friends of my father and mother, and were of the few who did not forget us in our adversity, but who were extremely kind. Their house in fact was a home to me, and to my eldest sister for three months, until I could take breath and make up my mind what to do. The place suited me well, at that particular crisis of my life. It was in the middle of the New Forest, surrounded by woods and commons on every side; and I had plenty of time for communion with my own heart alone, considering what it was best to do, and trying to adapt myself to my new circumstances. Nothing could be kinder than Colonel and Miss Thornhill, in fact they showed far more feeling, than many nearer blood relatives. But kindness alone could do but little for me, and certainly it was one of the most miserable times in my life; and I felt like Jacob, 'all these things are against me'.[12] My mother was in London all this time with my Uncle Edward Hurt, very ill.

[12] Genesis 42:36.

My father was up in Cheshire, assisting in winding up the affairs of the estate. Finally he and my mother settled down at Anglesey near Gosport, directly opposite Ryde, about the end of the year 1841, and there lived for the rest of their lives.[13]

I always distinctly remember in concluding this most painful chapter in my life's history, how few were actively helpful or friendly in all the circle of those I had known and loved. Most seemed silent, shocked, and stunned, and neither said nor did anything at all. The Rock House Arkwrights were all very kind, and feeling, and old Peter Arkwright especially was very helpful to my father; so also was my Uncle Edward Hurt; in little ways too my cousins were very kind to me. So also was John Thornycroft, William Courthope, Coote, and one or two more whom I could name. But I felt strongly that they all regarded it as a complete shipwreck, and desperate case, and for the rest of my life I must swim for myself, and should have no one to help me. And as I expected, so it has been. Thus ends the blackest chapter in my life.

In closing the chapter I wish to make one general remark. I believe that God never expects us to feel no suffering or pain when it pleases Him to visit us with affliction. There are great mistakes upon this point. Submission to God's will is perfectly compatible with intense and keen suffering under the chastisements of that will. Troubles in fact not felt, are no troubles at all. To feel trouble deeply, and yet submit to it patiently is that which is required of a

[13] Anglesey (also known as Anglesey Ville) was a fashionable Georgian development in the parish of Alverstoke, on the Hampshire coast, built in the 1820s and named in honour of Henry Paget, first marquess of Anglesey (1768-1854). The Ryles lived at No. 1 Eastern Terrace, an eight-bedroom property, with their unmarried daughters Emma and Mary Anne. After John Ryle's death in 1862, the contents were auctioned off, including a library of about 1,000 volumes; a harp designed by Johann Andreas Stumpff; valuable oil paintings by Domenichino, Carlo Maratta, Jan Miense Molenaer, Bartolomé Murillo and Andrea Sacchi; rare engravings; 240 bottles of fine wine; and mahogany furniture (see *Hampshire Telegraph*, 14 June 1862).

Christian. A man may submit cheerfully to a severe surgical operation, in the full belief that it is his duty to submit, and that the
operation is the likeliest way to secure health. But it does not follow
that he does not feel the operation most keenly, even at the moment
that he is most submissive. It was a wise saying of holy Baxter when
he was dying of a painful disease, 'I groan, but I do not grumble.'[14] I
ask my children and anyone who may read this Autobiography not
to forget this. I ask them to remember that I felt most acutely my
father's ruin, my exile from Cheshire with the destruction of all my
worldly prospects, and I have never ceased to feel them from that
day to this; but I would have them know, that I was submissive to
God's will, and had a firm and deep conviction that all was right,
though I could not see it, and feel it at the time.

[14] Ryle quoted the same saying from Richard Baxter (1615-91) in his *Expository
thoughts on the gospels: for family and private use: St John volume II* (London, 1869),
p. 144 (comment on John 8:51), *St John volume III* (London, 1873), p. 520 (comment
on John 21:18). The source is not known, but another of Ryle's favourite puritans,
Thomas Brooks (1608-80), tells of a godly army officer shot in battle who said, as a
bullet was cut from his wound, 'though I groan, yet I bless God I do not grumble.'
See Thomas Brooks, *The silent soul* (London, 1660), p. 46; reprinted in *The works of
Thomas Brooks* (Banner of Truth Trust edition, 6 vols, Edinburgh, 1980), vol. 1, p.
306. The same anecdote is found in Philip Goodwin, *The evangelicall communicant
in the eucharisticall sacrament* (London, 1649), p. 482.

Engraving of Exbury Chapel, in the New Forest, where Ryle was curate for two years, December 1841 to November 1843.

CHAPTER 9

EXBURY

I n December 1841, I was ordained as a Minister of Christ, as curate of Exbury in the Parish of Fawley, in the New Forest, Hampshire.[1] The Bishop who ordained me was Sumner, Bishop of Winchester,[2] and the Rector whose curate I became was the Revd W. Gibson, Rector of Fawley, famous for marrying in succession two cousins; first the daughter of the Bishop of Chester; secondly the daughter of the Bishop of Winchester.[3] The circumstances

---

[1] Fawley was a wealthy living, worth £1179 a year, in the gift of the bishop of Winchester. The previous incumbent was Thomas de Grey, fourth Baron Walsingham (1778-1839), rector of Fawley 1806-39, archdeacon of Surrey 1814-39, appointed by his father-in-law, Brownlow North (1741-1820), bishop of Winchester 1781-1820, a famous nepotist.

[2] Ryle was ordained deacon on Sunday, 12 December 1841, in the chapel at Farnham Castle, Surrey, residence of Charles Richard Sumner (1790-1874), bishop of Winchester 1827-69. He was ordained priest (that is, presbyter) in the same place on Sunday, 11 December 1842.

[3] William Gibson (1804-62), rector of St Bridget's, Chester 1832-39, of Fawley with Exbury, Hampshire 1839-62. He was married first in 1831 to Eliza Maria Sumner (1808-36), daughter of John Bird Sumner; and second in 1837 to her cousin, Louisanna Sumner (1817-99), daughter of Charles Sumner, who appointed Gibson to Fawley. Amongst the Gibson children born at Fawley rectory were Arthur Sumner Gibson (1844-1927), who in 1871 played for England against Scotland in the first rugby international; Edgar Charles Sumner Gibson (1848-1924), bishop of Gloucester 1905-22; and Alan George Sumner Gibson (1856-1922), coadjutor bishop of Cape Town 1894-1906.

under which I took orders were somewhat remarkable. I never had any particular desire to become a clergyman, and those who fancied than [*sic*] my self-will, and natural tastes were gratified by it, were totally and entirely mistaken. I became a clergyman because I felt shut up to it, and saw no other course of life open to me.

It is almost needless to say, that during the autumn I spent at Colonel Thornhill's at New Park in the New Forest, I was greatly exercised in my mind as to what was my duty. I saw clearly that I must take up some profession which would support me – and the question was, what profession it was my duty to take up. This was a point that occasioned me great anxiety. My father and mother, and all my family were perfectly helpless in the matter; they could suggest nothing, except that they hoped something would turn up. What this something was I do not believe any of them knew, and I soon saw that I must act for myself. What to choose, was an extremely anxious and soul-worrying question. I particularly dis-liked the idea of becoming a clergyman having a strong feeling that God did not intend all Christian men to become clergymen. But what to do besides was extremely difficult to discover. The idea of being a private tutor was loathsome to me.[4] The learned professions as a rule afforded no means of maintenance for several years. Civil engineering, or the law would not have brought in a penny for 4 or 5 years. Every avenue seemed shut against me. I was nibbled at about being private secretary to Gladstone, but I felt no confidence in him, and would not have it for a moment.[5] In short I could see

---

[4] In late 1841, Ryle was invited by John Bird Sumner (1780-1862), bishop of Chester 1828-48, archbishop of Canterbury 1848-62, to become private tutor to his son, Robert George Moncrieff Sumner (1824-85), who was preparing for Oxford University, but Ryle declined. See Mary Bache Thornhill to Sir Robert Peel, 4 June 1843, British Library, MS Add. 40529, fos 371-72.

[5] When Sir Robert Peel formed his new government, in September 1841, Gladstone was appointed vice-president of the board of trade. In later years Ryle frequently clashed with Gladstone, and in private called him 'a terrible infliction on this country' (Fitzgerald, *Herbert Edward Ryle*, p. 132).

nothing whatever before me but to become a clergyman because that brought me in some income at once. Unexpectedly I received the offer of Mr Gibson's curacy, and made up my mind to accept it, though with a very heavy heart. My father and mother neither of them liked it at all, though they were quite unable to suggest to me anything better, and the whole result was that I was ordained by the Bishop of Winchester at Farnham Castle in December 1841.

My first and only Rector was Mr Gibson, Rector of Fawley in the New Forest, a large Rural Parish, occupying the triangular piece of the New Forest which lies between Southampton water and the Solent. In this Parish I undertook the charge of the chapel of ease and district of Exbury, containing about 700 people. I lived at a small house in the hamlet of Langley half way between Exbury Church and Fawley. It was a very dreary, desolate, solitary place. This house and 100£ a year formed my stipend, but as I had to pay the preceding curate 16£ a year for the furniture, my real remuneration consisted of 84£ and a house.[6]

My work was to take the entire charge of a district about 3 miles wide by 2 miles broad. To do two full duties on Sunday in Exbury Church alone; to hold two cottage lectures every week on Wednesday and Thursday, in small crowded cottages reeking with peat smoke. To teach and superintend the Sunday school upon Sunday, and to keep up regular Pastoral visitation all the week. The district was a very wild and dreary one, containing many commons and heaths. A great number of the people had been brought up as poachers and smugglers, and were totally unaccustomed to being looked after or spoken to about their souls. A yatchting [*sic*] man of large fortune, and indifferent character lived close by Exbury Church.[7] A

---

[6] The previous curate, William Buckley Graham (1817-42), was ordained at Durham in July 1840 before moving to Langley in early 1841. After Ryle took charge of Exbury, Graham continued as curate of Fawley until his death in August 1842.

[7] Probably a reference to Henry Reveley Mitford (1804-83) of Exbury House,

coast guard station with a Lieutenant of the Navy, married, lived on the sea shore;[8] with these exceptions there was not a single gentleman in the Parish. Drunkenness and sin of every kind abounded; the Baptists and the Methodists had carried off many of the people. The climate was very unhealthy and relaxing,[9] from the quantity of undrained land. Snakes, vipers and adders, were frequently to be met with, when walking about during summer and autumn, and sometimes even crept into the houses. I never knew a time when cases of ague, scarlet fever, and typhus were not to be found in the district.

My house was reputed to be haunted, and was a very long mile from the Church. I had one maid-servant, one boy, one dog, one cat, and one pig. The maid-servant turned out a bad character and though she was 30 years of age she married the boy who was in his 17th year. The cat died of bleeding of the nose, the pig died of string-halt and was buried in a waste piece of ground on the other side of the road, and a grave made over it.[10] The maid-servant for some time received the money to pay the bills for me, but did not pay them. The Rector went away to Malta, and was absent the greater part of the time that I was there.[11] My sisters Mary Anne and Emma occasionally called to see me for a week or two. Mr Drummond of Cadlands, who married the Duke of Rutland's sister, came

who inherited the estate in 1827 from his grandfather William Mitford (1744-1827), historian of ancient Greece and MP. Henry Mitford was great-grandfather of the notorious Mitford sisters.

[8] George Frederick Westbrook (c. 1799-1878), naval officer, lived on the coast at Lepe.

[9] That is, enervating.

[10] String-halt is a muscular disease, usually affecting horses, causing spasmodic contractions of the hind legs.

[11] William Gibson was absent from Fawley between October 1842 and July 1843, during which period his parochial duties were taken by Thomas Burne Lancaster (1805-81).

to see me and showed me some civility.[12] The yatchting [*sic*] man quarrelled with me, and complained of me to the Bishop because I spoke against cricket matches late on Saturday night. Altogether my residence of 2 years as curate was not a very cheerful one.

As to work I took it as a matter of course, and just went right on with it from day to day and week to week, after a manner in which I see no curates work in the present day. My regular work was to prepare two written sermons for every Sunday, prepare two extempore expository lectures for every Wednesday and Thursday, and to visit, confer with, and distribute tracts among 60 families every week. As to the tracts, I used to get them from the Religious Tract Society at Southampton and stitch them up myself in brown paper.[13] I was too poor to give any away. I was obliged to lend and change them. I kept a regular account of all the families in the parish and was in every house in the parish at least once a month. Occasionally I lectured at the Coast guard station, but it was hard work; it was a mile and a half from my house, and 11 o'clock in the morning was the only time that suited them, as the men were generally up all night rowing guard on the coast, and had to sleep great part of the day.

As for doctoring the people's bodies, of course I could do little, being a young and ignorant man; also being unmarried I did not pretend to touch the women's cases, and left them alone. I cured many ague cases by administering first an Emetic of Ipecac and Syrup, and afterwards Tincture of Quinine. I saved many lives in Scarlet fever by supplying them with large quantities of very strong

---

[12] Andrew Robert Drummond (1794-1865) of Cadland House near Exbury, partner in Drummonds Bank. He was nephew of the evangelical prime minister, Spencer Perceval, who was assassinated in 1812. In 1822 Drummond married Lady Elizabeth Frederica Manners (1801-86), daughter of the fifth duke of Rutland.

[13] The Religious Tract Society, founded in 1799, was an interdenominational society which aimed to disseminate evangelical literature in the form of tracts, books and magazines. The headquarters were in London, but it had depots across the country.

Beef Tea, made from concentrated essence, and insisted on their swallowing it, as long as their throats kept open. However 10 per cent of the population had the Scarlet fever and 10 per cent died, chiefly children. As to Typhus fever I had no faith in anything but Port Wine, and this I used to give away in great quantities with great effect. As to Viper bites, I used to recommend Olive Oil, but I think the people had more faith in ointment made of viper fat. To give an idea of the number of vipers there were, I mention the simple fact that the lord of the manor paid 2d per head for every viper that was killed. The parish clerk had the payment of this money, and I have frequently seen half a dozen large vipers lying dead at his door in one day which had been brought there by those that had killed them.

As to spiritual matters, I was not at Exbury long enough, to speak very decidedly about them. Two years is not long enough for a minister to know what people really are. The Church was soon filled upon Sundays, and the people seemed interested, but the farmers were a rich, dull, stupid set of people, and the labourers had been in the habit of living in such utter neglect of God that it seemed as if nothing could turn them. However I worked away, and when I left at the end of two years, I think the people were sorry.[14]

I had very little rest or relaxation while I was curate of Exbury. About once in three months I used to go for a few days to see my father at Anglesey. Occasionally I paid a visit to Colonel Thornhill, and once I went to Rock House for a fortnight; with these exceptions I was always at work. Mr Drummond of Cadlands occasionally asked me to dine as a matter of civility but my opinions were evidently too strong for them, and when upon two separate occasions I declined to play at cards, or to dance with a large party after dinner, I do not think the curate of Exbury was very acceptable

---

[14] For Ryle's 'parting words' to his Exbury parishioners, see Appendix 5.

there. A Mr Bradley of Leamington who had a yacht in Southampton water and a pretty house in Fawley showed me much kindness. His wife used regularly to attend Exbury Church.[15] On the whole however I think I was regarded as an enthusiastic, fanatical, mad dog of whom most people were afraid. My Rector when he resided was extremely kind to me, and I really believe esteemed me very highly. But he was eaten up with caution, and seemed to me so afraid of doing wrong, that he would hardly do right. I have little doubt too that he was much under the influence of his wife, who always thought me a dangerous, extreme man, and struck me as very much inclined to keep in with everybody.

As for the people I think they would have done anything for me, and I believe the influence I had among them was very great indeed. On one occasion I remember being called in late at night to interfere in a pitched battle between two men on a green not far from my house, where two or three hundred men were present. I remember walking into the ring suddenly between the two combatants and insisting on their stopping. I told them they might do what they liked to me, but I would not have it if I could prevent it; the result was that the fight was stopped. The affair made a great noise at the time, and I do not know that perhaps I acted prudently, but I remember having no feeling about it at the moment but to stop the fight whatever the consequences might be. At any rate it taught me what power one man has against a multitude as long as he has right on his side.

I resigned the curacy of Exbury in November 1843, in consequence of ill health.[16] The district thoroughly disagreed with me and

[15] On Henry and Mary Bradley, see below.
[16] In June 1843, Mary Thornhill lobbied the prime minister, Sir Robert Peel, on Ryle's behalf in hope of securing for him a crown living, perhaps Eckington in Derbyshire which was then vacant. She described him as 'a young friend of mine … of rare abilities, and high attainments; & moreover, a most promising, & exceedingly zealous Clergyman. … He is not only excellent in character, but one

was really very unhealthy; it was well called Faux-lieu, or Fawley.[17] Constant headache, indigestion, and disturbance of the heart then began, and have been my plagues, and have disturbed me ever since that time, and will probably be my end at last; they always remind me of my curacy at Exbury.

On resigning the curacy, the Bishop of Winchester at once offered me the Rectory of St Thomas', Winchester – population 3000, income 100£ and a house.[18] This I at once accepted upon the understanding that I was not to go to it till December. I then went to Leamington, and put myself under Jephson and was there a month.[19] Being as poor as a rat, I was too happy to avail myself of the kindness of the Bradleys, who lived at Leamington, and insisted on my staying with them for a whole month. Mr Bradley had inherited an immense fortune from an ironmaster uncle, and was a kind of weak, good-natured man, with a great deal of good in him, who kept greyhounds, and staghounds, and was a kind of horse and dog man; but he had a great respect for me and would have done anything for me. Mrs Bradley had a good deal more religion than her husband, and neither cared for horses or dogs, and I had a great respect for her. But considering that she had only been ladies' maid to Mr Bradley's sisters, and he had run away with her, it would be vain to say that she was a thorough lady. Nevertheless considering

---

of the best & *most useful* Preachers I ever heard; & tho' an Oxford Man, is entirely opposed to Puseyism, & the Oxford Tract Divinity … I have known him from his Childhood … I love him as tho' he were my own Son.' See Thornhill to Peel, 4 June 1843, British Library, MS Add. 40529, fos 371-72. She described Exbury as 'a damp unwholesome situation'; Thornhill to Peel, 15 November 1843, MS Add. 40536, fo. 36.

[17] 'Faux lieu' is 'false place'.

[18] The bishop's mandate for Ryle's induction to St Thomas's, Winchester, is dated 1 November 1843 (Hampshire Record Office, 35M48/6/1410). According to the *Clergy List*, the living was valued at £145 a year, better than Ryle remembered.

[19] Henry Jephson (1798-1878), fashionable and prosperous physician at Leamington Spa, where patients went to 'take the waters'. He retired in 1848 after going blind.

all things, she was a wonderful person.[20]

Altogether these were miserable times for me. I never felt so utterly what a miserable thing it is, for a man to be first rich, and then poor. People who have never known what it is to be anything but poor cannot understand it in the least. Those only who have been rich till they were 25, and then became poor can comprehend what endless mortifications your circumstances entail upon you and you are compelled to submit to them.

Jephson was very kind to me, would never take a fee excepting every other visit, and would never allow me to come to him excepting twice a week. Blue pill to begin with for a week, and then Sulphuric Acid, dandelion, Leamington waters, and frequent cold shower baths were his medical treatment.[21] For diet, he allowed neither wine, beer, or spirits, in fact nothing but water. No vegetables, pastry, puddings, or cheese, or fruit. Nothing in short but mutton chops at 1.30 and again at 6.30, with a little boiled rice, and not a drop of anything to drink from 6.30 till bedtime. This system he ordered me to keep up for a year, and longer if I could. I think it did me good at the time. I saw few people at Leamington that I knew,[22] and indeed shrunk from society as much as possible.

[20] Henry Bradley (1802-70) was son of John Bradley (1769-1816), a prosperous ironmaster at Stourbridge, whose wealth he inherited. He joined the family firm in partnership with his uncle, James Foster (1786-1853), but retired in 1837 for a life of leisure, especially hunting and yachting. The bulk of Foster's substantial fortune was bequeathed to Bradley's cousin, William Orme Foster (1814-99), ironmaster and MP for South Staffordshire 1857-68. See further, Norman Mutton, 'The Foster family: a study of a Midland industrial dynasty 1786-1899' (PhD thesis, University of London, 1974). Bradley was married in 1828 to Mary Stokes, who had been ladies' maid to his four sisters.

[21] Blue pill was a medicine containing mercury, used as a purgative. To further cleanse the bowels, Jephson's favourite prescription was Epsom salt, iron sulphate, liquid dandelion, and diluted sulphuric acid, mixed with water; see 'Jephson's tonic aperient mixture', in Thomas J. Graham, *Modern domestic medicine: a popular treatise* (11th edition, London, 1853), p. 128.

[22] Ryle does not mention his evangelical friends in Leamington, William Marsh

I felt that I was a poor, penniless, despicable beggar, and I shrunk as much as possible from the society of rich people. My visit to Leamington did its appointed work, and I was glad to get away.

(1775-1864), perpetual curate of St Mary's, Leamington 1839-51, or his daughter Catherine Marsh (1818-1912), philanthropist and author. They had been bereaved in August 1843 of William Marsh's second wife.

CHAPTER 10

WINCHESTER

I began my work as Rector of St Thomas', Winchester, early in December 1843, in a very cold pinching winter. My establishment was just the same as it was at Exbury, and indeed in a pecuniary view, I was not a bit better off than I was there. With this exception, that by the kindness of two or three of my father's friends, I was able to furnish my house. My house though small was a tolerably good one, and there I settled down, with one elderly woman servant, and one boy, and a dog.

I found the Parish had been under the charge of an Evangelical Clergyman for some years, and so far as I could make out he seemed to have done but little, and when I called upon him, found him in slippers and dressing gown in the middle of the day.[1] I made up my mind that I should find that little had been done in the parish. The only person who seemed to be doing any good, was a Miss Althea

---

[1] The two previous incumbents of St Thomas's, Winchester, were Charles Drake Isdell (*c.* 1774-1841), rector 1800-41, and William Douglas Veitch (1801-84), rector 1841-43. Veitch was an evangelical, but had only been rector of St Thomas's for two years before his appointment in September 1843 as principal of the short-lived Hebrew College, Jerusalem (a missionary training college for Jewish converts to Christianity) and examining chaplain to Michael Solomon Alexander (1799-1845), first Anglican bishop in Jerusalem 1841-45. Veitch was afterwards vicar of St Saviour's, Paddington 1862-73.

Engraving of St Thomas's Church, Winchester, where Ryle was rector for a few months, November 1843 to February 1844. The church was demolished and rebuilt soon after his departure.

Wickham, a middle aged lady, who really appeared to be the life of the whole place, and the mainspring of anything good.[2] The Church was a very old tumble down kind of building, holding about 600 people, with old fashioned pews, and all its arrangements of the same character. The congregation was a tolerable average town congregation, containing a good many respectable people, and a good many poor. My work consisted of two full services, morning and evening, on Sundays. I found there had been no lecture in the weekday and I at once began an Expository lecture in the Infant school room which was very well attended. Beside this there was plenty of visiting every day of the week, and a district visitors society to superintend.

The whole place struck me as being in a very dead state like most Cathedral towns. The influence of the Cathedral body was as bad as possible, and worldliness reigned supreme in the Close.[3] Keble lived close by Winchester, and had an influence in the place.[4] Moberly, now Bishop of Salisbury, was head master of Winchester school and necessarily had considerable power.[5] Wilberforce, now Bishop of Winchester, was a Canon of the Cathedral, and had an influence too.[6] There were about six parishes in Winchester besides my own,

[2] Althea Maria Wickham (1805-75), daughter of a prominent Winchester surgeon, William Nicholas Wickham (1769-1846). Her nephew, Edward Charles Wickham (1834-1910), was headmaster of Wellington College 1873-93 and dean of Lincoln 1894-1910.

[3] The dean of Winchester from 1840 to 1872 was Thomas Garnier (1776-1873). His sons included the evangelical clergymen Thomas Garnier junior (1809-63), dean of Lincoln, and John Garnier (1813-38), curate of St Ebbe's, Oxford.

[4] John Keble (1792-1866), leading Tractarian, professor of poetry at Oxford University 1831-41, vicar of Hursley, near Winchester, 1836-66.

[5] George Moberly (1803-85), headmaster of Winchester College 1835-66, bishop of Salisbury 1869-85, a close friend of Keble.

[6] Ryle took a poor view of Winchester cathedral, and the baneful influence of men like Samuel Wilberforce. However, amongst the eleven canons in the cathedral chapter, were several senior evangelicals, including William Dealtry (1775-1847), chancellor of Winchester 1830-45, archdeacon of Surrey 1845-47; Charles

most of them occupied by unsatisfactory incumbents, while those who were Evangelical, were cautious proper men, who were dreadfully afraid of going into extremes. On the whole I saw that my position was not a very pleasant one. However, the story of my life has been such, that I really cared nothing for anyone's opinion, and resolved not to consider one jot who was offended and who was not offended by anything I did. I saw no one whose opinion I cared for in the place, and I resolved to ask nobody's counsel, in the work of my Parish, or as to the matter or manner of my preaching, but just to do what I thought the Lord Jesus Christ would like, and not to care one jot for the face of man.

With these feelings I set to work tooth and nail, and having youth on my side, nothing but my work to think about, no wife or children at home, I soon filled my church to suffocation, and turned the Parish upside down. Of course it must be remembered that I was a new broom, and therefore swept very clean. Moreover, I was an unmarried young man of 27, tall and thin and in good favour with the Bishop. No sensible person therefore will wonder, that preaching as I did however youthful and inexperienced, with a great deal of fire and energy, after a manner that was quite new at Winchester, I made a very great sensation. How long it would have gone on I cannot say, but I did not stay at Winchester more than five months.[7] During that time I believe and hope much good was done, though I did not know it at the time.

James Hoare (1781-1865), archdeacon of Winchester 1829-47, of Surrey 1847-65; Gerard Thomas Noel (1782-1851), vicar of Romsey 1840-51, brother of Baptist Noel; and William Wilson (1783-1873), vicar of Holy Rood, Southampton 1824-73.

[7] Ryle was inducted at Helmingham on 14 February 1844 (see *Bury and Norwich Post*, 10 July 1844), and the bishop's mandate for the induction of his successor at St Thomas's, Winchester, is dated 5 March 1844 (Hampshire Record Office, 35M48/6/1424), so if Ryle began in December 1843 he was there for less than three months. He was followed by a fellow evangelical, George James Cubitt (1804-55), former East India Company chaplain, rector of St Thomas's, Winchester 1844-55.

It was anything but a happy period of my life in many ways; though comparatively well and strong, I was obliged to be very careful about my health and to live by rule. I was up every morning long before it was light, and used to walk three miles before breakfast in the dark on the Andover road. I had a strong sense of the extreme awkwardness of my position, as a young unmarried Rector in a town like Winchester, but I saw no remedy for it; and this made me constantly anxious, and uncomfortable. I was quite determined that nothing should ever induce me to think of being married, unless I had a clear 500£ a year, as well as a house to offer to anyone. Actuated by this feeling, I studiously avoided all young ladies in company, and gave no one the slightest pretext for ever spreading a report about me. This however was a very unnatural and uncomfortable state of things. What the end would have been I cannot tell had I remained longer at Winchester, but my residence there was cut short by the unexpected offer of the Rectory of Helmingham in Suffolk.[8]

I left Winchester very unwillingly. I did not like Suffolk particularly, and did not at all fancy going to a small parish of 300 people, and leaving behind me a town part with 3000, where apparently I was very acceptable. But what could I do? As usual, at that time of my life, poverty was my constraining motive. I did not see how I could stay on at Winchester without being a burden to my father. Helmingham on the other hand, was a clear 500£ a year, and of

---

[8] Edmund Bellman (*c.* 1771-1843), rector of Helmingham from 1812, died on 26 December 1843. The living was in the patronage of the lord chancellor, but John Tollemache (the major landowner in the village) petitioned Sir Robert Peel because he was alarmed to discover that 'strenuous efforts' were being made to procure the living for a clergyman of 'Ultra High Church principles' who would do 'mischief' in the parish. Peel praised Tollemache as 'a very good friend of the Government', and the lord chancellor granted Tollemache permission to nominate a rector of his own choosing. See Peel to Baron Lyndhurst (lord chancellor), 7 January 1844, British Library, MS Add. 40442, fos 173-74; Tollemache to Peel, 8 January 1844, MS Add. 40538, fos 146-47.

course made me comparatively independant.[9] This turned the scale, and I decided to go. Nevertheless I must honestly say that I went very unwillingly, and of all the steps I ever took in my life, to this day I feel doubts whether the move was right or not. I sometimes think that it was want of faith to go, and I ought to have stayed. Certain it is, that as soon as my going was announced, the inhabitants of St Thomas', Winchester, offered to raise my income to 300£ a year, and to build a new Church.[10] This of course would not do at all, and the offer came too late.

I have often wondered since that time what would [have] happened to me if I had remained in Winchester. I have reason to believe that the Bishop had determined to promote me, and had intended to send me to St Mary's, Southampton.[11] The whole course of my life would undoubtedly have been altered, but whether it would have been good or bad for me I cannot tell. But I have never ceased to wonder whether I was right or not. I only know that my chief desire was to set my father free from any charge on my account, and so I tried to hope it was all right. But I think the doubt afflicted my spirits heavily for two or three years.

I ought to mention that during my residence at Winchester, Bishop Wilberforce then Canon of Winchester showed me great

[9] In the *Clergy List* for 1844 the living of Helmingham was valued at £461 per annum, with a population of 284.

[10] During 1844 there was an architectural competition to design a new church for St Thomas's parish, and the old medieval church was pulled down in 1845.

[11] The prestigious and wealthy parish of St Mary's, Southampton, was in the patronage of the bishop of Winchester. The rector from 1797 to 1850 was Francis North (1772-1861), sixth earl of Guilford, son of Bishop Brownlow North, and nephew of Lord North (1732-92, prime minister 1770-82). Francis North also held other rich livings, as rector of Alresford, Hampshire, and master of St Cross Hospital, Winchester, the inspiration for Anthony Trollope's *The Warden* (1855). If Bishop Sumner did intend to promote Ryle to St Mary's, Southampton, it was presumably as one of the two curates who looked after the parish in North's permanent absence – a previous curate, John William Reeves (*c.* 1816-62), left in March 1844.

kindness, occasionally attended my Church, and tried hard to get an influence over me. This lasted till one memorable night when he had a long discussion with me till a late hour about Baptismal Regeneration, in which he tried hard to turn me from Evangelical views on that subject; but it had no effect.

My preaching at Winchester on Sundays, consisted entirely of written Sermons, of a style that I should not care to preach now, because they were far too florid, and far less simple and direct than I afterwards learned to preach. Moreover there was not that amount of deep thought, and matter, and illustration in them which I afterwards found valuable. Nevertheless, they were all thoroughly Evangelical, and being well composed, and read with a good deal of earnestness and fire, I have no doubt they sounded very fine and very effective, but I should not care to preach them now.

Helmingham Hall, home of the Tollemache family, photographed by Henrietta Ryle in 1864.

CHAPTER 11

HELMINGHAM

I began my work at Helmingham, at Easter 1844. I found the Rectory in a most dilapidated condition,[1] and by the desire of Mr and Mrs Tollemache I lived at Helmingham Hall for a year, while my house was being repaired and put in order. This was a bad arrangement, and I did not quite like it myself at the time; but there really seemed no help for it, and I was driven to consent by sheer necessity. Poverty as usual, settled the question. Mr Tollemache was then in Parliament, and was down at Helmingham for a few weeks at Easter, and a fortnight at Whitsuntide, and for August and September when Parliament broke up. It was his practice to have his house continually full of visitors, chiefly from London and Cheshire, and a continual stream was passing through the house of individuals and families who came for a week or ten days; seldom less than 18 or 20 sat down to dinner, and were mounted or put in carriages at 2 o'clock every afternoon. With all these people of course I became intimately acquainted especially as I had to act as Chaplain every morning and evening, to a congregation of at least 40 persons. On Sundays too, I had always to preach to a good many

[1] The previous incumbent of Helmingham, Edmund Bellman, had served concurrently from 1801 to 1843 as rector of Pettaugh, a neighbouring parish, which may have been his preferred residence.

people in a high position, so that my place was not a very easy one. About the people that came there as visitors I will only remark that they were very various. Some were very worldly, one or two about the loosest, most unsatisfactory characters that I ever met. Some of them however were very thorough Christians chiefly brought there by Mrs Tollemache's influence, and I shall always feel thankful for the friendships and acquaintances I then made. Among these latter I particularly mention Admiral Harcourt and his family,[2] Admiral Sir Henry Hope, Captain George Hope and his family,[3] the Marquis of Cholmondely [*sic*] and his wife, Lord Henry Cholmondely [*sic*] and his family,[4] Robert Bevan,[5] the late Bishop Villiers,[6] the Longs,[7] the Sheppards,[8] Archbishop Sumner, beside a good many others. Most of them are now dead and gone to heaven. I always thank God that I met them, and think their acquaintance did me good. I feel nevertheless it was an unfortunate thing that I was obliged to stay

[2] In June 1845, Ryle buried Frederick and Marcia Vernon Harcourt's infant daughter, Louisa Charlotte, in the Tollemache family vault at Helmingham.

[3] George Hope (1801-93), naval officer, younger brother of Admiral Sir Henry Hope and brother-in-law of John Tollemache. He was married first to Charlotte Tollemache (*c.* 1815-37), with whom he had two daughters, and second to Katherine Frances Leveson-Gower (*c.* 1806-80).

[4] George Cholmondeley, second marquess of Cholmondeley (1792-1870), and his brother, Henry Cholmondeley, third marquess (1800-84), were both prominent patrons and supporters of evangelical societies. Their estates were Cholmondeley Castle in Cheshire and Houghton Hall in Norfolk.

[5] Robert Cooper Lee Bevan (1809-90), partner of the private banking firm, Barclay, Bevan and Co. (known as Barclays Bank), evangelical philanthropist.

[6] Henry Montagu Villiers (1813-61), rector of St George's, Bloomsbury 1841-56, bishop of Carlisle 1856-60, of Durham 1860-61.

[7] William Long (1802-75) of Hurts Hall, Saxmundham, Suffolk, and his wife Eleonora Charlotte Montagu Long (1812-1900), sister of Sir Edward Poore, baronet.

[8] John George Sheppard (1824-82) of High House, Campsea Ashe, Suffolk, and his wife Harriet Anne Sheppard (c. 1824-1903), daughter of Sir Thomas Tyrwhitt-Jones, baronet. Sheppard was high sheriff of Suffolk for 1859-60 and appointed Ryle as his chaplain (see *Ipswich Journal*, 19 March 1859). Long and Sheppard were both prominent supporters of evangelical societies in Suffolk.

in Helmingham Hall so long, but as I said before I know not how I could have avoided it.

My work in the Parish was very simple. There was neither village street, public house, beer shop, or shop of any description. To visit 300 people within a mile of the Church on every side was of course very easy work, and I had plenty of spare time.[9] There was no school, excepting a dame school at the lodge, and that was kept entirely in Mrs Tollemache's hands.[10] The Church was in perfect order having been restored and put in complete repair and highly decorated, when I first came.[11] The people were not interesting, living in fact in a state of servile subjection to Mr Tollemache, who owned every acre of the Parish, and not daring to have an opinion of their own about anything. There were however a few Christians among them of a very high order, especially old Mr and Mrs Nixon, the gardener and caretaker of the house.[12] But there really was little to be done, and I had more time for reading and thinking and storing my mind than I have ever had before, or since.

[9] At the Church Pastoral Aid Society in 1850, Ryle compared his small rural parish with the large urban districts of Liverpool, Manchester, and Birmingham: 'I cannot speak of the thousands committed to my charge, for I have but 300 people in my parish, and have every thing calculated to make the work of spiritual superintendence smooth. ... I find in the spiritual cure of the 300 souls committed to my charge, not, perhaps, sufficient, but, certainly, much work to be done; sin, I find, is always rife among them, and with all the preaching and all the care I can bestow, many still, I am sorry to say, remain unconverted; and, notwithstanding all the appliances of tracts, preaching, and teaching, many yet remain without God and without Christ.' (*Abstract of report and speeches at the fifteenth annual meeting of the Church Pastoral-Aid Society* (7 May 1850), p. 16; copy at Cadbury Research Library, Birmingham.)

[10] A new school was opened in Helmingham in 1854, at John Tollemache's expense.

[11] Ryle decorated the walls of Helmingham church with numerous Bible texts, painted in large letters, such as 'By grace are ye saved through faith' and (above the pulpit) 'Woe is unto me if I preach not the Gospel'.

[12] Thomas Nixon (*c.* 1781-1852), gardener at Helmingham Hall, and his wife, Martha Nixon (*c.* 1792-1873), housekeeper. They were both originally from Cheshire, and followed the Tollemaches to Suffolk.

After a few months I became acquainted with most of the Evangelical men in the county, and commenced the habit of going about speaking and preaching in all directions, which I kept up for 17 years, with little intermission.[13] I must honestly confess, that I never felt drawn to be socially intimate with any of the clergy, or their families. I soon got the reputation which I never lost of being unsocial, distant, reserved and indisposed to encourage friendship, and not at home anywhere except in the pulpit or on the platform. The plain honest truth is, that I did not feel at all drawn towards the families of the clergy whom I saw. Their wives and daughters did not attract me in any way, and being a young unmarried man I fought very shy of them. In fact it was a common practice of mine for many years to preach a sermon or make a speech, and afterwards go away without sitting down to tea or supper, often driving 15 or even 20 miles home. This of course made me immensely unpopular in many quarters, but I could not help it. As a rule I did not at all like the women whom I met, and I was determined not to be dragged into being intimate with any of them. The only way I saw to avoid this was to abstain from eating and drinking with them. As to visiting people or holding social intercourse with them for dining, or calling, or any other purpose except preaching, or speaking, it was a sort of thing I never dreamed of for a moment. I was ready to go anywhere, or any distance to speak or preach for Christ and never refused however great the inconvenience or fatigue; but if people asked me to dine or tea, or sup or lunch, or spend a day or two with them merely for society's sake I always flatly declined, and said I had no time for it. Of course this made me immensely unpopular, and people thought me a very odd person. Looking back now after an interval of five and twenty years, I am not prepared to

---

[13] That is, throughout Ryle's ministry in Helmingham from 1844 to 1861, before his move to Stradbroke.

defend all that I did, and I believe I did some harm, but after all, I think it was a fault on the right side; and my observation is that the young clergy are far more apt to err in the opposite direction. Besides I must honestly confess, things might have been different if I had seen any chance of meeting really attractive Christian ladies by going in society, but these I soon found were not to be met with and I came to the conclusion that what was called social intercourse was an immense waste of time. I fear that I did not adorn my profession much by this conduct, and caused my religion to be evil spoken of as wanting in courtesy, but these were the principles on which I acted, and the extreme to which I ran was at all events not a common one.

In the summer of 1844 [*sic*],[14] I moved into Helmingham Rectory, the house having been completely repaired and furnished. My establishment was not a very large one, consisting of a cook and housemaid and one labouring man out of doors who acted as gardener and looked after my one horse. As usual I found the place in a miserable condition, and it cost me a great deal of money to put it into decent order, which I was ill able to afford, again as on 50 other occasions, I found the misery of being a poor man.

In October 1844 [*sic*], I was married to Matilda, eldest daughter of J. P. Plumptre Esquire, M.P. for East Kent, I being 28, and she being 22.[15] About this and my other two marriages, I take occasion to make the general remark that the great thing I always desired to

[14] Ryle means the summer of 1845. In this chapter, almost all his dates are incorrect by one year.

[15] Ryle was married on 29 October 1845 to Matilda Charlotte Louisa Plumptre (1824-48) at Nonington parish church, Kent. Ryle was 29 and his bride 21. Matilda's father was John Pemberton Plumptre (1791-1864), MP for East Kent 1832-52, who was converted about 1815 through the ministry of Daniel Wilson at St John's, Bedford Row. For a tribute to Plumptre's evangelical faith, see Richard Glover, *The friend of Jesus, and the inheritor of the promises: two sermons on the occasion of the death of John Pemberton Plumptre, Esq ... preached in Christ Church, Dover, Sunday, January 17th, 1864* (London, 1864).

Helmingham Rectory, photographed by Henrietta Ryle in 1862.

find was, a woman who was a real Christian, who was a real lady, and who was not a fool. Whether I was successful or not, others must judge better than I can, but I can call God to witness these were the three points I always kept steadily in view.

We lived very quietly at Helmingham Rectory, and indeed could not afford to live in any other way, as we had barely 700£ a year between us. I do not think marriage made any difference in my manner of living, and I just worked and preached on as I had done before. My connexion with the Plumptres had certainly one great advantage, that it made me acquainted with several very Christian people of a gentler kind than I had seen before among men and I shall always be thankful for having known my wife's father, and his two brothers Charles and Western.[16] They were certainly three of the most amiable men I ever knew.

In May 1845 [*sic*], my only brother Frederic died, after a very short illness. He had been curate to Samuel Wilberforce, Rector of Alverstoke, now Bishop of Winchester, for two or three years, and I fear that this made a little coolness between us.[17] Not that there was ever anything like a quarrel or division, though it was impossible to feel thorough oneness of heart when we manifestly did not agree as to what was true religion. His death was a very heavy blow to my mother, and I think she never got over it, as he was her favourite in the family. My brother was a singularly amiable, good tempered, gentle creature, without any strong points in his character and a person who I suppose never had an enemy, without making any

[16] Charles Thomas Plumptre (1799-1862), rector of Wickhambreaux, Kent 1842-62; and Henry Western Plumptre (1803-63), rector of Eastwood, Nottinghamshire 1827-63.

[17] Frederic Ryle was ordained on 15 December 1844 as assistant curate of Alverstoke, with a stipend of £80 a year (bishop's licence, Hampshire Record Office, 21M65/E6/13/525). Samuel Wilberforce gave him responsibility for the chapel of ease at Elson (consecrated in August 1845), but Ryle died on 1 May 1846, aged 25, from peritonitis caused by constipation.

great mark in the world. We all felt his death very much; it was the first gap in our family. He was buried at the little district Church of Elson, of which he was the first incumbent. The grave is at the east end of the Churchyard under the Chancel window; and my mother lies by him.

I may here remark, that Wilberforce's influence about this period upon all my family at Anglesey, with the exception of my father, was extremely pernicious. They naturally looked up to him as Rector of the Parish; he was extremely fascinating in private society, and pleasant in intercourse; he was in the prime of life and in the fulness of intellectual vigour; preaching with great ability, stirring up everything round him, and turning a neglected parish upside down. I repeat, with the exception of my father, all my family seemed fairly carried away by him. To me when I visited Anglesey he was always studiously civil, though I suspect he secretly disliked me, and was a little bit afraid of me as a dangerous person; but he always asked me to preach whenever I was there on a Sunday, and tried to talk as if we were all agreed in the main. Trench, now Archbishop of Dublin,[18] and Burrows of Christ Church, Albany Street, London,[19] were then his curates, and worked with him might and main. Manning his brother-in-law, and Henry Wilberforce his brother (both of them since perverts to Rome) were frequently visitors at his house; and the whole result was such a tide and currant [sic] in the direction of Ritualism as fairly carried most of the people in the Parish off their legs.[20] It could not be wondered that unestablished and uninformed

[18] Richard Chenevix Trench (1807-86), curate of Alverstoke 1841-44, professor of divinity at King's College, London 1847-56, dean of Westminster 1856-63, archbishop of Dublin 1864-84.

[19] Henry William Burrows (1816-92), curate of Alverstoke 1840-48, vicar of Christ Church, Albany Street, London 1851-78 after the first incumbent (William Dodsworth) seceded to the Church of Rome, vicar of Edmonton 1878-82, canon of Rochester 1881-92.

[20] Henry Edward Manning (1808–92), archdeacon of Chichester from 1840

Church people, who had never seen zeal and earnestness before, were completely carried away by it, and the harm done in the whole district round Gosport was immense. As for myself, I thoroughly distrusted and disliked the whole set and their system, and they knew it and did not much trust me; yet whenever I visited my father I used to be asked to preach, and was allowed to preach just what I liked without any remonstrance. The effect must have been some-what ridiculous when I mention that Henry Wilberforce and myself have preached in Alverstoke pulpit in the same day. I mention these things by the way, and I wish it to be understood that the state of things I have spoken of went on for several years after my father and mother first settled at Anglesey. My poor brother, my eldest sister and Emma in my belief, all suffered greatly from it.[21]

In July 1845 [*sic*], Mrs Tollemache died at Leamington, after an illness of two or three hours.[22] She had always been delicate, had eleven children, of whom only two grew up, and had a life of much hurry and anxiety. In fact I often think she would not have died if she had not been hurried off from Helmingham Hall by her husband to see Jephson, because she complained she did not

---

until his conversion to Rome in 1851, Roman Catholic archbishop of Westminster 1865-92, cardinal from 1875; Henry Wilberforce (1807-73), vicar of East Farleigh, Kent, from 1843 until his conversion to Rome in 1850. Samuel and Henry Wilber-force, and Manning, all married daughters of the evangelical clergyman, John Sargent (1780-1833), author of a memoir of Henry Martyn.

[21] Emma Ryle wrote to Manning, 15 October 1850, expressing 'the unhappy, unsettled state my mind is in', concerning her position in the Church of England. She addressed him as 'My dear father in Christ', and declared: 'My old Evangelical friends, with all my deep, deep love for them, do not succeed in shaking me in the least. ... My brother has just published a book called *Regeneration*, which all my friends are reading and highly extolling; it has a very contrary effect to what he would desire *on my mind*.' See Edmund Sheridan Purcell, *Life of Cardinal Manning, archbishop of Westminster* (2 vols, London, 1896), vol. I, pp. 457-58.

[22] Georgina Tollemache died at the Regent Hotel, Leamington, on 18 July 1846, aged 37. Her death certificate records five hours of convulsions, after suffering 'disease of the brain' for fourteen months.

feel quite well. Her sudden death was a great blow to all the Tolle-mache family, and made a great sensation. To her husband it was an irreparable loss, and he never was the same man again in religion. To myself it was an enormous loss, she was always most kind and friendly to me, and I believe really delighted in my ministry; had she lived it might have made a great difference in the course of my after life. When she died, I soon saw Helmingham was no longer the same place that it had been. I shall never forget her funeral, and I shall never forget the crowds that attended when her funeral sermon was preached.[23] Her loss to my wife was also very great, she was a wise and most kind adviser to young women and just such an one my wife needed. I take occasion to say that taking her for all in all, she was the brightest example of a Christian woman I ever saw. Her position was a very trying one, and I never expect to see rich people so consistent as poor ones, but considering her position, she was a wonderful woman.

In 1846 [*sic*], in the month of April, my first child Georgina was born, at Helmingham Rectory;[24] her mother was with her;[25] she got through her confinement very well, but within ten days owing to the extreme mismanagement of her mother, she became extremely ill. As an example of what I mean by mismanagement, I may mention that she read her 15 letters one morning, from the foolish anxiety to show her how much everyone was interested about her. The result was that her life was soon despaired of; two physicians had to be called in besides the doctor who attended her

[23] J. C. Ryle, *'Be not slothful, but followers': a sermon, preached in Helmingham Church, on Sunday, July 26, 1846; being the day following the funeral of Georgina Louisa Tollemache, the beloved wife of John Tollemache, Esq., M.P.* (Ipswich, 1846). See Appendix 6.

[24] Georgina Matilda Ryle was born on 13 April 1847, and baptised at Helming-ham on 27 June. She was probably named after Georgina Tollemache.

[25] That is, Ryle's mother-in-law, Catherine Matilda Plumptre née Methuen (*c.* 1788-1886), who cared for his wife at the birth.

J. C. Ryle's great-grandfather, Thomas Ryle (c. 1720-79),
who moved from Manchester to Macclesfield.

J. C. Ryle's grandfather, John Ryle (c. 1744-1808), silk manufacturer and supporter of the evangelical revival.

J. C. Ryle's father, John Ryle (1783-1862), member of parliament and banker, as a young man.

J. C. Ryle as a young man at Eton College in 1834.

*Sketch from 1845, probably of J. C. Ryle's first wife, Matilda Plumptre.
She died three years later, aged 24.*

J. C. Ryle's younger brother, Frederic Ryle (1820-46),
painted in 1841 by George Richmond.

J. C. Ryle's middle son, Herbert Ryle (1856-1925), wearing the insignia for the Order of the Garter, painted by Richard Jack.

J. C. Ryle's youngest son, Arthur Ryle (1857-1915),
painted in 1907 by Richard Jack.

confinement, puerperal mania came on,[26] from which she did not recover for 4 months, and her constitution received a general shock from which it never recovered.

I take occasion to remark, as a general rule, that mothers-in-law are seldom wise, and seldom add to the happiness of their daughters in reality. With the best of intentions and out of excessive affection they often do a great amount of mischief, interfere in matters they had far better let alone, and cause a vast quantity of family squabbling and unhappiness. I ask my children particularly to notice this, it is the result of long observation of a great many cases in life. It is my deliberate conviction when a young woman once marries and leaves her home, that the more she and her husband are let alone and the less they are meddled with and interfered with by third persons the happier and the better it will be for them.

My wife's illness cost me an immense sum of money. I paid one of the doctors 113£ alone. When she became well enough to travel the doctors ordered that she should go from home with her child, whom of course she could not nurse, and to see as little as possible of me for 3 or 4 months. Mr Plumptre took a house at Tunbridge Wells and there I used to go about every three weeks to see her for a few days from Helmingham. I used then to see her for about 20 minutes or half an hour a day, and at first her intellect seemed like that of a little child and not of a grown up woman. Slowly and gradually her mind entirely recovered, and in September she was able to come back with me to Helmingham. Those were miserable days in many ways, but when she got back, I think she was really happier than ever she had been before. In the month of October, her health seemed to fail, and she began to be troubled with a cough before getting up in the morning. Not getting any benefit from

---

[26] That is, mental illness, including psychotic symptoms, following childbirth.

Ryle's first father-in-law, John Pemberton Plumptre,
evangelical politician,
photographed at Clifton in 1862.

medical advice in Suffolk, by Dr Durrant's advice[27] I took her up
to London to see Dr Latham,[28] who pronounced her right lung to
be in an unsatisfactory state, and advised her going immediately to
either Hastings, Torquay, or Ventnor. I decided on Ventnor chiefly
because it was near my father at Anglesey, and to Ventnor we went
about the middle of December, without my wife even returning
home.[29]

I ought here to mention, that my wife's only surviving sister
at the beginning of this year had married my old Eton friend
A. Coote, then Rector of Marsh-Gibbon in Bucks.[30] He was then
staying at his father's house, Sir C. Coote's in Connaught Place and
we went to stay there when we consulted Latham.[31] It was a dreary
cold miserable winter, and certainly was a very uncomfortable time
of my life. I thought I had had trial enough already in that year, but
I saw pretty clearly there was more yet to come. My wife's mother
thought little of her illness as usual, but I never had but one opinion
about it.

We settled at Ventnor about the middle of December 1846 [*sic*],
myself, my wife, the maid who acted as parlour-maid and housemaid, Georgina and her nurse. We had a small house to ourselves,
and a temporary cook. I did not like the place at all, and it did not
strike me as good for an invalid, from the immense quantity of sea

[27] Christopher Mercer Durrant (1814-1901), physician to East Suffolk and
Ipswich Hospital.

[28] Peter Mere Latham (1789-1875), physician-extraordinary to Queen Victoria.

[29] During Ryle's long absence from Helmingham, December 1847 to October
1848, his parish duties were partly covered by Charles Francis Champneys (1814-
74), whose brother William Weldon Champneys (1807-75) was famous for his
evangelical ministry in the slums of St Mary's, Whitechapel 1837-60, and as dean
of Lichfield 1868-75.

[30] Matilda Ryle's older sister, Cecilia Plumptre (1822-78), married Algernon
Coote at Nonington parish church in February 1847.

[31] No. 5 Connaught Place, London, on the edge of Hyde Park, near Marble
Arch.

fog. Moreover living in an Island one felt cut off from all the world. It was a long tiresome drive to Ryde and in rough weather it was a very disagreable passage to Portsmouth. Mr Coleman[32] was then the clergyman, a worthy old Evangelical man who thought it his duty to preach to the invalids in the morning expository sermons on the book of Revelation, or expatiate by the hour to poor dying creatures about seals, viols [sic], and trumpets. A more deplorable instance of want of common sense I never saw in my whole life. There were 30 clergymen at Ventnor that winter, either on their own account, or on account of the illness of some of their families. We knew hardly anybody there, except Mr Somerville Hay, brother of Lady Jane Wodehouse, since dead.[33] Altogether it was a very melancholy winter. My wife seemed to me to get continually worse, and cough and weakness seemed continually to increase. At the end of February 1847 [sic], in consequence of my reports, Mr and Mrs Plumptre came to Ventnor, and stayed there till we left. In the beginning of May we moved to Anglesey and we remained in my father's house for a fortnight. We then moved to Tunbridge Wells, and remained there nearly a month. We then moved to Fredville, and at the end of June my wife died. A blood vessel gave way at length in her lungs as Dr Martin at Ventnor predicted would be

[32] John Noble Coleman (1791-1872), first incumbent of St Catherine's Church, Ventnor 1837-55. His publications included *Papal Rome, the foretold and foredoomed apostasy, anathematized of God, and under the ban of divine excommunication: a sermon* (Ventnor, 1850), and *The Bible, the whole Bible, and nothing but the Bible* (London, 1870).

[33] Somerville Hay (1817-53), vicar of Netherbury with Beaminster, Dorset 1844-52, son of the seventeenth earl of Erroll; see *Remains of the honourable and reverend Somerville Hay, comprising sermons, tracts, and letters*, ed. T. J. Graham (London, 1854). His half-sister was Ducibella Jane Wodehouse née Hay (1793-1885), wife of Charles Nourse Wodehouse (1790-1870), prebendary of Norwich, rector of Morningthorpe, Norfolk 1815-50, of North Lynn 1850-60.

the case,[34] and she was dead in a few minutes.[35] She was buried in Nonington Church in the family vault, and a white marble slab in the north side of Nonington Church tells all about her.

I do not pretend to speak more precisely or minutely of the details of this last six months before she died, it is useless to attempt it, and would do no good. Mr Plumptre was kindness itself all the way through. Mrs Plumptre never believed her illness was dangerous, and always said it was only a cough. My wife's only sister, Mrs Coote, I suppose depended on her mother for information; the consequence was that she never came to Fredville till my wife was dead, and in fact never saw her again from the time we departed from Connaught Place the previous December. I have observed that some people never will believe that their relatives are ill, or that they are going to die.

After my wife's death, I stayed at Fredville for 3 months, with the exception of three weeks in August, when I went to Scotland with Mr Plumptre and Mr Coote by way of change. In October 1847 [*sic*] I returned to Helmingham, alone, leaving Georgina at Fredville, as it seemed the only natural course to take. To have her alone at Helmingham was of course out of the question. I used to go to Fredville once a month from Monday to Saturday in order to see how Georgina was going on; with this exception my work went on at Helmingham as usual, throughout the whole year 1848 [*sic*], broken only by an occasional visit to Anglesey. During the Summer and Autumn the Tollemaches were at Helmingham and their house was very full of Christian people, and I shall always remember with

[34] George Anne Martin (1806-67), physician at Ventnor from 1836, enjoyed the patronage of Sir James Clark (1788-1870), physician-in-ordinary to Queen Victoria.

[35] Matilda Ryle died on 25 June 1848, aged 24, at Fredville, Nonington, home of the Plumptre family. Her death certificate records that she suffered pulmonary disease for six months, and towards the end coughed up blood for thirty hours – longer than the 'few minutes' given by Ryle.

gratitude the great kindness that the Harcourts and others showed me at that time. It was indeed a solitary, dreary, miserable period, and I often felt as if everything was going wrong, and as if everything I touched must come to no good.

In February 1849 [*sic*] I was married to my second wife, Jessy Walker, eldest daughter of John Walker Esquire, of Dumfriesshire in Scotland.[36] She was Georgina's godmother,[37] and a great favourite of Mrs Tollemache's, and my first wife had always liked her very much. We were married at Torquay where her father was then living, and at once settled down at Helmingham.

During the whole ten years during which my second married life lasted I lived at Helmingham. These ten years were a very remarkable period of my life, and were years of singular trials, as well as years in which I came very much before the public. As to trials, death made very great gaps in the circle of those that I knew. Within this period died, my brother-in-law William Courthope after being insane for two years.[38] My mother;[39] my wife's mother Mrs Walker at Clifton;[40] her sister Ellen and her brother Charles at Madeira;[41] her father at Nice;[42] and my sister Caroline Innes, who married again

[36] Ryle was married on 21 February 1850 to Jessy Elizabeth Walker (1821-60), eldest daughter of John and Jessy Walker of Crawfordton, Dumfriesshire. The wedding service was conducted by John Thornycroft.

[37] For further details of godparents, see Appendix 1.

[38] According to his death certificate, William Courthope died at Lewes on 7 March 1849, aged 33, from convulsions, after suffering with 'disease of brain' for two and a half years.

[39] Susanna Ryle died at home in Anglesey on 1 April 1852, aged 71, of hypertrophy of the heart (which she had suffered for ten years) and colon cancer. J. C. Ryle's father, John Ryle, lived another decade until his sudden death from 'apoplexy' on 21 April 1862, aged 77, during a visit to his brother-in-law, Charles Wood, at Leamington.

[40] Jessy Walker died at Clifton on 30 July 1851.

[41] Charles Walker died on 3 October 1852 and Ellen Wallace Walker on 6 February 1855. Both were buried at Funchal, Madeira.

[42] John Walker died at Nice on 6 July 1857, aged 64. On leaving Stradbroke, Ryle

after William Courthope's death;[43] besides others, who were great friends of mine, and whose loss I felt very deeply. The worst trial was my wife's continued ill health. We had not been married six months before she became very unwell, and from that time till she died, a period of nearly ten years, she really never was well more than three months together. She was confined five times, and on account of her state of health we had to go to London for every confinement. On these occasions we never were there less than two months, and once we were there from December to May. On two occasions we stayed the whole time with her Uncle Mr Johnston, and Miss Johnston in Onslow Square.[44] Once we were with Mr Walker in Onslow

---

reflected that geographically separated Christians would meet again in heaven: 'I often think how various are the resting-places of God's people here below, and take comfort in the thought that in the gathering together we shall all meet again. My late wife's family I shall never forget. Two are buried at Madeira, one at Clifton, one at Rugby, two at the Isle of Wight, one at Nice, and one in Helmingham churchyard. They were all beloved while they lived, and all lamented when they died. They were all buried in different graves, but what a blessed thought that we shall all meet again in that day of gathering together. It matters little where we are buried, but it does matter greatly where we shall meet together afterwards.' ('Farewell sermons by the bishop of Liverpool, at Stradbroke', *Ipswich Journal*, 22 June 1880.) Jessy Ryle's brother, John Walker, was a pupil at Rugby School when he drowned in August 1841, aged 16, trying to save the life of a schoolfellow.

[43] Caroline Innes died at Brighton on 6 June 1857, aged 38, a few weeks after giving birth to a son, George Cecil Innes, who died on 23 July 1857, aged four months. She left three orphaned children from her first marriage to William Courthope, including William John Courthope (1842-1917), professor of poetry at Oxford University 1895-1900.

[44] Jessy Ryle's uncle John Johnston (c. 1804-83), solicitor, and aunt Eliza Johnston, lived at No. 35 Onslow Square, Kensington. Her first two children were born there – Jessy (or Jessie) Isabelle Ryle, born on 2 May 1851 and baptised at Helmingham on 15 June; and an unnamed daughter, born on 2 January 1853, more than two months premature, who died after about an hour. During Ryle's long absence from Helmingham in spring 1853, his parish duties were covered by Robert Allan Blomefield (1826-77), son of Sir Thomas Blomefield, baronet. Robert's brother, John Blomefield (1824-1908), was in India as Bishop Daniel Wilson's domestic chaplain 1850-56; see Andrew Atherstone (ed.), *The journal of Bishop Daniel Wilson of Calcutta, 1845-1857*, Church of England Record Society vol. 21 (Woodbridge, 2015).

Square;[45] once from December to May, we had a house of our own in Onslow Crescent;[46] and once when Arthur was born we had a house of our own in St Leonard's Terrace, Chelsea, opposite Chelsea Hospital.[47] How much discomfort, inconvenience, and expense all this occasioned, I cannot pretend to describe; in fact, without Mr Walker's kind assistance we could not possibly have managed to get through. But he was the most unselfish, generous man I ever met with, and was always helping us.

One result of these long residences in London was, that I became acquainted with all the leading Evangelical clergy and laity in London, was brought forward continually as a speaker and preacher, in every part of the Metropolis.[48] I once reckoned that I preached in no less than 60 church pulpits, in London, and might have had a Church there myself, half a dozen times over if I had liked.[49] But I never liked London as a Ministerial Sphere. I always

[45] Herbert Edward Ryle was born at No. 51 Onslow Square on 25 May 1856, and baptised (by his father) at St Luke's, Chelsea on 24 June. The evangelical rector of St Luke's from 1836 to 1860 was Charles Kingsley (1781-1860), father of the more famous Charles Kingsley (1819-75), Christian socialist and novelist.

[46] Reginald John Ryle was born at Onslow Crescent on 5 December 1854, and baptised (by his father) at St Luke's, Chelsea on 15 April 1855. During his long absence from Helmingham, Ryle's parish duties were covered by Wilmot Guy Bryan (c. 1820-1906), previously curate of Freston, near Ipswich.

[47] Arthur Johnston Ryle was born on 10 September 1857, and baptised at Helmingham on 20 October. The Royal Hospital, Chelsea, opened in 1692, is a home for army veterans or 'Chelsea pensioners'.

[48] Some of Ryle's earliest published lectures date from this London ministry. For example, in February 1853, shortly after the premature birth, and death, of his third daughter, he lectured three times to different audiences: J. C. Ryle, 'Baxter and his times', in *Lectures delivered before the Young Men's Christian Association in Exeter Hall, from November 1852 to February 1853* (London, 1853), pp. 361-403; J. C. Ryle, 'Occupy till I come': A lecture on the unexpected delay of the kingdom of God; delivered at St George's, Bloomsbury, London, Feb. 11*th*, 1853 (Ipswich and London, 1853); J. C. Ryle, 'Bishop Latimer', in *Lectures delivered before the Church of England Young Men's Society for Aiding Missions at Home and Abroad, in Freemason's Hall, January and February 1853* (London, 1853), pp. 153-205.

[49] In March 1852 it was falsely reported in the press that Ryle had been appointed

made a very bad 'lion',[50] and I always felt that 'popularity' as it was called was a very worthless thing, and a very bad thing for a man's soul. Why I was popular I really do not know, for I am certain that my preaching was very inferior to what it was after I was turned 50. But it was always bold and downright, and I suppose was very unlike what London congregations generally heard, and therefore was popular. When my wife got well enough, we always returned to Helmingham, and there work went on much as before, with the addition of more writing.

The last three years of my second married life were made additionally uncomfortable by a breach between myself and Mr Tollemache, and a complete suspension of all friendly relations between us. I will not say more about this painful subject excepting that he never was the same man after he lost his first wife.[51] This breach I need hardly say, as the whole parish of Helmingham belonged to him, made our position at Helmingham extremely uncomfortable, and decided me to leave whenever an opening should offer.

In the year 1860 my wife died, in the month of May, after a long and lingering illness of Bright's disease, which was not detected till two months before she died.[52] I can never help thinking that her case was misunderstood for three or four months, and if she had been treated for Bright's disease from the very first, her life might very probably have been prolonged a little – but it is easy to be wise after the event. For four or five years, she had painfully little enjoyment of life, and was neither able to fill her position as a mother or

as incumbent of Park Chapel, Chelsea, in succession to the popular evangelical preacher, William Cadman (1815-91); see *Morning Advertiser*, 11 March 1852; *Morning Chronicle*, 24 March 1852.

[50] That is, a celebrity.

[51] John Tollemache married again, in 1850, to Eliza Georgiana Duff (1829-1918).

[52] Jessy Ryle died at Helmingham rectory on 19 May 1860, aged 38. Bright's disease, first described by physician Richard Bright in the 1820s, is disease of the kidneys.

as a mistress,[53] to her own great sorrow, and of course to the general discomfort of the whole household. She was buried in Helmingham Churchyard, at the North side of the Church,[54] and I was once more left a widower with five children, the eldest only just 13; and altogether more disconsolate and helpless than ever.[55]

Few can have any idea how much wear and tear and anxiety of mind and body I had to go through for at least five years before my wife died. I very rarely ever slept out of my own house, in order that

[53] That is, with oversight of the servants at the rectory.

[54] Ryle's evangelical friend and neighbour, Charles Shorting (1810-64), rector of Stonham Aspal 1836-64, officiated and preached at Jessy Ryle's funeral; see J. C. Ryle, 'Comfort one another', in Robert H. Groome and J. C. Ryle, *Two sermons, preached in Stonham Aspal church, on Sunday, May 8ᵗʰ, 1864, on occasion of the death of the Rev. Charles Shorting, M.A.* (London, 1864). She was buried on 24 May, the day before Herbert Ryle's fourth birthday, and his earliest memory was of being held up by his nurse at the rectory attic window, next to the church, to watch the funeral proceedings; see Fitzgerald, *Herbert Edward Ryle*, p. 11. Just as the walls of Helmingham church are covered in exhortations from Scripture, so Ryle also designed his wife's gravestone as a sermon. It declares that she 'fell asleep in Christ' and 'rests in hope, waiting for the coming of our Lord Jesus Christ and our gathering together unto him'. The gravestone bears five Bible texts: 'With Christ which is far better' (Philippians 1:23); 'God shall wipe away all tears from their eyes, and there shall be no more death, neither sorrow, nor crying, neither shall there by any more pain' (Revelation 21:4); 'Come, Lord Jesus' (Revelation 22:20); 'Christ is all' (Colossians 3:11); and, most poignantly, 'Say unto her: Is it well with thee? Is it well with thy husband? Is it well with the child? And she answered, It is well' (2 Kings 4:26).

[55] In 1867, reflecting on the death in 1767 of the wife of the evangelical clergyman, Henry Venn, Ryle wrote: 'Mrs Venn was a woman of rare prudence, calmness, good sense, affection, and sympathy. She was, in fact, her husband's right hand. When she died, such a load of care and anxiety was accumulated on his head, that his health gradually gave way. People who have not been placed in similar circumstances, may probably not understand all this. Those who have had this cross to carry, can testify that there is no position in this world so trying to body and soul as that of the minister who is left a widower with a young family and a large congregation. There are anxieties in such cases which no one knows but he who has gone through them, anxieties which can crush the strongest spirit, and wear out the strongest constitution.' J. C. Ryle, 'Henry Venn and his ministry; or, England a hundred years ago', *The Family Treasury of Sunday Reading* (July 1867), p. 416; republished in *Christian leaders of the last century* (London, 1869).

I might be in the way if my wife wanted anything. I have frequently in the depth of winter driven distances of 12, 15, 20, or even 30 miles in an open carriage to speak or preach, and then returned home the same distance immediately afterwards, rather than sleep away from my own house. As to holidays, rest or recreation, in the year I never had any at all; while the whole business of entertaining and amusing the three little boys in an evening, devolved entirely upon me.[56] In fact, the whole state of things was a heavy strain upon me both in body and mind, and I often wonder how I lived through it.

[56] Ryle was not without assistance: at the 1861 census he was employing a live-in governess for his children – Louisa Lacell Harris (1835-1922), daughter of George Harris, Congregational minister of Ringwood, Hampshire – and five live-in servants: a housekeeper, a nurse, a parlour maid, and two housemaids (The National Archives, RG9/1156, fo. 35).

Early photographs, c. 1860, of J. C. Ryle's children,
Isabelle (left, born 1851) and Herbert (right, born 1856).

J. C. Ryle, his third wife, Henrietta, and his three sons, in July 1863.

The Ryle family on holiday at Lowestoft in September 1863.

Budding cricketers: Ryle's three sons, Arthur (aged 6), Reginald (aged 8), and Herbert (aged 7).

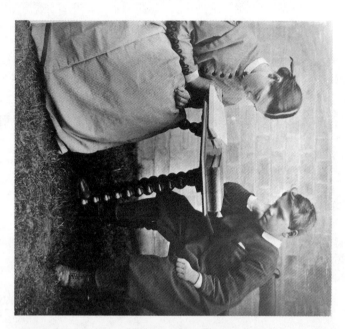

The Ryle children in 1865: Isabelle and Reginald (left), Arthur and Herbert (right).

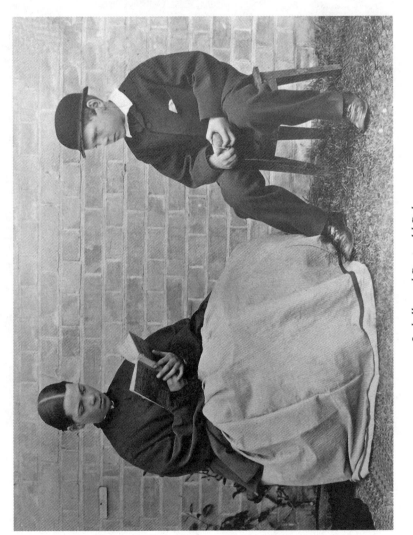

Isabelle and Reginald Ryle.

Georgina, Isabelle, and Henrietta Ryle, at Stradbroke Vicarage in 1865.

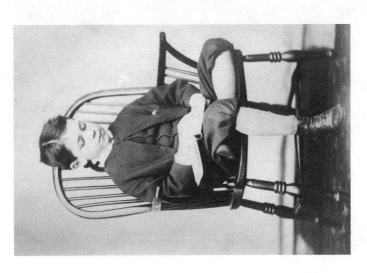

Arthur Ryle in 1866.

J. C. Ryle with Arthur and the family dog.

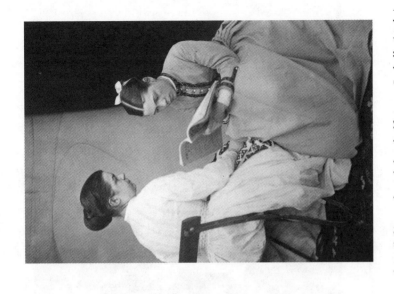

Georgina Ryle, known to her family as Gina, in 1867, aged 20 (left), and with her half-sister, Isabelle (right).

Isabelle Ryle in 1868. She lived with her father for half a century, in Suffolk and Liverpool, latterly as his private secretary.

Henrietta Ryle enjoyed photography, and her family often posed in tableau scenes, in costume. Here J. C. Ryle poses in 1866 as Martin Luther discovering the Bible in the Erfurt monastery.

A scene from John Bunyan's *Pilgrim's Progress*: J. C. Ryle (*with false beard*) poses as Christian reading the Bible.

Pilgrim's Progress: Christian (J. C. Ryle) knocks at the gate (left); he is welcomed at the Palace Beautiful by Piety (Isabelle).

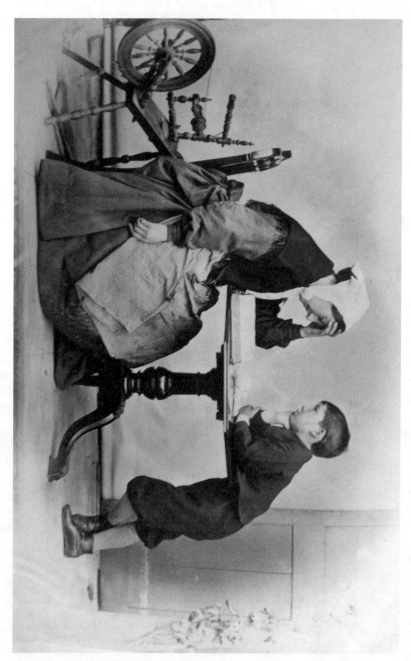

Pilgrim's Progress: Christiana (Henrietta Ryle) repents.

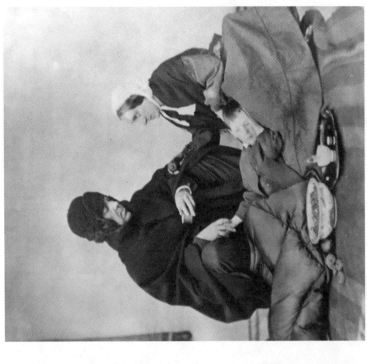

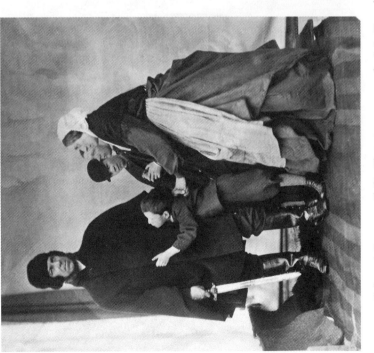

Pilgrim's Progress: (left) Christiana persuades Mr Greatheart (J. C. Ryle) to go with them; (right) Matthew (Arthur Ryle) falls sick after eating fruit from the devil's garden but is healed by Dr Skill (J. C. Ryle).

J. C. Ryle was always fond of pets.

APPENDICES

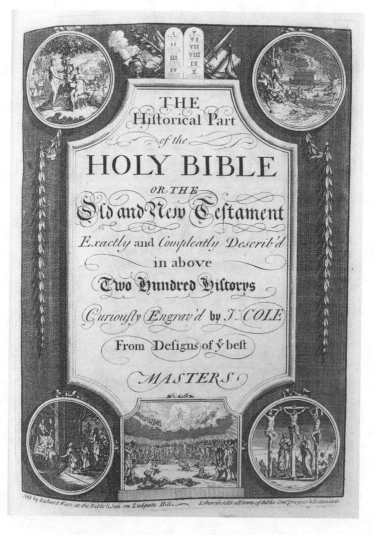

THE
Hiſtorical Part
of the
HOLY BIBLE
OR THE
Old and New Teſtament
Exactly and Compleatly Deſcrib'd
in above
Two Hundred Hiſtorys
Curiouſly Engrav'd by J. COLE
From Deſigns of ẏ beſt
MASTERS

Frontispiece from the Ryle Family Bible.

APPENDIX 1

THE RYLE FAMILY BIBLE

The Ryle Family Bible first belonged to J. C. Ryle's grandfather, John Ryle senior (*c*. 1744-1808), and the blank leaves in front and back were used to record the births of Ryle descendants for almost two centuries. The volume was initially two, both published at Oxford by Thomas Baskett, the king's printer – the *Book of Common Prayer*, with metrical Psalms and the Thirty-Nine Articles of Religion (published 1747), and the Old and New Testaments, including the Apocrypha (published 1752). These were bound together and resold as a single volume by Richard Ware, a printer at Ludgate Hill in London, with over two hundred additional engravings of biblical scenes, and a concordance (published 1745). John Ryle was a keen supporter of the eighteenth-century evangelical revival, and of early Methodism in Macclesfield, but the fact that his Bible was bound with the Prayer Book and Articles demonstrates his continued loyalty to the Church of England.

At the front of the Bible, John Ryle senior recorded the births of his nine daughters and four sons between 1773 and 1794 – J. C. Ryle's aunts and uncles. The Bible passed to John Ryle junior, who added the births between 1811 and 1820 of his four daughters and two sons. J. C. Ryle continued the tradition by adding details of his own six children between 1847 and 1857, and on his death he bequeathed the volume to his middle son, Herbert Ryle, whose descendants continued to add names up to the birth of J. C. Ryle's great-great-great-grandson, Rupert Ryle-Hodges, in 1961. Only the first three generations are published in this Appendix.

These details extend our knowledge of the Ryle family, with unique information not available elsewhere, but are not just of genealogical interest. Especially important is the record of baptism sponsors (godparents) for J. C. Ryle, his siblings and his children.[1] This reveals not only the strength of familial ties, but also the identities of some of Ryle's closest evangelical friends. His national allies in evangelical mission and politics are part of the public record, whether collaborators in print, platform or committee, but the Family Bible as a private document sheds new light on his personal friendships. He declared that to be a godparent to his 'beloved children' was 'an office I never asked any one to fill unless I believed him to be a man of God, and one whom I could trust'.[2]

Of the eighteen godparents chosen in Macclesfield by Ryle's father and mother, all but one were close relatives. In stark contrast, in the next generation, of the fifteen godparents chosen in Helmingham by Ryle and his wives, only four were close relatives, and none from Ryle's side of the family. This is a further indication that he made theological convictions paramount. Five times he invited local evangelical clergymen in Suffolk to stand as sponsor – Henry Lumsden (minister of St Peter's, Ipswich), Robert Groome (rector of Monk Soham), Herbert James (previously curate of Aldeburgh), Charles Shorting (rector of Stonham Aspal), and Frederick Evans (curate of Saxmundham). He also included two evangelical friends from Eton College days – Algernon Coote (his brother-in-law) and Arthur Kinnaird.

---

[1] The rubrics of the *Book of Common Prayer* require two godmothers and one godfather for a girl, and two godfathers and one godmother for a boy, but their names are very seldom recorded in baptism registers.

[2] Ryle, 'Comfort one another'.

The James family was particularly intimate with the Ryles. Ryle officiated in July 1854 at the wedding in Helmingham of Herbert and Mary James, and two years later the couple both stood as godparents for Herbert Ryle – perhaps named after Herbert James. The James children, including Sydney R. James (later headmaster of Malvern College and archdeacon of Dudley) and Montague R. James (later provost of King's College, Cambridge and of Eton College, best known for his ghost stories), enjoyed holidays in the Stradbroke vicarage. Archdeacon James recalled his impressions from the early 1870s:

> Mr Ryle, with his gigantic figure and stentorian voice, was perhaps rather formidable to a youthful visitor, but he was very kind and hearty, and I soon felt at home. The boys, each in his way, were delightful companions. The atmosphere of the house was, like that of my own home, devotional: daily Bible readings, somewhat lengthy family prayers, and a good deal of religious talk. But all was quite wholesome and unpretentious, and I don't think any of us were bored, much less inclined to cavil at the régime, at any rate at the time.[3]

They stayed in touch, and when Ryle became bishop of Liverpool, he chose Herbert James as one of his first examining chaplains.[4]

Charles Shorting in Stonham Aspal, the neighbouring parish to Helmingham, was one of Ryle's closest colleagues-in-arms. Shorting was appointed as rector in 1836, aged 26, and soon came under the influence of the prominent Suffolk evangelical, Charles Bridges (rector of Old Newton), author of the popular handbook, *The Christian ministry: with an inquiry into the causes of its inefficiency*

[3] Fitzgerald, *Herbert Edward Ryle*, p. 11.
[4] For Herbert James's doctrine, see, for example, 'Justification by faith; with especial reference to the ways in which the doctrine is corrupted in the present day', in *Thoughts for churchmen* (London, 1868), pp. 1-28; 'Evangelical churchmanship: what it is bound to teach', *The Record*, 19 January 1883, pp. 55-56.

(1829). By the early 1840s Shorting was firmly committed to evangel-icalism, and his views were said to be 'entirely assimilated to those of his excellent teacher'.[5] He threw his weight particularly behind the Church Missionary Society and each year hosted a missionary tea meeting, for 700 or 800 people from across Suffolk, in a large tent in his rectory garden.[6] Ryle and Shorting often stood side by side on the same evangelical platforms, in Ipswich and beyond. When Ryle's second wife died in 1860, Shorting officiated and preached at her funeral. When Shorting himself died in 1864, Ryle rushed back from his speaking engagements in London's Exeter Hall to deliver a funeral tribute. He praised his friend as 'a genuine Suffolk Protestant of the good old school of the Reformation'.[7]

Another person chosen as godfather because of his faith was Robert Holden, a leading evangelical layman. Holden and Ryle first got to know each other on the cricket field in the late 1830s, before Holden's conversion and his energetic commitment to evangelism in Nottinghamshire and Derbyshire. He became an advocate for the British and Foreign Bible Society, and other similar mission agencies, and when he died unexpectedly in November 1872, Ryle penned a tribute to his faith:

> When I first knew him, he certainly cared far more for the world that now is, than that which is to come. But, from the time that he felt the power of true, vital religion in his soul, till the time of his death, a period of more than twenty years, he lived more thoroughly and entirely for God than any layman that I ever was acquainted with. I frankly and unhesitatingly avow, that I never in my life saw a more remarkable instance of the converting power of the grace of God. ... He was one of those peculiar men who are full of fire, and steam, and energy, and can do nothing by halves. Well do I

[5] Groome and Ryle, *Two sermons*.
[6] 'Funeral of the Rev C. Shorting', *Ipswich Journal*, 7 May 1864.
[7] Ryle, 'Comfort one another'.

remember, in days when I knew little more of true religion than he did, what kind of a man he was in a ball-room, or in the cricket field. That very same zeal, after his conversion, he threw into all his work for Christ. ... In religious opinions he was thoroughly whole-hearted and unmistakable. He was a most decided Evangelical Churchman; he did not halt between two opinions. ... Few who have heard him speak on a Bible Society platform will ever forget the loving, tearful earnestness with which he would speak to a meeting, in words of true unadorned eloquence, and tell people what Bible religion had done for his own soul.[8]

These were the characteristics – personal conversion, evangelical doctrine, missionary zeal – which Ryle admired most amongst his friends. These were priorities he sought to instill in his children, through the witness of their godparents, whose identities are revealed here for the first time.

In this Appendix no attempt has been made to reproduce the original layout from the Ryle Family Bible. The names are collected in family groupings, with titles added. Abbreviations are expanded and capitalization sometimes altered, to aid readability.

---

[8] J. C. Ryle, 'Prefatory memoir', in *'A book of remembrance': being recollections of the late Colonel Holden of Nuttall Temple, Nottingham* (London, 1873), pp. ix-x, xii-xiv.

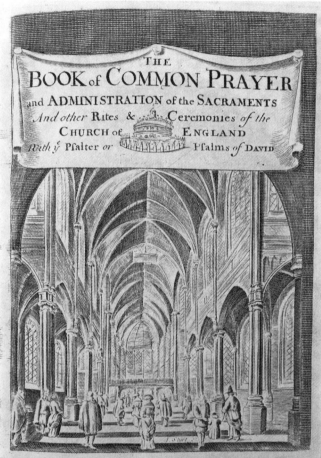

THE
BOOK of COMMON PRAYER
and ADMINISTRATION of the SACRAMENTS
And other Rites & Ceremonies of the
CHURCH of ENGLAND
With ỹ Pfalter or Pfalms of DAVID

Printed and Sold by Richard Ware at ỹ Bible & Sun on Ludgate Hill.
A Curious Set of Cuts for all Sorts of House Bibles Engrav'd by I Sturt. to which is aded Six Maps of
Sacred Geography 1 Shewing the Situation of Paradise 2 the Peopling the World by the Son of
Noah 3 The Plan of the City of Jerusalem 4 The Holy land divided into 12 Tribes of Israel & our
Saviour's Travels 5 The land of Canaan 6 The Travels of St Paul & the rest of the Apostles.

Frontispiece from the Book of Common Prayer,
attached to the Ryle Family Bible.

The Text

Children of John and Mary Ryle[9]

Elizabeth Ryle, born December 23rd 1773, at 6 o'clock in the morning, Wednesday.

Martha Ryle, born June 28th 1775, Tuesday, at two o'clock in the morning.[10]

Mary Ryle, born April 1st 1777 at 10 o'clock in the forenoon.

Thomas Ryle, born June 10th 1778 at 5 o'clock in the afternoon.

Katherine Ryle, born June 8th 1779 at 2 o'clock in morning. Died January 29th 1780, aged 7 months.

Ann Ryle, born June 16, 1781, Monday, quarter past 5 afternoon. Died July 4th 1781, aged 16 days.

Sarah Ryle, born October 20th 1782, at eleven o'clock, Sunday forenoon.

John Ryle, born December 9th 1783 at 12 o'clock, Wednesday fore[noon].

Joshua Ryle, born September 3rd 1785 at 12 o'clock at night, Saturday.

[9] For a similar list of John and Mary Ryle's thirteen children (but without times of birth, and with Katherine spelled Catharine), see Christ Church, Macclesfield baptism register (1775-1812), p. 3, Cheshire Record Office, P84/1.

[10] Martha Ryle, J. C. Ryle's aunt, died on 24 April 1799, aged 23. For an account of her deathbed, and her evangelical faith, see R. R. [Richard Reece], 'A short account of the death of Miss Ryle of Macclesfield', *Methodist Magazine* vol. 23 (March 1800), pp. 115-19. She and her siblings, Catharine (d. 1780), Ann (d. 1781), and Thomas (d. 1791), are commemorated on the same memorial at Christ Church, Macclesfield, alongside their grandparents, Thomas Ryle (*c.* 1720-79) and Martha Ryle (*c.* 1717-87).

A son still born August 24th 1789.

Thomas Ryle died January, Monday, the 10th of January 1791, aged twelve years and six months.

Frances Ryle, born January 22nd 1791 at 2 o'clock afternoon.

A daughter still born September 1793.

Jane Harriet Ryle, born December 11th 1794 at 5 o'clock in the afternoon.

Children of John and Susanna Ryle

Mary Anne
>Born October 30, 1811, at eight o'clock in the morning
>Sponsors: Mrs Ryle Senior,[11] Miss Watson, Mr C. Hurt[12]

Susan
>Born March 11, 1813, at 10 minutes before four in the afternoon
>Sponsors: Mrs C. Hurt,[13] Mrs Wood,[14] Mr Daintry[15]

Emma
>Born October 22, 1814, at half past one o'clock in the afternoon
>Sponsors: Mrs S. Wood,[16] Miss F. Hurt,[17] Mr Wood[18]

[11] J. C. Ryle's grandmother, Mary Ryle.
[12] J. C. Ryle's grandfather, or uncle, Charles Hurt.
[13] Probably J. C. Ryle's grandmother, Susanna Hurt.
[14] J. C. Ryle's aunt, Mary Wood.
[15] J. C. Ryle's uncle, John Smith Daintry.
[16] J. C. Ryle's aunt, Sarah Wood.
[17] J. C. Ryle's aunt, Frances Hurt.
[18] J. C. Ryle's uncle, Charles Wood or Samuel Wood.

John Charles

Born May 10, 1816, at five o'clock in the morning

Sponsors: Mrs Daintry,[19] Mr C. Hurt,[20] Mr John Daintry Junior[21]

Caroline Elizabeth

Born August 23, 1818, at nine o'clock in the morning

Sponsors: Mrs Hurt Senior,[22] Mrs Holcombe,[23] Mr Edge[24]

Frederic William

Born August 2, 1820, at quarter before six o'clock in the afternoon

Sponsors: Mrs Peter Arkwright,[25] Revd Dr Holcombe,[26] Lieutenant Colonel Thornhill[27]

---

[19] J. C. Ryle's aunt, Elizabeth Daintry.

[20] J. C. Ryle's grandfather, or uncle, Charles Hurt.

[21] J. C. Ryle's cousin, John Daintry (1795-1869), son of John Smith Daintry and Elizabeth Ryle, undergraduate at Trinity College, Cambridge 1812-17, perpetual curate of Shidfield, Hampshire 1832-41, rector of Patney, Wiltshire 1841-48, perpetual curate of North Rode, Cheshire (of which he was patron) 1849-68.

[22] J. C. Ryle's grandmother, Susanna Hurt.

[23] J. C. Ryle's great-aunt, Catherine Holcombe née Hurt (c. 1754-1841), wife of George Holcombe.

[24] J. C. Ryle's great-uncle, Thomas Webb Edge (c. 1756-1819) of Strelley Hall, Nottinghamshire.

[25] J. C. Ryle's aunt, Mary Anne Arkwright.

[26] George Holcombe (c. 1756-1836), rector of Matlock, Derbyshire 1780-1836, of Osgathorpe, Leicestershire 1796-1836, of East and West Leake, Nottinghamshire 1804-36, prebendary of Canterbury 1815-22, of Westminster 1822-36.

[27] William Thornhill.

Daughter of John Charles and Matilda Charlotte Louisa Ryle

Georgina Matilda
>   Born at Helmingham Rectory, April 13, 1847
>   Sponsors: Revd H. Lumsden,[28] Mrs A. Coote,[29] Jessy Eliza-
>   beth Walker[30]

Children of John Charles and Jessy Elizabeth Ryle

Jessy Isabelle
>   Born at 35 Onslow Square, Brompton, May 2, 1851
>   Sponsors: Mrs Harcourt,[31] Mrs Sheppard,[32] Revd A. Coote[33]

A daughter
>   Born and Died, January 2, 1853

Reginald John
>   Born Onslow Crescent, Brompton, December 5, 1854
>   Sponsors: Eliza A. Walker,[34] Revd R. Groome,[35] Honourable
>   A. Kinnaird[36]

---

[28] Henry Thomas Lumsden (1808-67), perpetual curate of St Peter's, Ipswich 1837-57, of St Thomas's, Portman Square, London 1857-67, author of *Christ the substance of the gospel ministry: a sermon* (Ipswich, 1850).

[29] J. C. Ryle's sister-in-law, Cecilia Coote.

[30] J. C. Ryle's second wife.

[31] Marcia Vernon Harcourt.

[32] Harriet Sheppard.

[33] J. C. Ryle's brother-in-law, Algernon Coote.

[34] J. C. Ryle's sister-in-law, Eliza Ann Walker, author of *Hymns and thoughts in verse* (London, 1864) and other evangelical literature from Ryle's publisher, William Hunt.

[35] Robert Hindes Groome (1810-89), rector of Monk Soham, Suffolk 1845-89, editor of *The Christian Advocate and Review* 1861-66, archdeacon of Suffolk 1869-87.

[36] Arthur Kinnaird.

Herbert Edward
> Born Onslow Square, Brompton, May 25, 1856
> Sponsors: Revd Herbert James,[37] Mrs James,[38] Revd C. Shorting[39]

Arthur Johnston
> Born St Leonard's Terrace, Chelsea, September 10, 1857
> Sponsors: Miss Octavia Plumptre,[40] Revd F. Evans,[41] Robert Holden Esquire[42]

[37] Herbert James (1822-1909), curate of Aldeburgh, Suffolk 1848-52, of Christ Church, Dover 1852-55, perpetual curate of Goodnestone, Kent 1855-65, rector of Livermere, Suffolk 1865-1909, one of Bishop Ryle's examining chaplains 1880-91.

[38] Mary Emily James née Horton (1818-98), daughter of Rear-Admiral Joshua Horton, wife of Herbert James.

[39] Charles Shorting.

[40] Matilda Ryle's aunt, Octavia Anna Plumptre (1807-90).

[41] Frederick Evans (c. 1808-68), curate of Saxmundham, Suffolk 1853-62, rector of Linstead, Suffolk 1862-68.

[42] Robert Holden (1805-72) of Nuttall Temple, near Nottingham.

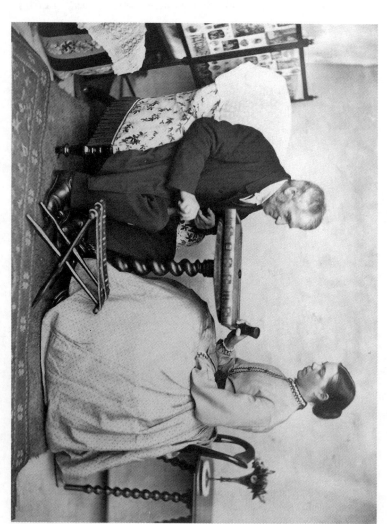

Frederick Evans playing a game with Isabelle Ryle, July 1866. He was godfather to

J. C. Ryle's youngest son.

APPENDIX 2

THE ETON SOCIETY

T he Eton Society was an exclusive debating and social club for pupils at Eton College, founded in 1811. Membership was limited to twenty-five senior boys, who met each Saturday for debate, and it proved an excellent training ground for those from Eton who entered public life as politicians and opinion-formers. Amongst its most illustrious early participants were Edward Stanley and William Gladstone, both of whom later served as British prime minister. The society deliberately reflected the House of Commons, in miniature, where boys referred to each other as 'honourable members' and could test their skills in oratory and rhetoric. The debates were often passionate and boisterous, displaying a mix of earnest argument, barracking, humour and petty rivalries. It was here that Ryle cut his teeth as a public speaker, initially ambitious to follow his father into parliament. At the Eton Society he gained invaluable experience later put to good use from pulpit and platform as a popular preacher, lecturer, and evangelical spokesman.

Ryle wrote in his autobiography, 'the old Chronicles of the Society must be at the present day very interesting documents'.[1] Indeed they are! The minute books survive in the Eton College

[1] See above, p. 40.

Archives, detailing the society's activities, including transcriptions of many of the speeches. According to the rules, new members were elected by existing members, but a candidate was rejected if he received five or more 'blackballs' (negative votes) in the ballot. During Ryle's penultimate year at school he was proposed for election five times. At the first attempt, in September 1832, he received six blackballs.[2] He was turned down again in February 1833 and twice in May, with six blackballs on the last occasion, before finally being elected in June with only three blackballs.[3] It was thus during his final academic year that he played a part in the society, soon taking a leading role.

Ryle's Whiggish political sympathies were often evident. For example, in October 1833 the Eton Society discussed which newspapers and magazines should be taken by their small reading room. Ryle proposed that they turn out *The Standard* (a pro-Tory newspaper, founded in 1827) and subscribe instead to *The Times*. George Lyttelton (later Baron Lyttelton) answered that 'since Mr Ryle had come forward as a professed Radical, he must caution the House against any paper proposed by him (Cheers).' Likewise Thomas Phinn (later a barrister and MP for Bath) warned that

> he saw a strong wish in some hon. gents. to turn out every Tory paper, & bring in such radical, nay, he might say, such *rascally* papers. (Tremendous cheers, & violent cries of No, No, from Messrs Carter, Ryle, & Mills.) He could support this by saying that he had known these papers write against the King, for the abolition of the House of Lords, & every sort of infringement of the constitution. (Cheers.)

When another member proposed that the *Morning Post* be replaced by the *True Sun* (a short-lived pro-Whig newspaper, founded in

[2] Eton Society Minute Book 1830-32: 29 September 1832, p. 350.
[3] Eton Society Minute Book 1832-33: 23 February, 4 and 11 May, 15 June 1833, pp. 110, 130, 133, 151.

1832), Phinn dismissed the *True Sun* as 'the worst paper of the worst set. It advocated universal suffrage, vote by ballot, & annual parliaments, & he had heard a person connected with the paper say that it was the worst in London.' Yet Ryle replied that anything was better that 'the fashionable humbug of the Morning Post'. Next Ryle proposed that they take William Cobbett's *Political Register* in lieu of the *John Bull* (founded in 1820). Lyttelton believed that the Eton Society would be 'disgraced, were it to take the abominable, abusive trash of the greatest political blackguard of the present day (Cheers)', to which Ryle retorted that he would consider Lyttelton 'a very clever fellow could he write with half the talent of Mr Cobbett'.[4] Although political rivalries divided the Eton Society, Ryle won unified backing a few months later when he proposed they subscribe to *Bell's Life in London*, a sporting newspaper with excellent coverage of rowing and cricket.[5]

The minute books also reveal other aspects of Ryle's character, such as his rough teasing and independence of mind. For example, in February 1834, Theodore Thring brought a complaint against Ryle and two others for their 'very dastardly conduct' in mistreating him in the reading room. Ryle replied that the extent of their violence was only to knock Thring's hat off three or four times. It was a mere 'trifle', said one, compared to a previous occasion when a member of the Eton Society had been thrown out of the window. Ryle escaped with a caution, rather than a fine.[6] His willingness

[4] Eton Society Minute Book 1832-33: 12 October 1833, pp. 202-204. For more on *The Times* as 'a rascally paper', see 26 October 1833, pp. 234-37. For Ryle's next attempt to get rid of the *Morning Post*, see 10 May 1834, p. 85. In later life, Ryle continued to recommend that young preachers imitate the clear and direct style of William Cobbett who 'wrote the finest simple Saxon-English the world has ever seen'; J. C. Ryle, *Simplicity in preaching: a few short hints on a great subject* (London, 1882), p. 44; republished in *The upper room: being a few truths for the times* (London, 1888), and by the Banner of Truth Trust 2010.

[5] Eton Society Minute Book 1833-34: 28 June 1834, p. 114.

[6] Eton Society Minute Book 1833-34: 1 February 1834, pp. 41-44.

to swim against the flow, a major theme in his autobiography, was shown in May 1834 by interjections during a debate on whether MPs ought to vote according to the dictates of their conscience or the wishes of their constituents. Ryle's future brother-in-law, William Courthope, opened with a warning that if parliament-arians were pledged to mirror the views of the electorate, then they would become

> a mere set of puppets, who would move to this side or the other according as their constituents pulled the wires (Loud laughter, & Hear, Hear, from all parts of the house, especially Messrs Ryle, Charlton and Ritchie) than which conduct sure nothing could be more disgraceful. And here he would observe, without wishing to hurt the feelings of any honourable members, that it would be better if the Eton Society did not expose themselves to a like charge by the greater part of it always voting in unison with influential members without consulting their own opinions (Loud cheers from Messrs Ryle & Charlton, & Cry of Question from Mr Phinn).

Phinn then proceeded to rebuke Courthope for having 'publicly insulted the House by his comments on their behaviour (No, No from Messrs Ryle and Ritchie).'[7] Ryle's habit of speaking his own mind, however bluntly, was a hallmark of his later ministry, even if it meant challenging the Anglican or evangelical *status quo*.

Debates at the Eton Society covered a wide range of subjects. Often they tackled questions of statesmanship, national virtue and civic duty, in the guise of classical or British history – discussing the character and achievements of Philip of Macedon, Julius Caesar, Pompey, Cicero, Richard the Lionheart, Cardinal Wolsey, Mary Queen of Scots, Bonnie Prince Charlie, Sir Robert Walpole, and many others. They debated the Crusades, chivalry, colonialism, monasticism, the Glorious Revolution, the relative benefits of agri-

[7] Eton Society Minute Book 1833-34: 31 May 1834, pp. 92-93.

culture and manufacturing, alongside topics such as 'Are riches or poverty most beneficial to genius?' (May 1832) and 'Are literary or political talents most useful to a country?' (July 1833). Sometimes they broached moral conundrums, such as whether the theatre was pernicious, whether flogging was beneficial in the army and navy, and whether capital punishments should be abolished. Occasionally there was a direct echo of contemporary questions in the House of Commons. In January 1832, eighteen months before the Slavery Abolition Act was passed, the Eton Society debated, 'Ought slaves to be entirely emancipated?' In September 1834, shortly before the Great Western Railway Company was incorporated by Act of Parliament, the Eton boys asked whether railroads were detrimental to the country.

Ryle spoke in eight debates, six times as opener. These included his proposals that naval supremacy is of greater advantage than military (December 1833); that Achilles is a more admirable figure than Hector in *The Iliad* (May 1834); and that Africa was circumnavigated by the Phoenicians (July 1834). The chronicles of the society offer only the briefest summary of these speeches, once with the lazy but formulaic excuse that the scribe 'regrets his inability to do justice to Mr Ryle's elegant oration'.[8] The Society for the Prevention of Cruelty to Animals (founded in 1822 by moral reformers including the evangelical abolitionist William Wilberforce) was lobbying parliament in the cause of animal welfare, resulting in the 1835 Cruelty to Animals Act, which banned bear-baiting and cock-fighting. This was pre-empted at the Eton Society in May 1834 by a debate on the motion: 'Ought the amusements of bull and badger baiting, cock fighting, and prize fighting, to be encouraged as tending to excite the spirit of, or suppressed as tending to demoralize, the English

---

[8] Eton Society Minute Book 1833–34: 7 December 1833, 10 May and 12 July 1834, pp. 27, 82, 117.

people?' Ryle opened the debate and – remarkably, in the light of his later evangelical sentiments – spoke in favour of these sports. Unfortunately his speech was not recorded.[9]

Four of Ryle's speeches were recorded in full, on successive Saturdays in November 1833. They are the earliest surviving examples of his public oratory, for which he later became famous. Though the themes are diverse, they are bound together by questions of moral leadership. Ryle's speeches were presumably expressive of his own opinions, but his longest, on the virtues of duelling, was largely plagiarized from the *United Service Journal and Naval and Military Magazine*. In this edition, abbreviations have been expanded.

[9] Eton Society Minute Book 1833-34: 24 May 1834, p. 90.

The Texts

Saturday, 9 November 1833: 'Has the progress of arts and sciences contributed to corrupt or purify manners?'[10]

Mr Ryle opened the debate, amidst loud cheers from all sides of the house:

Mr President,

As it is, I believe, the first time this subject has been brought before the house, I must regret that it has fallen to the lot of one so inexperienced as myself to open the debate of this evening; I must still further regret that it has not been in my power to obtain any information on it from any book in my possession, and consequently whatever opinions I may bring forward are my own humble theories. I hope therefore, that the house will pardon any ignorance I may shew, any inability to define a subject requiring such nice discrimination, as the one we are at present about to consider. Before however we enter into any discussion on it, I would wish to inform those Honourable Members, who are not aware of the circumstance that it was for an essay on this subject, that the celebrated Jean Jacques Rousseau received a prize in the year 1750 from the Academy of Dijon, and by that essay commenced his literary career:[11] (Hear) this work some Honourable Member may have seen, or even have in his possession; if so he has the advantage of me, for I have not only not seen it, but do not even know which side of the question the illustrious Frenchman espoused; I can only hope that I shall be clear from the imputation of differing in opinion from so highly

---

[10] Eton Society Minute Book 1832-33, pp. 272-76.

[11] Jean-Jacques Rousseau (1712-78), French philosopher, author of *Discours sur les sciences et les arts* (Geneva, 1750), in which he argued that scientific progress corrupts human morality.

talented a man. (Hear.) To say the truth, it was a long time before I knew which side of the question to take; there seemed so much to be said either way, such numberless arguments, such weighty considerations, such cogent reasons for adopting this or that mode of thinking that I had some difficulty in coming to a determination. (Hear, Hear.) Now however, I think I may safely say, (not to be obnoxious to the Honourable Members on the opposite side of the question) (here the honourable gentleman was interrupted by loud laughter and cheers occasioned by some latent cause) that I have come to this conclusion that the progress of arts and sciences has decidedly tended to corrupt the manners of men. (Hear.) It would of course lead to endless discussion, were I to endeavour to prove this by entering into the minutiae of each different art and science, but this is not the line of argument that I intend to pursue. I think it will not be denied, that, from the time when a taste for the arts and sciences first influenced mankind, there has been hardly a single nation that has attained a preeminence by its progress in civilisation [*sic*], without finally and suddenly sinking to a lower level after reaching a certain pitch: so that nation has succeeded nation, differing from each other only in magnitude, like one great wave following another. (Hear.) For it would seem that after the arts and sciences had been directed for some time to objects of public utility, during which period most states enjoyed the greatest prosperity, they became subservient to luxury and pleasure, and invented means by which a simple life was forgotten, and the trouble of laborious occupations was taken from the richer portion of the inhabitants and when luxury had once taken root, effeminacy soon followed, under whose influence that fortitude, those virtues which had secured to each state her former power and independence, were soon overwhelmed; and thus each empire in turn, though perhaps long supported by money and mercenaries, or even by the power of her name, became the prey of internal seditions, or the spoil of the first invader. (Hear.) For I should think, that as long as real purity of manners existed, no state could sink into insignificance, but would remain on the contrary unmoved by adversities, and invincible to any visible enemy; for I am not aware that there is a single instance of any state that came to an end before her own inhabitants, by prostituting the arts and sciences to the service of pleasure and luxury, had wrought their own ruin. (Hear.) It would detain the house too long to bring forward the numberless instances which go to prove this; but the history of the rise and fall of every great empire that has existed on earth puts the fact beyond a doubt. Did not the Romans flourish while they directed their attention to objects of public utility, while their study was to perfect the art of war and the science of taking and fortifying cities, to improve the morals of their countrymen and put a stop to anything approaching to luxury? Do we hear of Roman defeats and adversities, of battles lost and provinces revolted, until the effeminate rule of the emperors had directed the talents of men of science another way, had brought in the art of living well, and the science of inventing new pleasures, with a total disregard for the administration of public affairs? (Hear.) But judging from the events of all ages from the commencement of civilisation [*sic*] down to the present day, the greatest purity of manners seems to have prevailed in the early beginning of each state's prosperity, when the arts and sciences tended to what was useful to the community at large, to the improvement of morals, to the keeping up of simplicity and virtue, to the encouragement of fortitude and patriotism: (Hear) but the farther they progressed, the less they seem to have purified, and the more to have corrupted and tainted the general character of the people. Let us however hope that in our lives at least they may not so contribute to corrupt the manners of this nation, as to bring about that final ruin, which, I trust, is as yet far distant.

The honourable Gentleman then resumed his seat amidst loud cheering. ...

Saturday, 16 November 1833: 'Was the partition of Poland an act that demanded the active interference of Great Britain?'[12]

... Mr Ryle rose amidst deafening applause, and addressed the house as follows:

Mr President,

This subject must, I think, be considered by all one of great importance, when we reflect that on it depends the great question, 'whether one state has a right to interfere in the affairs of another', (Hear, Hear), and it always seems to me that the historians of that period have passed it over with less attention than it deserves, which we can only attribute to the circumstance that the year which witnessed the partition of Poland, witnessed also other events of stirring interest: it was the year which commenced those unhappy disputes between England and the American states, that led to an unnatural war and a final separation between the mother country and her rebellious colonies.[13] (Hear, Hear.) But with all becoming deference to those Demosthenic abilities which the Honourable Opener and Mr Ritchie have so amply displayed in their orations,[14] I must say that I cannot view the question in the same light that they have; for without the smallest desire to be obnoxious to them, (here the Honourable Gentleman was interrupted by loud cheers, intermingled

---

[12] Eton Society Minute Book 1832-33, pp. 305-309. Ryle was the fourth speaker.

[13] The Polish-Lithuanian Commonwealth was forcibly divided in 1772 between Austria, Prussia, and Russia. Although King Stanisław II August appealed for help from Western Europe, none was forthcoming.

[14] The debate was opened by Ryle's friend, Thomas Charlton, supported by William Ritchie (1817-62), later a barrister, advocate-general of Bengal 1856-62, member of the supreme council of India 1861-62.

with some coughing from Mr Lyttelton, by which that Gentleman is supposed to have expressed his disapprobation of the use of the word 'obnoxious') I decidedly think that the partition of Poland by no means deserved the interference of England. (Hear.) Much I am aware may be said on the injustice of such an act, such a flagrant violation of the universal law of 'meum' and 'tuum';[15] much may be urged against so open an abolition of the constitutional liberty of a country, such an aggrandisement of one state at the expense of another; but if we examine the case calmly and dispassionately, if we take into consideration the state of this country at that period, both in her foreign and domestic relations, I flatter myself that at any rate some few Honourable Members will side with me in the view that I take of the question. (Hear, Hear, Hear.) It was no time to talk of distant interference, even supposing that the government had been so inclined, when a war of dangerous and vital importance might every day be expected to break out; not a war by which advantage might be gained or laurels won, but a revolutionnary [*sic*] war, a war of kindred against kindred, in which the hope of freedom and independence and the fear of a disgraceful death would nerve the arm and invigorate the heart of each enemy: it was in a word, a war against a revolted province, in which much might be lost and nothing gained by this country. (Hear, Hear.) And at that time any man of common sagacity might see, that it would be the interest of France to assist the revolted Americans with all the means in her power, in the event of a rupture; which was afterwards fatally proved by her active cooperation with them during the whole course of the war, a cooperation without which the American success must have been rather doubtful. (Hear.) I have perhaps attached too much importance to the condition in which this country was at the time that

---

[15] That is, the law of ownership: mine and yours.

the partition of Poland took place; ('No' from Mr Phinn)[16] but even supposing that no war had impended, that our affairs had been in the highest state of prosperity, I cannot think that any interference in behalf of Poland, would have been an act of policy, or worthy the labour and expense attending such an undertaking. (Hear.) It is well to talk of fighting for the sacred cause of liberty, of putting a stop to the power of tyrannical despots, but acting and carrying these ideas into effect is quite another thing. (Hear, Hear, Hear.) The first steps of course would have been to enter a protest against the proceedings of the three nations which committed the injustice, which protest they would most likely have totally disregarded: we should then I suppose have declared war, and I think it is almost certain that in it we should have incurred an immense expenditure of blood and treasure to no purpose; for against the combined power of three such great continental states as Austria, Russia and Prussia, our small military force, brave and highly disciplined as it was, could have effected little or nothing: (Hear) our naval supremacy would have been no advantage to us, since these three states had no distant colonies to be taken, little commerce or shipping to be destroyed, and few seaports that could receive any material injury from the efforts of our marine; so that we should have had the miserable satisfaction of seeing the wretched Poles overwhelmed by surrounding armies of their oppressors, and punished with additional cruelty for daring to rely on the vain hope of our assistance.

In conclusion I must repeat that although in my opinion the partition of Poland was a most unjust and despotic infringement on the sacred liberties of a free people, I think notwithstanding that any interference in her behalf on the part of England would have been a useless act of ridiculous Quixotism. (Hear, Hear, Hear.)

The Honourable Gentleman resumed his seat amidst loud cheers …

[16] Thomas Phinn (1814-66), barrister, MP for Bath 1852-55.

Saturday, 23 November 1833: 'Was Chatham or Pericles the greatest statesman?'[17]

... Mr Ryle then addressed the house amidst loud cheering:

Mr President,

I am perfectly aware, that in all such comparisons as that which forms the subject of this evening's debate, we should come to the point in consideration, unprejudiced by any sense of pride for the honour of our countryman, unbiassed [*sic*] by any natural unwillingness that we feel to give superiority to a character of so ancient a date, in preference to a statesman of comparatively our own standing. (Hear, Hear.) And this must more especially be kept in mind in the debate of this evening, when we reflect that the civilisation [*sic*] of the era of Chatham was as much beyond that of the age of Pericles, as the manners of the polished Grecian himself were superior to those of the period when arts and sciences were first cultivated by mankind. (Hear.) But as I know that many talented and honourable Members of this society have so far overcome, what I should suppose to be the natural bias of their feelings, as to maintain that Pericles was a greater statesman than Chatham, I shall not, I think, be accused of prejudice, when I affirm that the Athenian, highly talented as he was, was decidedly inferior to the Englishman, in all those qualifications which make a man an able administrator of government. (Cheers.) This question can of course be only proved by comparing the different acts of policy, by which these two great lights of their respective countries distinguished themselves during their public career: and in this also we should bear in mind the respective magnitude of their two countries at the period when

[17] Eton Society Minute Book 1832-33, pp. 340-45. Pericles (*c.* 495-429 BC) was the leading statesman and general during the Athenian 'golden age'. William Pitt the Elder, first earl of Chatham (1708-78) was British prime minister 1766-68.

they flourished; for although Chatham proved himself amply able to wield the destinies and direct the complicated movements of a mighty nation like ours, it remains doubtful whether Pericles could have done it, however fit he may have been for the administration of a small state like Athens. (Indications of disapprobation from Mr Courthope.)[18] Great as Pericles unquestionably was, there are many circumstances, that would seem to militate against his reputation as a statesman: let us in the first place consider his inconsistency, a fault, which, inexperienced as I am, (loud cries of No, No from certain polite Members) I should think every public character, who must expect to have all his words and actions accurately observed, should carefully avoid. (Hear.) When he first brought himself before the notice of the Athenians, in order to oppose the authority of Cimon,[19] he endeavoured to obtain the favour of the people, and by use of the public treasury in his own service, by distributing money among the lower orders, (Hear from Mr Phinn)[20] by increasing the fees paid for their attendance in the courts of judicature, and other donations, he finally established his power: but when the banishment of Thucydides[21] put a period to the two factions, and Pericles became sole master of Athens, he adopted a totally different line of conduct. (Hear, Hear.) His manners were totally changed; he was no longer obsequious to the people and ready to gratify all their capricious desires; nor did he administer the government by courting popular favour and indulging the passions of the multitude: in fact he flattered the people so long only as he thought he might profit by it. As soon as he was once established in the good graces

[18] William Courthope spoke next in the debate, focusing on Pitt's failures and Pericles's abilities.

[19] Cimon, Athenian statesman and political opponent of Pericles.

[20] Phinn had opened this debate.

[21] Thucydides, Athenian historian, author of the *History of the Peloponnesian War*, which was fought between Athens and Sparta 431-404 BC.

of the aristocracy the natural bias of his mind became evident. (Hear, Hear, Hear and Cheers.) Much also as I admire in him that firmness of mind, that prudence, which restrained the Athenians within their walls at a time when the Lacedemonians were ravaging their country,[22] I cannot also admire the mode of carrying on the war which he recommended to his countrymen; it was a system, which, even if they had been victorious, would have reduced them to such a state of weakness and exhaustion, as would have rendered them an easy prey to the first invader; it was by boldness alone that Athens could hope for success, such boldness as the narrow-minded policy of Pericles would have condemned as temerity. (Hear, Hear, and Cheers intermingled with signs if disapprobation from Mr Courthope.) His vicious partiality for the celebrated courtezan [*sic*] Aspasia cannot I think be defended on any principle whatever; for making all due allowance for the weakness of human nature, and the strength of our passions, to undertake an unjust war, like that against the Samians, at the instance of a depraved female, seems to me an act unworthy of a statesman. (Hear, Hear, Hear and Cheers.) A war having taken place between Samos and Miletus on account of the city Priene, in which the latter of the states was defeated, Aspasia (a Milesian by birth) so far influenced the conduct of Pericles as to induce him to declare a war against Samos in the course of which the inhabitants of that country were punished with the utmost cruelty.[23] (Hear.) The Athenians too had reason to execrate the memory of a man, who by his example corrupted the purity and innocence of their morals, who made licentiousness respectable, and the indulgence of every impure desire the qualification of men of the highest ranks. For when he had lost all his legitimate children

[22] That is, the Spartans.

[23] Aspasia was born in Miletus, but migrated to Athens where she became Pericles's lover. In the Samian War (440-439 BC), Athens intervened on the side of Miletus to defeat Samos.

by the pestilence, to call a natural son by his own name, he went so far as to repeal a law which he had made against spurious children,[24] and which he had enforced with the greatest severity. (Hear, Hear.)

Let us however now turn to Chatham, a character that no one can examine without a feeling of pride, as one of the brightest ornaments of this country. The Honourable Opener with his accustomed eloquence has so amply expatiated on his act that it will be amply sufficient for me to give a short sketch of his life. He commenced his public career at the early age of 27, and for twenty years exerted his talents in the service of his country; in 1757 defeat and disgrace having fallen on his country, the unanimous voice of the people compelled the sovereign to place him at the head of the administration: under his auspices Britain was during four years triumphant in every quarter of the globe.[25] Thwarted in his measures by the want of cooperation in his colleagues, after the accession of George 3rd, he resigned an office, which he could no longer hold with honour to himself or advantage to the nation. To the end of his life, though suffering severely from disease at the latter part of it, he continued to speak in Parliament upon all important occasions. The American war in particular he opposed with all his wonted vigour and talent; it was while speaking on this subject, that he fell into a convulsive fit, which finally proved fatal; and thus died as he had always lived in the service of his country.[26] (Hear, Hear.) He well deserves, I think, the character that Grattan, the able Irish orator, gives of him: 'There was in this man something that could create, subvert, or

[24] That is, illegitimate children.

[25] In 1756, at the start of the Seven Years' War, Britain was humiliated by France in the Battle of Minorca, which led to the court-martial and execution of Admiral John Byng. However, during the next four years from 1757 to 1761, when Pitt was secretary of state in a coalition with the Duke of Newcastle, Britain won a series of decisive military victories, especially in North America.

[26] Pitt collapsed while speaking in the House of Lords on 7 April 1778, and died on 11 May.

reform; an understanding, a spirit, and an eloquence, to summon mankind to society, or to break the bonds of slavery asunder, and to rule the wilderness of free minds with unbounded authority; something that could establish or overwhelm empire, and strike a blow in the world, that should resound throughout the universe.'[27] (Hear, Hear, Hear and Cheers.)

The Honourable Gentleman then resumed his seat amidst great applause. …

Saturday, 30 November 1833: 'Is duelling beneficial to society?'[28]

Mr Ryle opened the debate as follows:

Mr President,

I am perfectly aware of the weakness of the side that I am about to support, of the multitudinous and forcible arguments that may be brought against it, and I must therefore regret my inability (cries of No, No, from certain hyper-urbane members) to do justice to a question of such importance as the present one, a question, which, by some indiscreat [*sic*] action, some hasty expression of temper, may at a future time be of the deepest interest to any one of us. (Hear.) For I maintain, Sir, that duelling is not only beneficial to society, but even absolutely necessary for the preservation of politeness and good-breeding, for that distinction between gentleman and black-

---

[27] Henry Grattan (1746-1820), Irish parliamentarian. See 'Character of Mr Pitt' (1772), in *Miscellaneous works of the Right Honourable Henry Grattan* (London, 1822), p. 10.

[28] Eton Society Minute Book 1833-34, pp. 1-12. Most of Ryle's speech was lifted, often word-for-word, including the classical references, from 'On duelling', *United Service Journal and Naval and Military Magazine* (February 1831), pp. 145-53, and 'J. M. on duelling, in reply to his critics', *United Service Journal and Naval and Military Magazine* (May 1831), pp. 100-102.

guard, which has always been the pride of this country. (Cheers.) Let us in the first place consider its antiquity; for it would seem no small argument in favour of the custom, that it has prevailed through so many centuries, that after the lapse of so many ages, after the improvements that civilisation [*sic*] has made in every era, duelling has still been kept up, as the last resource of an honourable man against injury and insult. (Hear.) It is a mistake to suppose that duels were not known to the ancients; for we find in Plutarch, that during the Indian expedition Hephaestion and Craterus drew their swords on each other, and fought till separated by Alexander himself:[29] a duel also is mentioned and described in the seventh book of Quintus Curtius,[30] (Hear and Laughter) to which without resorting to the Iliad, others might no doubt be added. But as a practice sanctioned by law and custom, duelling can be traced no further back than the judicial combats of the Germans. The laws of these nations ordained, that in all doubtful cases, when the judges were unable to decide and pass sentence, the parties themselves should be allowed the trial by battle, in order to settle their differences sword in hand. These combats were unknown in Germany at the time of Tacitus, who makes no mention of the practice;[31] but owing to the total absence of all efficient laws they appear to have spread with great rapidity over the least barbarous parts of Europe soon after the fall of the western empire. But it was in the ages of chivalry that duelling increased most, when that romantic spirit, which had begun about the eleventh century, gave rise to extra-judicial combats, fought before judges selected only for the occasion, and often intended to settle mere points of honour. These combats, as long as they were confined to knights and nobles, were fought on horseback in the full panoply

[29] Plutarch, *Life of Alexander*, chapter 47.

[30] Quintus Curtius Rufus, *Histories of Alexander the Great*, book 9, section 7, records the duel between Dioxippus and Corratas.

[31] Tacitus, historian of the Roman Empire.

which distinguished the warfare of that period: but this mode of settling private quarrels did not long survive the flourishing period of the institution that gave rise to it; and in the middle ages we find duels fought with every description of arms and in every imaginable manner. Entire parties called each other to the field; and when hostile armies lay inactive near each other, it was not uncommon for officers of the contending nations to meet by appointment, each attended by a certain number of friends, in order to settle a private feud, or merely to fight, as they termed it, to keep their arms from rust. (Hear.) Latterly the custom was carried to such a pitch in France, that no less than four thousand people are said to have been killed by duels in that country alone, between the years 1594 and 1607. (Laughter and Cheers.) All these wild practices yielded however in the end to modern manners and customs, and very generally made way for the simplicity of our present duels, that partake more of the original trial by battle and knightly combats, than of the extravagances of the middles ages: being generally fought to decide cases which the law cannot reach in a satisfactory manner, or for the purpose of settling mere points of honour. Of these in their present form something must be said. Society very justly expects from all who move in a certain rank an amenity of manners, a fair, manly and upright line of conduct in the general intercourse and transactions of life, that no law can enforce; (Hear, Hear) it further demands from all such persons, a character for honour unblemished to a degree far beyond the protection afforded by the laws of the land; and inflicts the severest punishment that can befall a high-minded man, on all those who submit to conduct not sanctioned by the rules of polite society, or who allow the least stain or reflection to rest on their own character, or on the honour and reputation of those dependant on them for protection. (Hear.) These rules, as far as they go, are exceedingly just and proper, but they are after all found applicable only to exterior manner, so that society can be said to insist only on the strict observance of certain conventional rules, requiring indeed that the evil passions of the human heart should be varnished over, but pretending by no means to insist on their abolition. The consequence is that the passions and feelings of the worthless are constantly breaking through these slight and artificial trammels; and provided the offender only keeps beyond the reach of the criminal law, the offended party, however much he may have been injured and aggrieved, has not only no legal redress, but is himself severely punished, if he leave the wrong unredressed, the injury unavenged. The consequence naturally is, that where the law ceases to afford protection, men do their best to protect themselves, and appeal to arms as a matter of course; and society conscious of the dilemma in which men may be placed by this contradictory rule of manners, naturally refrain from punishing with severity such appeals to arms, except in cases where some glaring deviation from what is termed fair practice can be made out. For it seems to me, and I think on consideration it will seem to many Honourable Members too, that if a man is permitted by the laws of his country to defend a little paltry gold at the risk of slaying the aggressor, on what fair ground can he be prevented from defending his own reputation and the reputation of those, whose fame must be dearer to him than his own? (Hear, Hear, Hear.) In this opinion too [I] am borne out by no less a character that Dr Johnson himself (Cheers and Laughter) who expresses himself on this point as follows, 'I do not see that fighting is forbidden in Scripture; I see revenge forbidden, but not self defence. A man may shed the blood of a man who invades his character, as he may shoot him who attempts to break into his house.'[32] (Hear, Hear, Hear and Cheers.) It may be asked, cannot the practice of duelling, a practice

---

[32] A very loose quotation from James Boswell, *The life of Samuel Johnson* (2 vols, London, 1791), vol. 2, p. 450. It appears in this exact form in 'J. M. on duelling', p. 100.

avowedly derived only from the barbarism of our Gothic ancestors, be entirely abolished, as unworthy of an enlightened and refined age? Certainly not, as long as this age of refinement retains under a slightly gilded exterior, all those evil passions against which the age of barbarism, whose manliness of feeling we entirely want, instituted the practice. It is only by raising the standard of politeness and of moral conduct, and by insisting on its being acted up to by all ranks, that such an abolition can ever be effected. (Hear, Hear.) Till then all legal enactments will be in vain; for no high-minded man will consent to lose his station in society, and to bring disgrace on himself, his friends and his kindred, by submitting to insult or injury from the base and insolent without challenging the offender. (Hear.) Nor can it ever be the object of a sound system of morality or a just legislation, to render man regardless of shame, and indifferent to the opinion of his fellow men; for let a man be once suspected of timidity, and all the world immediately seeks to become heroes at his expense. Reputation and character cannot possibly be left so unguarded; for men of high and generous feelings have after all little left to lose in this world, when they have once lost even this world's esteem. (Hear, Hear, and Cheers.) And what remedy, what protection is there in many cases, but what is afforded by the precarious and uncertain law of battle; itself avowedly evil, rendered necessary by the evil passions of the human breast, that too often leave us nothing but a choice of evils. (Hear.) The Greeks and Romans of old, it may be urged by supporters of the opposite side of the question, had no higher standard of politeness and moral conduct than our own, yet did not on that account fight duels: there are also insolent and ill-behaved men at the present time among the Turks, yet they never challenge each other to single combat: why then should we, who pretend to be more refined, more civilized than these nations, suffer another shot to be fired in such an encounter? Simply because our more artificial state of society leaves openings for the commission of more extra-judicial offences, the repression of which renders some extra-judicial law of very general application indispensable; (here much laughter was occasioned by the Honourable Opener getting so entangled among his voluminous papers, as to be unable to proceed for some minutes) and also because, with no more virtues than the nations above mentioned, (though having, from our greater knowledge and civilisation [*sic*] perhaps, fewer gross vices) we have in point of manners acquired a higher degree of exterior polish, which the respect due to female delicacy and purity of feeling has tended not a little to keep up, since women have taken their proper station in society. (Cheers and Hear, Hear.) And here it may be added, that the protection, which the softer sex is always entitled to receive from us, gives rise to the most legitimate causes for which challenges may be sent and duels fought; not only because women are unable to protect themselves from calumny and insult, but because the least aspersion thrown upon their character, however false it may be, acts as a corrosive poison, the effects of which no atonement can ever entirely remove. (Hear, Hear.) For the rose, over which the pestiferous breath of the fiery wind of the desert has once passed, lifts not its head with the return of the healthful breeze; the particles of poison adhere insensibly but immoveably [*sic*] to the fibres of life, and the flower withers in its bloom. (Hear, Hear.) Even so has many a kindly heart been crushed, and many a lonely head been bowed down in silent sorrow by the baneful effects of slander, long after the slanderer's voice had been stopped and put to shame and ignominy. For no law with its paltry shilling damages can redress such injuries as an attack on the character and reputation of a woman, and high-minded men can never let an insult to a female dependant on them for protection pass unavenged. (Hear, Hear, and Cheers.) Though I maintain the necessity of duelling, I do not pretend to say that I should think the fighting fifty battles a proof of a man's courage; for it does not, I know, require a high degree of fortitude to stand for a few seconds to be shot at; (Laughter and Cheers) but yet I think that the dislike, not to call it the fear, of fighting a duel has a salutary effect on the conduct of six persons out of ten; for I am of opinion that there are many people who agree with Lord Byron, in that he says,

> It has a strange quick jar upon the ear
> That cocking of a pistol, when you know
> A moment more may bring the sight to bear (Hear)
> Upon your body, twelve yards off or so.[33] (Hear.)

To conclude, let politeness bear proof of springing from the just feelings and impulses of the heart, instead of being, as it is at present in the fashionable world, a mere show of hypocrisy and humbug: let falsehood, meanness, coarseness and ignorance be as easily detected and as severely punished in the wealthy and powerful, as they are in the poor and unprotected: (Hear) let gamblers be consigned to the worthy fraternity of blacklegs, as a class of men, whose minds are of so low a cast as to attach all the interest they are capable of feeling on the turning up of a card or the roll of a die: (Hear) let the drunkard, who, by destroying the reason that has been given him for his guidance and conduct, debases himself beneath the very brute that retains its natural instinct, be pitied, prayed for, but avoided: (Hear) and above all let the least breach of faith or word, the least insult to a woman, even of the humblest rank, be branded with the heaviest stigma that society can inflict. (Hear, Hear, Hear.) When this is done and it may be done without the aid of legislative enactments, then, and not till then, will the world have a right to call for the abolition of the modern trial by battle. (Hear, Hear.)

The Honourable Gentleman resumed his seat amidst loud cheers …

[33] 'Don Juan', canto 4, stanza 41, in *The works of Lord Byron including the suppressed poems* (Paris, 1828), p. 604.

HERBERT RYLE ON
HIS FATHER'S SCHOOLDAYS

Amongst the tributes and recollections published when J. C. Ryle died in June 1900 was an article by his son, Herbert Ryle, entitled 'The late bishop of Liverpool as an Eton boy'. It contains significant new information not in the autobiography, including an account of J. C. Ryle's two floggings at the hands of the headmaster, which the bishop enjoyed recounting with humour. The text was transcribed by Guthrie Clark in 1947, presumably from a newspaper or magazine cutting in the Ryle family archive, and is found at the back of the exercise book into which he copied the autobiography. The cutting has not been traced, nor the original source identified.

Clark also copied a short text giving Ryle's measurements as an 18-year-old and the measurements of Ryle's favourite dog, his Lyme mastiff called 'Caesar' (again the source has not been traced). Ryle was nicknamed 'Magnus' by his Eton contemporaries and his impressive physical build was often a source of comment. Archdeacon Sydney James, as has been seen, spoke of Ryle's 'gigantic figure'.[1] At the annual Church Congress at Swansea in 1879, a

---

[1] Fitzgerald, *Herbert Edward Ryle*, p. 11.

leading Anglo-Catholic ritualist, W. J. Knox-Little (rector of St Alban's, Cheetwood, in Manchester), quipped:

> Canon Ryle dropped a hint that he was ready to turn up his sleeves, and double his fists, and square his shoulders, against any one who should say a word in favour of [auricular] confession. ... Certainly I should not like to accept battle with him, for I am afraid, judging from the Canon's build, I should get, in plain English, an awful drubbing.[2]

Nevertheless, Ryle's size was sometimes exaggerated. His son claimed: 'He was a man of magnificent physique, standing 6 ft 3½ inches in height, and as straight as an arrow.'[3] J. I. Packer described him as 'massive', 'nearly six feet four and strong as a horse'.[4] Yet the measurements published here give more accurate, marginally shorter, dimensions. In Ryle's own words, as an octogenarian, 'I now stand six feet two in my shoes'.[5]

---

[2] 'Best means of promoting internal unity in the church', *Nineteenth annual meeting of the Church Congress, held at Swansea on October the 7th, 8th, 9th, & 10th 1879* (London, 1880), p. 397.

[3] 'The dean of Westminster in Macclesfield: centenary commemoration at the parish church', *Macclesfield Courier and Herald*, 21 October 1916, p. 3; followed by Martin Wellings (ed.), 'J. C. Ryle: "First words". An opening address delivered at the first Liverpool diocesan conference, 1881', in Mark Smith and Stephen Taylor (eds), *Evangelicalism in the Church of England c.1790 – c.1900: a miscellany*, Church of England Record Society vol. 12 (Woodbridge, 2004), p. 289.

[4] J. I. Packer, 'Preface', in J. C. Ryle, *Holiness: its nature, hindrances, difficulties, and roots* (centenary edition, Welwyn, 1979), p. viii.

[5] Ryle at Bootle (January 1897), quoted in Machray, *The first bishop of Liverpool*, p. 13.

The Texts

John Charles Ryle was born on the 10th of May 1816. He was the eldest son of John Ryle, a well-to-do banker at Macclesfield and M.P. for that borough. At the time when the future Bishop of Liverpool was born his father lived at Park House in Macclesfield, a solid well-built brick house standing in its own grounds. Later on he moved to a large country seat called Henbury, where there was a large Park with beautiful trees and extensive pieces of water. It was only a little distance out of Macclesfield and was therefore very convenient for business purposes. The Bishop always looked back upon Henbury with great affection.

After a brief period at a county preparatory school, the banker sent his eldest son to Eton, where his tutor was Rev. E. C. Hawtrey, who afterwards became headmaster. Hawtrey was an excellent tutor; and in later days the Bishop used often to say that whatever he had of scholarship at Eton was due to the private work which Hawtrey did with his pupils. Young Ryle was probably in some respects an apt pupil; and though he used to declare that he was very idle and careless at school, there is no doubt that at least in his last years at Eton he shaped into an admirable scholar. His Latin composition and versification was good, his work was neat and orderly. He had a good knowledge of Homer, Sophocles and Thucydides, Horace, Virgil and Livy, by the time he left school. He had a fine memory. Like other famous Etonians he knew Horace by heart; and up to the last year of his life used to utter the half comic lament, 'If I only knew my Bible as well as my Horace.' And certainly he could 'cap' quotations from Horace with extraordinary readiness. He was wont to say that the Eton boys of his day had not half the minute and careful coaching which Arnold bestowed upon his sixth form pupils at Rugby. Keate 'impiger, iracundus'[6] was headmaster at Eton; he drove the school with the birch rod. But so far as young Ryle was concerned it was not Keate who put scholarship into him but Hawtrey, and after him Cookesley.[7] In 1834, his last year at Eton, he seems to have come out third in the Newcastle Scholarship Examination when Lonsdale was scholar[8] and Lyttelton (the famous classical scholar Lord Lyttelton, bracketed senior class[icist] with Vaughan in 1838) was second or medallist. It was a brilliant Eton year for Ryle, who was third, got a Craven Scholarship at Oxford only two years later.

When he first went to Eton he was a short square dumpy lad; and it is said that fears were expressed of his never growing any taller. If so, those fears were quickly dissipated. He grew rapidly at Eton and became a tall and remarkably powerfully built young fellow. He was so big that his companions dubbed him 'Magnus'; and forty years afterwards when Lord Lyttelton met Canon Ryle, as he then was, in the playing fields of Eton, he addressed him familiarly by his old school name.

He excelled in cricket and hockey. He was very fond of both games, especially of cricket. He always maintained an intensely keen interest in cricket and even in 1899 was closely following the scores and averages of the leading cricketers and the contests of the chief elevens. At Eton he was in the eleven in 1833 and was captain in 1834 when Eton beat Winchester by 13 runs, and was beaten by Harrow by 13 runs. As a cricketer, he was a powerful hitter, having a commanding reach and immense strength; he was also a fast round-arm

---

[6] Horace, *Ars Poetica* II. 121, describes Achilles as 'impiger, iracundus, inexorabilis, acer' – that is, energetic, wrathful, implacable, impetuous.

[7] William Gifford Cookesley (1802-80), classical scholar, fellow of King's College, Cambridge 1824-31, master at Eton College 1830-54, perpetual curate of St Peter's, Hammersmith 1860-68, rector of Tempsford, Bedfordshire 1868-80.

[8] That is, James Gylby Lonsdale. Ryle only came fourth in the Newcastle scholarship, according to his autobiography (see above, p. 38).

bowler. He used to dwell with satisfaction upon a certain innings in the Upper Shooting Fields at Eton when he got a six off the first ball by hitting a half volley to leg that pitched into the water by Sheep's Bridge.

As to his general life and behaviour at school it is not possible to record much. A younger contemporary of his, Bishop Hobhouse,[9] is said to have related his impression that Ryle was a great big masterful fellow, a very fine cricketer and a boy who set a good example and always lived a straight God-fearing life. He himself used to regard his school days as a time of thoughtlessness and utter spiritual neglect. Confirmation was the merest form; and according to his recollection at a later time, practically no attempt was made to look after the souls of the boys or to deepen their Christian life. Sermons were occasionally preached in college chapel by the fellows of the college. One sermon which was preached again and again was on the word 'Peter'; another which the boys welcomed as an old friend was on the text, 'And his mother made him a little coat.'[10] But beyond the peculiar joy which the boys appear to have derived from the eccentricities of the preachers, these sermons can hardly be said to have left any sort of useful impression. The Bishop always spoke highly of one of the masters named Edward Coleridge, afterwards a fellow of Eton, who in the midst of many difficulties, and in spite of much misunderstanding, seems to have sought to promote the religious welfare of the pupils.

Probably the Bishop was an ordinary gentlemanly boy of high born and general good influence. He used to speak in terms of the profoundest contempt for certain lads who neither played hard nor worked hard, but skulked away up Windsor and smoked on the

---

[9] Edmund Hobhouse (1817-1904), pupil at Eton College 1824-30, fellow of Merton College, Oxford 1841-58, bishop of Nelson, New Zealand 1858-66, assistant bishop in Lichfield diocese 1869-81.

[10] 1 Samuel 2:19.

sly, and sought to imitate the least estimable ways of some young officers at the barracks. He was fond of relating how Keate flogged him. Keate had the reputation of having flogged every boy in the school; certainly on one occasion he flogged all the Confirmation candidates, their list having become accidentally substituted for the punishment list.

Keate twice flogged the Bishop, and on both occasions he said he richly deserved it. The first time it was for shooting with a pistol. Ryle and a young friend of his had procured this engine of war; and having spread a handkerchief on the side of a hedge, were busily engaged taking it in turns to endeavour to perforate their target. In the midst of the fun a heavy hand was laid on his shoulder, and the voice of Dupuis,[11] one of the assistant masters, was heard saying, 'Give up that pistol; what are your names? I shall report you to the headmaster!' Needless to say before 24 hours had passed both had become victims at the block.

The other occasion was a more serious affair. Ryle was playing in a cricket match in the playing fields; and the two elevens were excused attendance at the evening 'Absence', i.e. roll call. But the match happened to be over early. The cricketers thought they would notwithstanding avail themselves of their leave. They retired to Slough and greatly enjoyed a good supper of duck and green peas with other refreshments at some well-known hostelry. But as ill-luck would have it, one less hungry or more punctilious cricketer had not gone to Slough; and had shown himself at Absence and answered to his name. The matter was investigated. Keate was furious. That night the defaulting boys were extracted from their various rooms, brought to the headmaster and then and there soundly flogged, the

[11] George John Dupuis (1795-1884), fellow of King's College, Cambridge 1818-31, master at Eton College 1819-40, rector of Creeting St Mary, Suffolk 1840-62 (near Ryle at Helmingham), of Worplesdon, Surrey 1862-78, vice-provost of Eton College 1868-84.

whole lot of them; Keate interjecting between the strokes of the birch indignant spasmodic utterances such as 'Foolish boy', 'I am ashamed of you', 'You will bring down the grey hairs of your father with sorrow to the grave!' The Bishop used to tell the story with great laughter and enjoyment.

One of the old school fellows who was in the eleven with him and remained a life-friend, was the late Sir Algernon Coote, who only died a few months before the Bishop.

The Bishop's name is carved on the oak door on the left of the desk at the end of the Upper School. The names of his two Eton sons are carved immediately below his. The door was two years ago frequently photographed because on it is also carved the name of an older and more illustrious Etonian, W. E. Gladstone.[12]

The Bishop's picture painted at the headmaster's request on his leaving Eton hangs in the cloisters; and though he was only in his eighteenth year, the picture is that of a well-grown, distinguished-looking, young man, fashionably dressed, with thick wavy dark hair, clear complexion and an attractive look of thoughtful dignity.[13]

* * *

[12] Gladstone died in May 1898, two years before Ryle.
[13] See the colour portrait in this volume.

J. C. Ryle's measurements, aged 18

Perpendicular reach up	7 feet 9 inches
Height	6 feet 1 7/8 inches
Round the waist	2 feet 7 1/2 inches
Length of arm	2 feet 7 inches
Across the shoulders	1 foot 7 inches
Round the thigh	1 foot 10 inches
Round the wrist	7 1/4 inches
Round the neck	1 foot 3 1/2 inches
Length of leg from hip joint	3 feet 4 inches
Span of fingers	9 1/2 inches
Horizontal reach of both arms	6 feet 2 1/2 inches

Size of Caesar, a Lyme mastiff[14]

Length from nose to tip of tail	5 feet 10 1/2 inches
Height of shoulder	2 feet 7 1/2 inches
Round the waist	3 feet 2 1/2 inches
Round the neck	2 feet 1 inch
From tip to tip of ears	1 foot 6 inches
Length of head	11 1/2 inches

---

[14] For Ryle's fondness for Caesar, see above pp. 92-93.

APPENDIX 4

CANON CHRISTOPHER ON RYLE'S CONVERSION

The best-known account of Ryle's conversion is the story of how, as an undergraduate in 1837, he attended a parish church in Oxford where he was particularly struck by the Bible reading from Ephesians chapter 2, and the emphasis given to verse 8: 'By grace are ye saved – through faith – and that not of yourselves – it is the gift of God.' This narrative was first published in *The Record* newspaper in June 1900, a few days after Ryle's death, by Canon Alfred Christopher (1820-1913), rector of St Aldate's, Oxford.[1]

Christopher and Ryle were friends and allies in the promotion of evangelical theology, and Ryle preached frequently at St Aldate's in the years before his appointment as bishop of Liverpool. His first sermons there were in June 1865 and June 1866,[2] with repeat appearances the following decade in 1875, 1876, 1877 (twice), 1879, and

---

[1] John S. Reynolds, *Canon Christopher of St Aldate's, Oxford* (Abingdon, 1967).

[2] *Jackson's Oxford Journal*, 24 June 1865 and 9 June 1866. One undergraduate who heard Ryle in 1866 was Francis Chavasse (1846-1928), later his successor as bishop of Liverpool. See entries for 9-10 June 1866, in Andrew Atherstone (ed.), 'The undergraduate diary of Francis Chavasse 1865-1868', in Smith and Taylor, *Evangelicalism in the Church of England c.1790 – c.1900*, p. 188. For Chavasse's notes of Ryle's sermon, see Bodleian Library, MS Chavasse dep. 30, pp. 9-13.

Alfred Christopher, rector of St Aldate's, Oxford, in the 1860s and in old age.

1880 (twice), sometimes scheduled to coincide with Ryle's delivery
of the university sermon as 'select preacher'.[3] He also lectured twice
at Oxford Town Hall, in May 1871 on lessons from English church
history (Christopher was on the platform and opened in prayer),[4]
and in November 1877 on 'James II and the seven bishops' for
the local branch of the anti-ritualist Church Association at which
Christopher presided.[5] Therefore the two men had abundant opportunities to get to know each other. Christopher remembered that
it was during the first visit in 1865 that Ryle gave account of his
conversion, but he was subsequently able to check the details when
Ryle returned to Oxford. The story became 'a great favourite' of
Christopher's, one he often retold.[6]

Francis Jansen (1865-1947), vicar of Newton Solney near
Burton-upon-Trent, studied theology at Oxford in the mid-1880s,
and heard Christopher speak about Ryle's conversion 'more than
once'. Jansen repeated that Ryle 'dropped in to Carfax Church
one Sunday afternoon when a stranger happened to be officiating',
heard Ephesians 2 read in a distinctive manner, and 'there and then,
under an overmastering impulse, he sank on his knees and yielded
his heart and life to God, coming out of the church a changed
man'.[7] If this identification of Carfax Church is correct, then it is
highly significant, because Christopher did not name it in his published account and the location has long been shrouded in mystery.

[3] *Jackson's Oxford Journal*, 20 November 1875, 3 June 1876, 12 May and 24 November 1877, 15 November 1879, 24 April and 22 May 1880. See also, 'The Bishop-Designate of Liverpool at New College', *Jackson's Oxford Journal*, 29 May 1880; 'University Sermon', *Jackson's Oxford Journal*, 20 November 1880.

[4] 'Lessons from English Church History', *Jackson's Oxford Journal*, 6 May 1871.

[5] 'Church Association', *Jackson's Oxford Journal*, 1 December 1877.

[6] W. H. Griffith Thomas, 'Memories of Canon Christopher', *The Churchman* vol. 34 (September 1920), p. 511.

[7] 'The late Bishop Ryle', letter from Francis Jansen, *The Record*, 9 November 1916, p. 887.

Engraving from 1836 of Carfax Church, Oxford, probably the place where Ryle heard Ephesians 2 being read. It was demolished in 1896.

Carfax – formally known as St Martin's Church, Oxford – was the 'city church' (as opposed to the 'university church') in the patronage of the mayor and corporation, until its demolition in 1896. The rector during Ryle's undergraduate years, John Hyde (*c.* 1775-1838), was largely non-resident and left the church in the charge of a succession of curates. There was also a prestigious lectureship attached to St Martin's, founded in 1586, with a sermon delivered before the mayor and corporation twice each Sunday, morning and afternoon, by one of the four 'city lecturers'.[8] One of these clergymen may have been the 'stranger' who officiated when Ryle was present.

In the early twentieth century other authors picked up Christopher's published report. At a 'quiet day' for ordinands in the diocese of Worcester in December 1902, John William Diggle (1847-1920), later bishop of Carlisle, spoke of the significance of the public reading of Scripture, and took Ryle's experience as proof:

> Reading is even more important than preaching: for in preaching we are preaching our own words, but in reading the Lessons we are preaching the message of God Himself. It is better to read the lessons searchingly than to preach a sermon strikingly. ... Bishop Ryle owed his conversion to the reading of a lesson in church.[9]

Christopher's narrative was further popularized by W. H. Griffith Thomas (1861-1924), who had served as his curate at St Aldate's 1889-96. In Thomas's pastoralia lectures as principal of Wycliffe Hall, Oxford, published as *The work of the ministry* (1911), he took Ryle's conversion as an illustration for ordinands of their 'solemn responsibility to read God's own Word to the people'. The anecdote ran as follows:

---

[8] Carteret J. H. Fletcher, *A history of the church and parish of St Martin (Carfax) Oxford* (Oxford, 1896).

[9] J. W. Diggle, *Quiet hours with the ordinal: a series of addresses* (London, 1906), p. 72.

W. H. Griffith Thomas, principal of Wycliffe Hall, Oxford.

J. C. Ryle in academic dress.

Many years ago an Oxford undergraduate sauntered into an Oxford
Church, of which afterwards he was quite unable to remember the
name. At that time he was nearing his final examination and was
feeling somewhat depressed. As he entered the Church the second
lesson was being read (Ephesians ii), and the reader made somewhat unusual pauses as he read verse 8 thus: 'By grace – are ye saved
– through faith – and that, not of yourselves – it is the gift of God.'
The Divine Word went home to the undergraduate's heart, and led
to his conversion. His name was John Charles Ryle, and in later life
he became Bishop of Liverpool.[10]

Thomas embellished Christopher's account in four ways – first,
that Ryle's attendance was casual, even accidental (he 'sauntered'
in); second that Ryle could not remember the name of the church
(Christopher says only that Ryle did not know the name of the
clergyman); third that Ryle was depressed (according to Christopher he was in a 'more serious state of mind', that is, wrestling with
spiritual questions); fourth that Ryle was late for the service and
arrived as the lesson was being read. This third-hand account of
Ryle's conversion is therefore dubious. It was a casual lecture illustration, perhaps narrated from memory, not intended to supply
strictly accurate historical detail. Nevertheless, this version with
its various embellishments was carried over into subsequent biographies by Guthrie Clark and Marcus Loane.[11]

Thomas was more careful when attempting to write history.
He collected materials for a biography of Christopher, drafted but
never published, though an abridgement appeared in installments
in *The Churchman* during 1920. This time his retelling of Christopher's memories of Ryle stuck closely to the published account in
The Record and is therefore more trustworthy than *The work of the*

[10] W. H. Griffith Thomas, *The work of the ministry* (London, 1911), p. 185.
[11] Clark, *John Charles Ryle*, p. 10; Loane, *John Charles Ryle* (1953), pp. 13-14.

ministry.[12] What every account has in common, however, is the centrality of Ephesians 2:8. Thomas concluded:

> it is not too much to say that all the sermons, the addresses, the unique tracts, the *Expository Thoughts on the Gospels*, and all the other works written and published by J. C. Ryle in his long and honoured career as a country clergyman, an honorary Canon and a Bishop, were the fruit of God's work of grace in the heart of the undergraduate wrought by means of that never-forgotten verse.[13]

Loane, in more romantic mood, declared that 'that verse was like an arrow strung to the bow of an Archer Divine, and its flight was winged in mercy straight to the heart of the chosen mortal.'[14]

Christopher's original account remains puzzling because, at first sight, it appears to contradict Ryle's own narrative of his conversion in his autobiography. Ryle wrote: 'The circumstances which led to a complete change in my character were very many and very various … It was not a sudden immediate change but very gradual. I cannot trace it to any one person, or any one event or thing, but to a singular variety of persons and things.'[15] Among the various contributory factors, he makes no mention of Ephesians 2. Christopher, by contrast, presents Ryle as awakened suddenly and decisively by hearing a single verse read by a stranger – taken by Christopher, and by many preachers since, as a famous example of the power of Scripture. Did Christopher muddle or misunderstand the story? Did his memory become vague during the three and a half decades between first hearing the account in 1865 and publishing it in 1900, though he had often repeated it in the interim? He admitted it was queried

---

[12] Thomas, 'Memories of Canon Christopher', pp. 511-13. The unpublished typescript of Thomas's biography of Christopher is in possession of Andrew Atherstone. It was reworked by John Reynolds for his 1967 biography.

[13] Thomas, 'Memories of Canon Christopher', p. 511.

[14] Loane, *John Charles Ryle* (1953), p. 14.

[15] See above, p. 67.

by his friend, E. P. Hathaway (rector of St Ebbe's, Oxford), who had heard that Ryle's conversion came through a rebuke for swearing by Sir Charles Coote. This is recorded in the autobiography as taking place two years before Ryle's conversion, but there the rebuke was by Algernon Coote not Sir Charles.[16] This discrepancy in detail suggests Christopher's facts were not perfect. Nevertheless, he insisted that the converting impact of Ephesians 2:8 was confirmed by Ryle himself.

On closer inspection, Christopher's account fits well with Ryle's autobiography. According to the original lectionary for the *Book of Common Prayer* (in use until replaced by a new lectionary in 1871), most of the New Testament was read three times a year, and Ephesians 2 was a set reading at Evening Prayer on 25 February, 25 June and 22 October – which in 1837 fell on Saturday, Sunday and Sunday. The last two dates are both possibilities. Christopher reported that it was 'near the time of his final examination', which took place at the end of November 1837, so perhaps the memorable reading of Ephesians was in October, at the start of Ryle's last term in Oxford. Ryle recorded in his autobiography that evangelical doctrines

seemed to flash upon me like a sunbeam in the winter of 1837, and have stuck in my mind from that time down to this. People may account for such a change as they like, my own belief is, that no rational explanation can be given of it, but that of the Bible; it was what the Bible calls 'conversion', and 'regeneration'. Before that time I was dead in sins, and on the high road to hell, and from that

[16] See above, p. 68. In response to Christopher's article, Algernon Coote's widow wrote to *The Record* quoting a letter she received from Ryle in November 1899 following the death of her husband. Ryle had written: 'And now he is gone – the oldest, most godly, and most faithful friend I have ever had, to whom my soul was indebted sixty-five years ago! He was the first person who ever told me to think, repent, and pray, and I shall never forget him.' ('Bishop Ryle', letter from Constance Coote, *The Record*, 22 June 1900, p. 613.)

time, I became alive, and had a hope of heaven. And nothing to my mind can account for it, but the free sovereign grace of God.[17]

This emphasis upon the grace of God, and being 'dead in sins' and then 'alive' in Christ, is an echo of Ephesians 2, so Ryle may have been remembering the impact of that text, though he did not make it explicit.

Ryle explained in his autobiography that by the beginning of 1838 he was 'fairly launched as a Christian'. However, his conversion took place gradually over the previous six months, which may point to 25 June as the more likely decisive date. Ryle recalled:

> about Midsummer, a severe illness which I had at Oxford, of inflammation of the chest confined me to bed for some days and brought me very low for some time. That was the time I remember distinctly when I first began to read my Bible, or began to pray. It was at a very curious crisis in my life – it was just about the time that I was taking my degree, and I have a strong recollection that my new views of religion helped me very greatly to go through all my examinations very coolly and quietly. In short, from about Midsummer 1837, till Christmas in the same year, was a turning point in my life.[18]

Midsummer is traditionally reckoned as 24 June (the feast of St John the Baptist), so if Ryle heard Ephesians 2 read on Sunday, 25 June 1837, the dates are a perfect match. In that case, although not perhaps the conversion moment itself, it was the stimulus which brought Ryle to conversion over the succeeding weeks. It is curious that the autobiography does not mention this memorable incident, but Christopher's account certainly coheres well with Ryle's broader testimony. Furthermore at Ryle's death in 1900, Ephesians 2:8 – so significant in shaping his life and ministry – was carved upon his gravestone.

[17] See above, p. 73.
[18] See above, pp. 69-70.

The Text

'Canon Christopher's Reminiscences', *The Record*, 15 June 1900, p. 572

Canon Christopher sends us the following reminiscences of the late Bishop Ryle:

It was in 1865, seven years before he was appointed an Honorary Canon of Norwich Cathedral by Bishop Pelham,[19] that the Rev. J. C. Ryle, B.A., Vicar of Stradbroke, kindly accepted my invitation to stay with my wife and me, and preach in St Aldate's Church.

He had never set his foot in Oxford before since he took his B.A. degree in 1837, when he was in the First Class of the Final Classical School (*In Literis Humanioribus*) with the late Dean Stanley, having in the same year obtained a Craven Scholarship. During that twenty-eight years no one had invited him to come to Oxford, and he had never cared to take his M.A. degree. Sometime after his visit to me, the Dean of Christ Church, the late Dr Liddell, being Vice-Chancellor, and having formerly been Mr Ryle's tutor when he was an undergraduate at Christ Church, wrote to him nominating him to preach before the University one of the sermons for which the Vice-Chancellor selects the preacher.[20] Dr Liddell had

[19] John Thomas Pelham (1811-94), evangelical bishop of Norwich 1857-93, appointed Ryle as honorary canon of Norwich Cathedral in February 1872.

[20] There were ten 'select preachers', five appointed each year for a two-year term, whose responsibility was to preach occasional sermons before Oxford University. Nominations were made by a small committee – the vice-chancellor, the regius and Lady Margaret professors of divinity, and the two proctors – and were submitted to the university's Convocation for approval. During Liddell's time as vice-chancellor there was intense controversy over the nominations of Frederick Temple in 1871 and Arthur Stanley in 1872, both notorious 'broad churchmen', so Liddell's plan to nominate Ryle may have been a calculated attempt to deflect accusations of theological bias. On the controversy, see 'Protecting the university pulpit', in

to write next day saying, 'I find that you are only a B.A.' To preach before the University a clergyman must be an M.A. I then wrote to the B.A. and said, 'You must come up and take your M.A. degree.' He did so, and it was curious in 1871 to see this stalwart veteran of fifty-five among the young M.A.s taking his hitherto avoided M.A. degree.

Whilst he was my guest in 1865 he told me several things which I have remembered with interest ever since, and have often repeated. God opened his eyes to the Gospel in a very simple way. Not by a sermon, a book, a tract, a letter, or a conversation, but by a single verse of His Word impressively read by a clergyman unknown to him. It was in 1837, near the time of his final examination, that he was getting more serious than he had been in the earlier part of his undergraduate course. He was in the University cricket 'eleven', treasurer of the University Cricket Club, and treasurer of the Christ Church Cricket Club. He had lived in the undergraduate world, but his will was as strong as his body, and he read hard nevertheless, as his First Class in the Lit. Hum. School and his Craven Scholarship proved.

One Sunday, not long before he took his B.A. degree, his more serious state of mind led him into a parish church in the afternoon. A stranger read the prayers and lessons – whose name he never knew. He did not preach, and Mr Ryle told me that he remembered nothing about the sermon. But the stranger read the second chapter of St Paul's Epistle to the Ephesians very impressively, and placed a short pause between each two clauses of the eighth verse thus: 'By grace are ye saved – through faith – and that not of yourselves – it

Andrew Atherstone, *Oxford's protestant spy: the controversial career of Charles Golightly* (Milton Keynes, 2007), pp. 263-77. Ryle took his MA degree in June 1871, and was appointed a 'select preacher' for 1874-76, but was forced through illness to resign in May 1875 (see *Ipswich Journal*, 15 May 1875; *Jackson's Oxford Journal*, 22 May 1875). He was 'select preacher' at Oxford again in 1879-81, and his university sermons were published in *The upper room* (1888), chs 4, 8-11.

is the gift of God.' That verse, read so that each clause might sink into the mind by itself, showed the undergraduate the Gospel. That one verse of God's Word was the seed which, through the applying power of the Holy Spirit, produced his Gospel writings, sermons, speeches, pastoral conversations and parish-school teachings, and all that he did for the glory of God through his long, hard-working, and useful life. How much can God do by one verse of His Word!

My late beloved friend E. P. Hathaway[21] once said to me: 'Are you sure you are right in your story about Bishop Ryle's conversion? Coote tells me that his father was the instrument of his conversion.' When Bishop Ryle next visited Oxford I asked him to explain this matter. He said: 'The incident to which Coote refers took place two years before my conversion by means of the eighth verse of the second chapter of the Ephesians. I was with his father and others on a drag,[22] and I used some expression which I ought not to have used. Coote's father sharply rebuked me. I never used the same sort of expression again, but this was not my conversion.'

When he heard of his father's failure[23] he exclaimed: 'Now I shall go into the Church.' His father's failure is mentioned in several of the newspapers, so I need not keep back a very interesting fact connected with it.

When the beloved veteran, the late Canon Bardsley, Rector of St Ann's, Manchester, was in Oxford many years ago as deputation for the Church Pastoral-Aid Society,[24] he told me he knew that for

[21] Edward Penrose Hathaway (1818-97), barrister 1846-64, founder of the Oxford Churches Trust (an evangelical patronage trust), rector of St Ebbe's, Oxford 1868-73, of Holbrook, Suffolk 1885-92.

[22] That is, a drag-hunt, with hounds following a line of scent.

[23] That is, bankruptcy.

[24] James Bardsley (1805-86), rector of St Ann's, Manchester 1857-80, spoke in Oxford for the Church Pastoral Aid Society in 1866 and 1869; see 'Church Pastoral Aid Society', *Jackson's Oxford Journal*, 17 and 24 November 1866, 27 November 1869. His son, John Wareing Bardsley (1835-1904), was Ryle's first domestic chaplain, archdeacon of Warrington 1880-86, bishop of Carlisle 1892-1904.

many years, when Mr Ryle was Rector of Helmingham, he wore threadbare clothes, and denied himself many things, in order to pay off, so far as was possible, the small depositors at his father's bank. He was not himself a partner in the bank, and was not legally liable for anything. The failure took place through the establishment of a branch bank at Manchester, which did not succeed, and pulled down the parent bank at Macclesfield. Mr Ryle senior was a very honourable man, and sold off his houses and lands promptly at a great loss to pay his debts so far as this was possible. When I next saw Bishop Ryle, I asked him if Canon Bardsley's story was in all respects correct, and he was obliged to acknowledge that it was so.

There is no doubt that Bishop Ryle's remarkably forcible English style – short, clear sentences, always to the point – had much to do with his success in life. Old Dr Hawtrey, the late Provost of Eton, used to say, 'None but an Eton boy could write that English.'[25] But it was a strong sense of duty which had led him to adopt the style with which everyone who has read any of his tracts is familiar. He told me that when he was first ordained he made Melvill his model. When I was an undergraduate at Cambridge sixty years ago, I used occasionally to hear Melvill preach before the University in St Mary's Church.[26] The three deep galleries which then existed in that church were crowded with undergraduates, and the preacher's eloquent passages, abounding in long sentences, held us almost breathless. When he stopped to wipe his forehead everyone in the

[25] This comment by Hawtrey was originally told to Christopher in the 1860s by Lord Wriothesley Russell (1804-86), rector of Chenies, Buckinghamshire 1829-86, canon of St George's, Windsor 1840-86. See Christopher's speech in *The report of the conference of the Church Association, with deputations from the country, held in Willis's Rooms, London, on 26th and 27th November, 1867* (London, 1867), p. 69.

[26] Henry Melvill (1798-1871), incumbent of Camden Chapel, Camberwell 1829-43, principal of the East India College, Haileybury 1843-57, canon of St Paul's Cathedral 1856-71, rector of Barnes, Surrey 1863-71. He was a popular preacher, known as 'the evangelical Chrysostom', often invited to preach before Cambridge University and in other prestigious pulpits.

church moved, and there was a resulting noise which I could hear. I was not deaf then.[27] A style could hardly be conceived which would be a greater contrast to the mature style of Bishop Ryle. He used to write these early sermons in Melvill's style, in a small, neat hand, a great contrast to the handwriting of his after-life.[28] It was a sense of duty which led him to change his style of writing. He said to me: 'I found that I was doing the country people in my congregation no good whatever. I was shooting altogether over their heads; they could not understand my imitation of Melvill's style, which I thought so much of. I therefore considered it my plain duty to crucify my style and to bring it down to what it now is.'[29]

Thus from a sense of duty alone he gave up the style he liked, and adopted a plain one which he did not like, in order to make himself understood by uneducated country people, and the style he thus adopted from a sense of duty when ably used in his tracts made his reputation and led on to his elevation.

[27] Christopher was famously deaf, and used an ear-trumpet.

[28] Ryle's handwriting was notoriously illegible.

[29] This anecdote was confirmed by Henry Elliott Fox (1841-1926), clerical secretary of the Church Missionary Society 1895-1910, who as curate of St Ebbe's, Oxford 1869-73 heard Ryle address young clergy at Canon Christopher's mission room. Ryle explained that in his curacy, modelling his preaching on Melvill, he found himself 'miles over the heads' of the local farmers and their wives, 'And so I crucified my style, and became plain John Ryle.' See 'The late Bishop Ryle', letter from H. E. Fox, *The Record*, 16 November 1916, p. 906.

RYLE'S EARLIEST TRACTS

Du.uring his 36-year ministry in Suffolk, Ryle made his name as a prolific author of theological tracts. By some estimates, 12 million copies were in circulation during his lifetime, and many were translated into Welsh, Gaelic, French, German, Dutch, Portuguese, Italian, Norwegian, Swedish, Danish, and Russian, as well as 'Hindustani' and 'Chinese'.[1] Assorted collections were published as *Home truths* (1851-71), a series of eight volumes, and later under famous titles such as *Knots untied* (1874), *Old paths* (1877), *Holiness* (1877), and *Practical religion* (1878). When reflecting on Ryle's promotion to another sphere of ministry in 1880, *The Times* newspaper highlighted the special significance of his tracts:

> It is not as preacher or public speaker that Canon Ryle has carved out a niche for himself, but as a pamphleteer. Before journalism supplied a need which it has also in a great measure created, a pamphlet was the one open avenue to the public mind. The Oxford school of Tractarians recalled the half-dead tradition of the eighteenth century. With them the pamphlet became a party organ and voice, as in the days of Bolingbroke and Swift and Pulteney. As the

---

[1] Machray, *The first bishop of Liverpool*, pp. 43-44. See also, Alan Munden, 'J. C. Ryle: "the prince of tract-writers"', *Churchman* vol. 119 (Spring 2005), pp. 7-13.

weapon dropped from their hands, Canon Ryle picked it up, and tempered it to new and very different uses of his own. His pamphlets were sermons preached not from pulpits, but from room to room. Barbed with Evangelical theology, they yet were suffused throughout with a strangely individual tone. The writer was there in person, talking and arguing with his reader face to face, ready to listen to a retort and to answer it by anticipation. For many years Canon Ryle's pamphlets streamed forth on every point and question of theology, moral or doctrinal. They are numbered by the hundred, and constitute a special department of the theological literature of the present generation.[2]

Ryle's passion for tract distribution, and his desire to maximize its usefulness as a pastoral and evangelistic tool, was evident in the earliest years of his ministry, soon after ordination. During his curacy at Exbury in Hampshire, as he revealed in his autobiography, he borrowed literature from the local Southampton depot of the Religious Tract Society, and circulated it amongst his parishioners, though he was too poor to give the tracts away.[3] At the point of leaving for pastures new in November 1843, Ryle experimented for the first time with a tract of his own – a brief but heartfelt farewell, entitled *A minister's parting words to the inhabitants of Exbury*. It has a good claim to be the earliest surviving evangelical literature from Ryle's pen.[4] Just a thousand words, it was printed on two sides of paper, and presumably distributed amongst the households in Exbury and Langley.

---

[2] *The Times*, 6 March 1880, p. 9.

[3] See above, p. 101.

[4] Another possibility for Ryle's earliest surviving evangelical text is an undated sermon, preached at Exbury in support of an unnamed missionary society, and published as 'The compassion of Jesus', in J. C. Ryle, *The Christian race and other sermons* (London, 1900). Exbury is mentioned twice, pp. 227, 230. The sermon dates either from Ryle's curacy or from a later visit to the village.

After a brief interlude in Winchester, Ryle transferred to Suffolk. Had he remained in Winchester, a busy city-centre parish of 3,000 people, it is unlikely his writing ministry would have developed with such speed. Helmingham, by contrast, with less than 300 parishioners, allowed him the leisure to invest time in literary pursuits. As he confessed in his autobiography, his parochial responsibilities were 'very simple ... there really was little to be done', apart from reading and writing.[5] His first Helmingham sermon, in February 1844, was printed as a tract for local distribution. The following year he wrote for a wider audience for the first time, spurred into action by a terrible tragedy at Great Yarmouth, on the Norfolk coast, in May 1845. William Cooke's equestrian circus arrived in the town and as a publicity stunt the clown, 'Nelson', announced his intention to sail down the River Bure on Friday evening, 2 May, in a washing tub pulled by four geese. The tub was nicknamed *The Victory*, in mock homage to Admiral Nelson at the Battle of Trafalgar.[6] It was a rare feat, though not unprecedented amongst circus clowns,[7] and attracted thousands of spectators to the banks of the river, mostly young people and families. Too many congregated on Yarmouth suspension bridge for a better view, when some of the iron cables suddenly snapped, plunging hundreds of onlookers into the water. The *Norwich Mercury* reported:

> The children, poor little things, of whom there were very many, and had naturally gathered to the balustrade, were of course the first to sink, while the force with which the whole fell, caused those who were in the background to be hurled with terrific force into the water beneath, crushing and annihilating those under them.

[5] See above, p. 117.

[6] Handbills for 'Cooke's Royal Circus' (1845), at 'Yarmouth miscellanies', British Library, N.Tab 2012/6, vol. 7.

[7] For another example, by a clown from Astley's Amphitheatre in London, see 'Novel feat on the River Thames', *Illustrated London News*, 28 September 1844, p. 193.

Oh! who shall paint the one mighty simultaneous agonizing death-scream which burst upon the affrighted multitude around ... One instant and all was hushed, save the struggling of a few whose lives it pleased their Maker in his mercy to spare.[8]

Seventy-nine people were drowned, almost half of them children under the age of twelve.

Local clergy responded to this divine summons by exhorting their parishioners to repentance. The incumbent of Great Yarmouth, Henry Mackenzie (1808-78), later bishop of Nottingham, described the disaster as 'a judgment upon our sins ... God has sent down to us his destroying angel.'[9] As a permanent sign of the town's contrition, he launched a campaign to enlarge the parish church and to build a parish school where children would be 'reared in the nurture and admonition of the Lord'.[10] Likewise, Paul Johnson (c. 1789-1883), rector of Overstrand near Cromer, spoke of the calamity as 'a dispensation of God's providence ... a solemn and awakening lesson ... we are standing on the bridge that divides time from eternity. Think how awful, if we should be plunged into death, and being impenitent and unbelieving, perish for ever.' Taking as his text the collapse of the tower at Siloam, he urged his readers: 'unless ye repent, ye shall all likewise perish' (Luke 13:5).[11] From

[8] 'Fall of the Yarmouth suspension bridge', *Norwich Mercury*, 10 May 1845. For further reports, see 'The late dreadful accident at Yarmouth', *Norfolk Chronicle and Norwich Gazette*, 10 May 1845; 'Calamitous accident and loss of life at Yarmouth', *Illustrated London News*, 10 May 1845, pp. 297-98.

[9] Henry Mackenzie, *The restoration of God's church, a fitting recognition of God's judgments: sermon, preached on Whitsunday, 1845; being one of a series delivered after the fall of the bridge, at Great Yarmouth* (London, 1845), pp. 5, 9.

[10] Mackenzie, *The restoration of God's church*, p. 10. See also *The restoration of the parish church of St Nicholas, and for the establishment of a national school, at Great Yarmouth, Norfolk* (1845), at 'Yarmouth miscellanies', British Library, N.Tab 2012/6, vol. 7.

[11] Paul Johnson, *The downfal* [sic] *of the Yarmouth suspension-bridge: with serious reflections arising out of that fatal event* (Norwich, 1845), pp. 4-5.

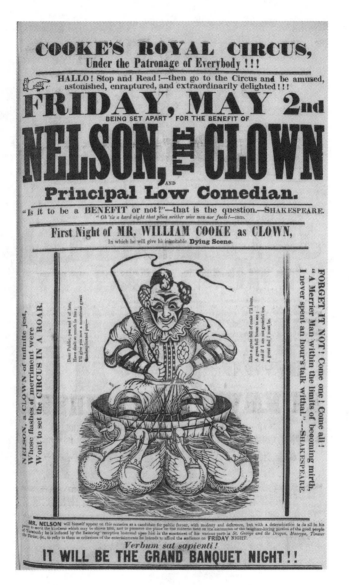

Circus handbill from Great Yarmouth, May 1845, advertising Nelson the Clown, pulled in a tub by four geese.

YARMOUTH SUSPENSION BRIDGE,

AS IT APPEARED AFTER THE ACCIDENT BY WHICH 79 LIVES WERE LOST,

ON FRIDAY EVENING, MAY 2, 1845.

Engraving of the collapse of Yarmouth suspension bridge.

Helmingham, forty-five miles from Great Yarmouth, Ryle also issued a call to repentance, written a week after the tragedy, on the very day that he read the extensive reports in the local newspaper. He signed his tract, only a thousand words, with the anonym 'A Spiritual Watchman'.[12] It was printed by Edward Hunt (1792-1862), bookseller and publisher in Ipswich, and sold in East Anglia and London at six pence per dozen, or three shillings and six pence per hundred.[13] This was the beginning of a long and fruitful relationship with the Hunts – first Edward, and then his son, William Hunt (1823-1901) – Ryle's publisher of choice for almost four decades until the company went bankrupt in 1883.

Soon a stream of tracts began to flow from the Helmingham rectory and Ryle's writing career was duly launched. His sermon in August 1845 to approximately 350 schoolchildren from the parishes of Helmingham, Otley, Framsden, Pettaugh, Ashbocking and Gosbeck, who attended a Feast supplied by the Tollemaches in Helmingham Park, was published as *Seeking the Lord early*.[14] His lecture to parents on bringing up children in the Christian faith was published as *Train up a child in the way he should go*.[15] Next followed a sermon, *Young men exhorted*.[16] Despite the national distribution of

[12] Guthrie Clarke, *John Charles Ryle*, pp. 14-15, mentioned the publication of this anonymous tract, presumably on the basis of documents he saw in the 1940s in the Ryle family archive. The title of the tract was first identified by Alan Munden, *Bishop J. C. Ryle*, p. 58.

[13] [J. C. Ryle], *A word in season about the awful accident at Yarmouth* (Ipswich, 1845), p. 4.

[14] J. C. Ryle, *'Seeking the Lord early': a sermon for children, preached in Helmingham church, August 2, 1845* (Ipswich, 1845); republished in J. C. Ryle, *Boys and girls playing, and other addresses to children* (London, 1881).

[15] J. C. Ryle, *'Train up a child in the way he should go': a sermon for parents, preached in Helmingham church, August 20, 1845* (Ipswich, 1846); republished in *The upper room* (1888).

[16] J. C. Ryle, *'Young men exhorted': a sermon to young men, preached in Helmingham church* (Ipswich, 1846); republished in *The upper room* (1888).

Ryle's Helmingham tracts, he continued to write often with his own 300 parishioners in mind. For example, his 6,000-word charge for New Year 1846, addressed to 'my beloved people', was printed 5,000 times within a few months and sold in bulk.[17] His 10,000-word address for New Year 1847 was even more widely circulated, and after being revised and 'adapted to all seasons' it reached its tenth thousand in 1849 under the new title *Consider your ways*.[18]

The five texts in this Appendix are amongst Ryle's earliest tracts, four of them addressed directly to his parishioners. Of all his multitudinous publications, these are amongst the rarest texts.[19] In this edition footnotes have been added, to demonstrate the range of Ryle's biblical quotations and allusions.

[17] J. C. Ryle, *A ministerial address for the beginning of the new year* (Ipswich, 1846).

[18] J. C. Ryle, *A pastor's address to his flock at the beginning of a new year* (Ipswich, 1846); revised as J. C. Ryle, *Consider your ways: being a pastor's address to his flock* (Ipswich, 1849); republished again as the opening chapter in J. C. Ryle, *Home truths: being miscellaneous addresses and tracts*, first series (Ipswich, 1850), pp. 7-41.

[19] Copies can be found in the British Library.

The Texts

(1) A Minister's Parting Words to the Inhabitants of Exbury (November 1843)[20]

Dearly Beloved in the Lord,

The time has come when my Ministry among you must end. My course is finished[21] – my work is done – it only remains for me to say a few parting words by way of Farewell!

In looking back on the time during which I have had the oversight of your souls, I do indeed feel great cause for humiliation and shame. How much have I left undone that I ought to have done[22] – how much unsaid that I ought to have said – how great have been my shortcomings – how small my wisdom, my faithfulness, my love! But it is too late to dwell on these things now – the Lord Jesus forgive me, and send you a better Minister than ever I have been.

I am going forth to another charge. I know not that I shall see your faces any more on this side of the grave. Suffer for the last time a word of exhortation – all that I have to say now I say from an affectionate concern about your souls.

(I.) I leave some among you with fear and trembling – I speak of all who are open sinners and breakers of God's commandments – of all despisers and neglecters of means of grace – of all worldly, prayerless, impenitent persons – of all who are self-righteous, proud, formalists and hypocrites. Are there none such among you? Judge ye what I say. I repeat, I leave you with fear and trembling – if the Bible be true, your souls are in fearful plight.

[20] A copy of this pamphlet was sent by Mary Bache Thornhill to Sir Robert Peel in November 1843, and survives among the Peel Papers in the British Library, MS Add. 40536, fo. 38.

[21] 2 Timothy 4:7.

[22] *Book of Common Prayer* (1662): general confession at morning prayer and evening prayer.

I know not what may happen before we shall meet again at the judgment-seat of Christ – with God all things are possible;[23] but sure am I, without a mighty change, the last day will be to you a day of weeping and lamentation, and mourning and woe.[24] Oh, that I had warned you more faithfully. Oh, that I had pleaded with you more earnestly! One thing at least you cannot say: I never told you sin was a light and trifling matter – I never told you there was any way to heaven but Jesus Christ and faith in Him – I never told you a man was a true christian [sic] whose heart was not converted and renewed by the Holy Ghost. The Lord grant that you may repent and be converted before it is too late!

(II.) But some, I trust, there are among you whom I can leave with hope – I speak of all who are really convinced they are sinners, and hate and mourn over their sin – of all who are resting only on Jesus Christ for salvation – glorying in nothing but the Cross of Christ – depending on nothing but the blood and work of Christ – I speak of all who show by their lives and conversation that they are indeed born of the Spirit and new creatures in Christ Jesus. You, I repeat, I can leave with hope, and in my Master's name I bid you God speed. I never told you you would have no temptations – never told you you would have no difficulties – never said you would meet with no persecutions – have to bear no cross – have to encounter no trials – find in yourselves no weakness, faintness, and shortcoming. But still I do bid you God speed.

Let not your hearts be troubled[25] – fear not – you have an everlasting covenant to look to, ordered in all things and sure.[26] Consider your Saviour and High Priest, Christ Jesus; He is mighty – able to save to the uttermost all them that come unto God by him;[27]

[23] Matthew 19:26.
[24] Ezekiel 2:10.
[25] John 14:1.
[26] 2 Samuel 23:5.
[27] Hebrews 7:25.

He is gentle and loving, He will not break the bruised reed nor quench the smoking flax.[28] Remember the death He died to save you – remember the blessed words of his own mouth, 'Come unto me, all ye that labour and are heavy laden and I will give you rest[29] – Him that cometh unto me I will in no wise cast out[30] – I know my sheep and they shall never perish, neither shall any man pluck them out of my hand.'[31] Fear not therefore, you have in Jesus exceeding great and precious promises;[32] fear not, but go forward.

But, brethren, I charge you, I beseech you for your own sakes to bear in mind, in this world you have a battle to fight, you are not yet at home. Watch then and pray without ceasing[33] – Be very jealous over your own souls – Put on the whole armour of God[34] – Be very diligent in reading your Bibles – very diligent in private prayer – very diligent in using all means of grace. Do not be always wavering and carried about from one place of worship to another – dread all divisions – keep steady to your Church – do not neglect her Sacraments – do not despise her Prayer book, the more you look at it, the wiser and the better that book will seem. Beware of evil company – beware of hypocrites and busybodies – beware of trifling with little sins. Beware of idleness, of the love of pleasure, of worldly-mindedness, of the fear of man. Beware of lingering, of lukewarmness, of spiritual sloth, of evil speaking, of want of love – Examine yourselves very often – Do not forget the souls of those about you – Strive to grow in grace, in charity, and in knowledge of the Lord Jesus Christ. Brethren, keep these things in mind, and ye shall do well.

[28] Matthew 12:20.
[29] Matthew 11:28.
[30] John 6:37.
[31] John 10:27-28.
[32] 2 Peter 1:4.
[33] Matthew 26:41; 1 Thessalonians 5:17.
[34] Ephesians 6:11.

And now, beloved, farewell – I commend you all to God and the word of His grace which is able to build you up and to give you an inheritance among all them that are sanctified.[35] The time is short.[36] The Lord is at hand.[37] A few short years and the Lord Jesus Christ will have come the second time, and separated the wheat from the chaff for ever.[38] At that great day I shall meet you all once more – the Lord grant it may be with joy and not with grief – the Lord grant I may see your faces on the right hand of your Saviour and not on the left.[39]

Brethren, I shall often think of you – your names will often come across my mind, and God forbid that I should sin against the Lord in ceasing to pray for you. But pray for yourselves – pray much for yourselves – and when you do it, remember my last request, pray also for me.

I remain, dearly beloved,

Your most affectionate Minister,

J. C. RYLE
Langley, November, 1843

[35] Acts 20:32.
[36] 1 Corinthians 7:29.
[37] Philippians 4:5.
[38] Matthew 3:12.
[39] Matthew 25:33.

(2) I Have Somewhat To Say Unto Thee (February 1844)[40]

Reader,

I do not know who you are. I know not whether you are old or young, rich or poor, learned or unlearned. I only know that you are a child of Adam, and have a soul to be lost or saved. And therefore I say, '*Hear me! I have somewhat to say unto thee!*'[41]

Reader, I have four things to say, and they shall soon be said. The Lord make them words in season to your soul.

I. Firstly, I have a word of *wishes and desires* for every one into whose hands these pages may fall.

I tell you it is my heart's desire and prayer to God for you, that you may be saved.[42] I want you to be convinced of your sinfulness in the sight of God, to feel your need of a Saviour, to know Christ by faith, and to have eternal life in Him.

I wish you to be one who knows his own lost condition by nature – his own corruption, guilt, and danger of eternal ruin – his need of a righteousness far better than his own, wherein to appear before God at the day of judgment.

I wish you to be one who actually applies to Christ for peace, and casts the burden of his soul upon Him – who believes on Him for forgiveness – who trusts Him for deliverance from all transgression, and forsaking all other hopes and confidence, draws from Him all his comfort and strength.

I wish you to be one who lives by faith,[43] stands by faith,[44] walks

---

[40] Ryle's first sermon in Helmingham was printed for private circulation. No copies of the original printing have been found, so the text is taken from a revised version in J. C. Ryle, *Home truths: being miscellaneous addresses and tracts*, third series (Ipswich, 1854), pp. 7-15.

[41] Luke 7:40.

[42] Romans 10:1.

[43] Romans 1:17; Galatians 3:11.

[44] Romans 11:20; 2 Corinthians 1:24.

by faith[45] – who receives with the heart that grand truth, 'He that believeth on Jesus is not condemned',[46] and rests securely upon it.

This faith is the only principle that produces inward peace and real holiness. This is the faith that sanctifies a man – that purifies the heart[47] – that overcomes the world[48] – that works by love[49] – that brings forth fruit. He that hath this faith is born of God and an heir of glory. He that hath it not, is not of God, knows little of true vital Christianity now, and will be lost for ever hereafter.

Reader, my best desire is that you may be a new creature in Christ Jesus[50] – led by the Spirit of God[51] – conformed to your Master's likeness, and not unto the world – loving much, because much forgiven[52] – having communion with the Father and the Son – one with Christ and Christ in you.

Then I should feel that you were *safe* – safe, though the Lord should come in glory, and heaven and earth be dissolved, and the elements melt with fervent heat[53] – safe, because ready for every condition. Judge for yourself, can I feel that for all who profess and call themselves Christians?

Then I should feel that you were truly *happy* – happy, because the springs of your happiness would be in heaven, and never dry – happy, because your peace would be that blessed peace which the world can neither give nor take away.[54] Judge for yourself, can I feel that for all who profess and call themselves Christians?

[45] 2 Corinthians 5:7.
[46] John 3:18.
[47] Acts 15:9.
[48] 1 John 5:4.
[49] Galatians 5:6.
[50] 2 Corinthians 5:17.
[51] Romans 8:14.
[52] Luke 7:47.
[53] 2 Peter 3:10.
[54] John 14:27.

Reader, I make no secret of my wishes, whatever you may think of them. God is my witness, these are my wishes, these are my desires for everybody.

II. Secondly, I have a word of *sorrowful warning* for some into whose hands these pages will fall.

Some of you know in your own hearts and consciences – though I could say it with weeping – you know well, that you are not walking with God.

You, to whom I now speak, know well that God's ways are not your ways – that although you profess and call yourselves Christians, your hearts are not right in His sight. You have no heart-felt hatred for sin. You have no heart-felt love for God's commandments. You have no delight in God's word. You have no pleasure in the company of His people. His day is a weariness to you. His service is a burthen. His ordinances are not precious to your soul. Your first and best thoughts are given to the life that now is – you spend but the wreck and remnant of them on the life to come. Your treasure is on earth and not in heaven.[55] Your affections are set on things below, and not on things above.[56] Your friendship is with the world, and not with God.[57]

Oh! reader, what has the Lord God done to you that you should treat Him in this fashion? What can the world do for you, that you should love it better than Christ? Would the world die for you? No! but Jesus did. Can the world put away your sins? No! Jesus alone can. Does the world give true peace in this life? No! but Jesus does. Will the world give comfort in death? No! but Jesus will. Can the world help you in the day of judgment? No! No! none can help you then but Christ!

[55] Matthew 6:19-20.
[56] Colossians 3:2.
[57] James 4:4.

Reader, what will you do when God riseth up, except you alter? – when He visiteth, what will you answer Him, except you change?[58]

Do you not know that whatsoever a man soweth he shall also reap? He that soweth to the flesh, shall of the flesh reap corruption. He only that soweth to the Spirit, shall of the Spirit reap life eternal.[59] The world you think so much of now passeth away. He only that doeth the will of God abideth for ever.[60]

But God, our Saviour, still loves you. God is not willing that any one should perish.[61] He sends you by my mouth a message of peace this day. Turn from the broad way and come unto Christ while there is yet time. Turn before the fountain is sealed, now open for sin and uncleanness[62] – before the Father's house is closed for ever and not one more allowed to enter – before the Spirit and the Bride cease to invite.[63] Be wise, repent, return, and come.

Reader, you cannot prevent my grieving over you, although you may be at ease yourself. God is my witness, this day I have given you a warning.

III. Thirdly, I have a word of *quickening and stirring-up* for all true believers, into whose hands this tract may fall.

Believing reader, I trust I may say of you, you love the Lord Jesus Christ in sincerity.[64] Know then that I want you to be a bright and shining light to those around you.[65] I want you to be such a plain epistle of Christ,[66] that all may read something of God on the

---

[58] Job 31:14.
[59] Galatians 6:7-8.
[60] 1 John 2:17.
[61] 2 Peter 3:9.
[62] Zechariah 13:1.
[63] Revelation 22:17.
[64] Ephesians 6:24.
[65] John 5:35.
[66] 2 Corinthians 3:3.

face of your conversation. I want you so to live that all may see that you are one of the people of Jesus, and thus to glorify your Father which is in heaven.[67]

Alas! I say it with shame, we many of us bring little glory to the Lord who bought us; we are far from walking worthy of our vocation.[68] How weak is our faith! How fleeting our sorrow for sin! How faint our self-denial! How soon spent our patience! How thin and thread-bare our humility! How formal our prayers! How cold our love! We are called God's witnesses, but truly our witness is often little better than silence – it is but an uncertain sound.[69] We are called the light of the world,[70] but we are – many of us – poor, glimmering sparks that can only just be seen. We are called the salt of the earth,[71] but we scarcely do anything to make our Saviour felt and known. We are called pilgrims and strangers,[72] but those who observe us might sometimes think this world was our only home. Often, too often, we prove to be one thing in name, and another in reality – high in our professions, but low in our practice – giants in our resolutions, but infants in our actions – angels and spiritual in our talking, heathen, or little better, in our doing – goodly, like Naphtali, in our words – unstable, like Reuben, in our works.[73]

Oh! believing readers, these things ought not so to be. We must not be content with a low measure of holiness. We must not rest satisfied with a *little* sanctification. We must not think it is enough, because we have attained a small degree of grace, and are just one step better than the world. No! indeed, we must go forward from

[67] Matthew 5:16.
[68] Ephesians 4:1.
[69] 1 Corinthians 14:8.
[70] Matthew 5:14.
[71] Matthew 5:13.
[72] 1 Peter 2:11.
[73] Genesis 49:4, 21.

strength to strength.[74] We must shine more and more unto the perfect day.[75] We must strive to bear *much* fruit.[76]

Christ did not give Himself to us that we should be a sleeping generation – trees that grow not – always standing still. He would have us be a peculiar people, zealous of good works[77] – valiant for the truth[78] – fervent in spirit[79] – living not unto ourselves, but unto Him.[80] Freely saved, we should freely and willingly labour. Freely forgiven, we should freely and cheerfully work. Freely redeemed from more than Egyptian bondage, we should count it a pleasure and a privilege to serve the Lord. Our lives should be books of evidences. Our acts should tell out whose we are. 'Ye are my friends', saith Jesus, 'if ye do whatsoever I command you.'[81]

Brother or sister, what do you in the world? Where is the proof of your growth in grace? Are you awake, or are you asleep? Are there no tempers you might keep under more strictly? Is there no sort of besetting sin you are shamefully sparing? Is there no time you might employ more usefully? Is there no kind of selfishness you are secretly indulging? Is there no good you have the means of doing, and leave undone? Are there no daily habits you might alter for the better? Are there no spots upon your spiritual garments which you never seek to have washed out? Are there no friends and relations you are letting alone in their sins? Oh! that you may deal more honestly with yourself than you have done hitherto! The Lord is at hand.[82]

[74] Psalm 84:7.
[75] Proverbs 4:18.
[76] John 15:5, 8.
[77] Titus 2:14.
[78] Jeremiah 9:3.
[79] Romans 12:11.
[80] 2 Corinthians 5:15.
[81] John 15:14.
[82] Philippians 4:5.

Brother or sister, look within. Take heed lest a deceitful heart, and an ensnaring world, and a busy devil, turn you out of the way. Study a tender conscience. Beware of indolence under the cloak of false humility. Make not the old Adam, and the devil, an excuse for little sins. Let the least things of your daily life be done well – like the shekel of the sanctuary, let them be good measure[83] – let them be even more than full weight. Remember the Apostle's advice 'Watch ye, stand fast in the faith, quit you like men, be strong' (1 Cor. xvi. 13). They that follow the Lord fully are those that follow Him most comfortably. Be zealous though the world may sleep.

Brother or sister, I give you this word of quickening in love. I would not have you be the least in the kingdom of heaven.[84] I would not like you to be the palest and dimmest amongst the stars in glory. I want you not only to be scarcely saved, and so as by fire,[85] but to receive a full reward.[86] Then lay these things well to heart.

IV. Fourthly, I have words of *advice* for every one that desires to be a real Christian.

One part of my advice is this – '*Search the Scriptures.*'[87] They only are able to make you wise unto salvation, through faith which is in Christ Jesus.[88] They are the truth of God. They must be fulfilled. They cannot be broken. And yet they are the book which many have, and very few read.

Reader, beware lest an unread Bible be an awful witness against you at the last day. If you would have your soul saved, read the Bible. If you would not be always wavering and carried about by

[83] Leviticus 27:25.
[84] Matthew 5:19.
[85] 1 Corinthians 3:15.
[86] 2 John 8.
[87] John 5:39.
[88] 2 Timothy 3:15.

every wind of doctrine,[89] read the Bible. Read it regularly. Read it all. Be a Bible-reading Christian, whatever the world may say. Make time for this, whatever others may do. Remember my advice. *If you would not lose your own soul, read the Bible.*

Another piece of advice is this – '*Pray without ceasing.*'[90] Prayer is the only way by which man can approach God. Prayer is the only messenger we can send to tell God what we want; and if we would have good things for our souls, we must ask for them. Prayer opens the treasuries of God's mercies like a key; if we ask, we shall receive.[91] Prayer is the means that every one can use if he will; and yet for all this many people never pray.

Reader, beware lest your neglect of prayer should prove your condemnation. If Jesus is to save you, you must pray. If your sins are to be forgiven, you must pray. If the Spirit is to dwell in your heart, you must pray. If you are to have strength against sin, you must pray. If you are to dwell with God in heaven, your heart must talk with God upon earth by prayer.

Oh! be not a prayerless Christian, whatever others may think right. Begin to pray this day if you never prayed before. Remember if you and I are to meet each other with joy at Christ's appearing, *you must pray.*

Another piece of advice is this – '*Attend regularly on the means of grace.*' Remember the Sabbath day, to keep it holy.[92] Go to some place of worship where the Gospel is preached. Faith cometh by hearing.[93] Those who never hear are never likely to believe the Gospel.

---

[89] Ephesians 4:14.
[90] 1 Thessalonians 5:17.
[91] Matthew 21:22.
[92] Exodus 20:8.
[93] Romans 10:17.

Reader, beware lest you are ruined for ever by neglecting the means which God has appointed for your salvation. Alas! it does not need to be a murderer, or an adulterer, or a thief, or a liar, in order to be in the way to hell. You have only to sit still, to do nothing, to profane the Sabbath, to refuse to listen to instruction, and in hell you will find yourself at last. Oh! do not let this be your end. Draw nigh to God and He will draw nigh to you.[94] Walk in the road where Jesus loves to walk, and who can tell but He will one day make you one of His believing people?

Reader, I commend these things to your special notice. I know they are worth thinking over.

The Lord grant, if you never thought of them before, that you may go on thinking, thinking, thinking about them till your soul is saved.

The Lord grant, if you have thought of them, that you may think of them more and more every year you live.

The more you think of them the happier you will be.

I remain,

your affectionate friend,

J. C. RYLE

[94] James 4:8.

(3) A Word in Season about the Awful Accident at Yarmouth (May 1845)

Reader,

Let me tell you a true story. An accident happened at Yarmouth last Friday Evening, by which seventy-five souls were taken out of the world at once. I will give you the particulars in the words of the *Norwich Mercury* newspaper:[95]

On the Afternoon of the day on which this narration bears date, Nelson, the clown at Mr Cook's [*sic*] circus,[96] had undertaken to swim in a tub, drawn by four geese, from the draw-bridge on the quay to the suspension-bridge across the North River – a foolish exhibition – but it was one which, from its novelty in Yarmouth, was calculated to attract the multitude. As early as 5 o'clock, when the train arrives from Norwich, although raining smartly, thousands of spectators had already assembled on both sides of the river to witness the feat. The bridge then was comparatively clear. The clown commenced his feat with the flood-tide, at the draw-bridge, and had entered the North River. There were many persons on the bridge, and as he drew near the multitude rushed upon it to obtain a full view as he should pass underneath. Already had he reached Bessy's [*sic*] Wharf,[97] not far from the bridge, when one or two of the rods were observed to give way. An instant alarm was given to quit the bridge. Alas! the caution came too late. The chains broke, and, quick as the passing thought, one entire side fell, and the whole mass of human beings, whose numbers are estimated at from 300 to 600,[98] were swept into the river below.

[95] This passage is copied from a long report, 'Fall of the Yarmouth suspension bridge', *Norwich Mercury*, 10 May 1845. Ryle's tract bears the same date, which suggests that he may have written it immediately upon reading the news.

[96] *Norwich Mercury* has the correct spelling, 'Mr Cooke's circus'.

[97] *Norwich Mercury* has the correct spelling, 'Bessey's Wharf'.

[98] *Norwich Mercury* has 'from three to four hundred'.

And out of this number, it is now certain, at least seventy-five persons, men, women, and children, were drowned.

Reader, I will say nothing of the occasion on which these crowds were gathered together. The less said of it the better. I will say nothing of those that perished. They have gone to their long home. They are past any change. Their present state none but God knoweth.

But I will ask you one question about yourself. Where would your soul be now, if you had been among the seventy-five who were drowned? And where will your soul go, if you are called away this Whitsuntide as suddenly as they were last week?[99]

You may say there is little likelihood of this. I answer, 'Boast not yourself of tomorrow, for you know not what a day may bring forth.'[100] Think not that health and youth and strength are things to be depended on; a man may have them all upon his side, and yet he is not beyond the reach of death. Examine, rather, your conscience, while there is time; search your heart while you have an opportunity. I warn you – It is a fearful thing to die unprepared to meet God.

I. What is your own life? Are you living unto God? Are you a true Christian? Have you really repented of your sins and turned from them? Have you actually come unto Christ and believed on Him for salvation? Are you walking according to the course of this world,[101] or are you renewed in the spirit of your mind?[102] Are your affections set on things below, or on things above?[103] Are you seeking first the kingdom of God,[104] labouring and striving after eternal life? Oh! judge yourself, lest you be judged of the Lord.[105] TAKE CARE!

[99] Whitsunday (Pentecost) was 11 May 1845.

[100] Proverbs 27:1.

[101] Ephesians 2:2.

[102] Ephesians 4:23.

[103] Colossians 3:2.

[104] Matthew 6:33.

[105] *Book of Common Prayer* (1662): exhortation at holy communion.

II. Remember the men of Noah's time – they were eating and drinking, marrying and giving in marriage, until the flood came and destroyed them all. Remember the men of Sodom – they did eat, they drank, they bought, they sold, they planted, they builded; but the same day that Lot went out from Sodom, it rained fire and brimstone from heaven, and destroyed them all.[106] Remember Belshazzar slain in the midst of his banquet, because he lived not up to his light – weighed in God's balances, found wanting, and cast away.[107] Remember Elah, king of Israel, killed while drinking himself drunk in Tirzah.[108] Oh! remember these things, and TAKE CARE!

III. Consider your own ways. Where will they lead you to? What will be their end? Sin may be sweet for a time, but it will be bitter in eternity. It may seem pleasant now – it will bite like a serpent hereafter. Beware of rioting and drunkenness, of chamber-ing and wantonness,[109] of revelling and uncleanness; they which do such things shall not inherit the kingdom of God.[110] And be not deceived; God is not mocked. Whatsoever a man soweth in the life that now is, he shall surely reap in the life which is to come. He that soweth to the flesh shall of the flesh reap corruption; but he that soweth to the spirit shall of the spirit reap life everlasting.[111] Oh! consider these things, and TAKE CARE!

Beloved reader, this is a time of especial temptation. I charge you, as ever you would have comfort in the day of judgment, I beseech you, come out from among the men of the world and be separate.[112] Have no fellowship with the unfruitful works of

[106] Luke 17:27-29.
[107] Daniel 5:27.
[108] 1 Kings 16:9-10.
[109] Romans 13:13.
[110] Galatians 5:21.
[111] Galatians 6:7-8.
[112] 2 Corinthians 6:17.

darkness, but rather reprove them.[113] Time is short, life is uncertain, the judgment is near, eternity is long. What shall it profit you if you gain the whole world, but lose your own soul?[114]

I do pray you in Christ's stead, be reconciled to God.[115] The Lord Jesus says to you, 'Come unto me and I will give you rest.'[116] Oh! do not refuse Him. The Spirit says, 'Enter not into the path of the wicked, and go not in the way of evil men; avoid it; pass not by it; turn from it and pass away.'[117] Oh! do not disobey Him.

Repent and be converted, and so iniquity shall not be your ruin.[118] Have a Bible hope, and live a Bible life; and then, whatsoever happens, you are prepared. Be not ashamed to confess Christ before men, and then He will confess you before his Father, in the day of His appearing.[119] That day may be drawing very nigh – Watch and be ready for it.

I remain,

Your affectionate friend,

A SPIRITUAL WATCHMAN

10th May, 1845.

[113] Ephesians 5:11.
[114] Mark 8:36.
[115] 2 Corinthians 5:20.
[116] Matthew 11:28.
[117] Proverbs 4:14-15.
[118] Ezekiel 18:30.
[119] Matthew 10:32.

(4) A Ministerial Address For the Beginning of the New Year (January 1846)

'The night cometh when no man can work.' – John ix. 4.
'Let every man prove his own work.' – Galatians vi. 4.
'Is it well?' – 2 Kings iv. 26.

My Beloved People,

The second year of my ministry among you has come to a close, and you and I are so much nearer to our latter end. Suffer me once more to address you in all affection about your souls. I feel it laid upon my conscience never to let this season pass unnoticed. Hear me then before the name of 1845 is quite forgotten – before the name of 1846 is quite familiar to your ears; hear me, while I try to speak a plain word about the things that are for your eternal peace. And may the Holy Spirit give a blessing to all I have to say.

Brethren, when I look back and consider how little I have done for you, as your minister, I find abundant reason to be humbled and ashamed. But one thing I can say, in spite of all shortcomings, and that with confidence – your souls are exceedingly dear to my heart. If I know anything of myself, it is my chief desire and prayer to God for you all, that you may be saved in the day of Christ: I should rejoice to see every man, woman, and child, amongst you, born again, washed, sanctified and justified in the name of the Lord Jesus, and by the Spirit of our God;[120] I have no greater happiness than to find any member of my congregation walking in the truth.

But I do trust you will always find me a truth-speaking and a faithful friend. I am sure it would be no mark of affection to keep back my opinion about your spiritual state. It is no sign of love to cry peace when there is no peace,[121] or, like a lying physician, to

---

[120] 1 Corinthians 6:11.
[121] Jeremiah 6:14, 8:11.

hold out hopes of life to souls ready to die. Bear with me, therefore, while I speak openly and unreservedly about your present condition in God's sight. I would fain say something that may apply to every class of character among you. Believe me, if I use great plainness of speech, I do it because I love you, and not because I like to give you pain. Knowing the terrors of the Lord I would persuade you to your profit,[122] and I earnestly pray that God may apply my words to all your consciences with power.

I. Firstly – *Let me say there are many of you about whom I feel strong fears.*

You are those who, judging from appearances, take no thought for your souls. Your treasure is all on earth. You live for this world only, and not for the world to come. Your attention is swallowed up by the perishable things of time. You go on as if resurrection and eternal judgment were not true but a lie; and as to grace, and justification, and redemption, they are things which, like Gallio, you care not for[123] – they are words and names which have manifestly no place in your minds. Sin is plainly not reckoned your deadliest enemy, nor the Lord Jesus your chiefest friend, nor the Bible your best counsellor, nor communion with God your highest comfort. Yet you are dying creatures, and time is short,[124] and the Lord is at hand,[125] and one more year has been taken from your day of grace. How can I help fearing about your souls!

And worst of all, the spirit of slumber has come over some of you, and you are at ease, self-satisfied, and content. You have got a Laodicean heart, and feel unconcerned. You fancy you are rich and increased with goods, and have need of nothing.[126] You have

[122] 2 Corinthians 5:11.
[123] Acts 18:17.
[124] 1 Corinthians 7:29.
[125] Philippians 4:5.
[126] Revelation 3:17.

closed your ears against God's counsel, and will have none of God's reproof; it may be all very good, but it is not wanted for you.

Brethren, the King of kings has spoken to you many a time, and you have given him no answer. By the weekly testimony of his sabbaths, by the trumpet of His ministers, by the hammer of His Word,[127] by the pleasant voice of mercies, by the smarting stroke of affliction – by all these He has been calling to you, but you have refused to listen. Jesus has knocked at the door of your hearts, but you have not opened.[128] The Spirit has striven with you, but you have resisted His hand. Nothing has touched you yet. You have been told of death, judgment, and eternity, and have remained unconcerned. You have been warned against sin, and have returned to it without shame. You have had Christ crucified for sinners set forth before you, and have gone away unmoved. There has been a place in your heart for almost every thing but God – room for business, room for pleasure, room for trifling, room for sin, room for the devil, room for the world; but, like the Inn at Bethlehem, no room for Him who made you, no admittance for the kingdom of God, no entry for Jesus – the Spirit – and the Word. Dear Brethren, how can I help fearing about your souls?

What do I fear for you? I fear everything. I fear lest you persist in refusing Christ till you have sinned away your own souls. I fear lest you be given over to a reprobate mind, and awake no more. I fear lest you grieve the Spirit till He leave you alone and strive no longer. I fear lest you come to such deadness and hardness of heart, that nothing but the voice of the archangel and the trump of God shall break your sleep. I fear lest you should never read your Bible, or begin to pray till it be too late; lest when you take up the Bible it seem a sealed book, in which every promise is shut up, and every

[127] Jeremiah 23:29.
[128] Revelation 3:20.

page condemns you; lest you be brought to that melancholy confession, 'I have tried, but I cannot pray.' I fear lest you cling to this deceitful world so closely, that nothing but death shall part it and you – lest you live without peace, die without comfort, rise again without hope, and receive judgment without mercy.

But I must warn you, though I seem, like Lot, as one that mocks.[129] I do solemnly warn you to flee from the wrath to come.[130] I entreat you to remember that the Word of God is all true, and must be fulfilled; that the end of these things is death;[131] that without holiness no man shall see the Lord;[132] that not only the wicked shall be turned into hell, but also all the people that forget God;[133] that the Lord shall one day take account of all your doings; that Christless sinners can never stand in His sight, for He is holy and a consuming fire.[134] Oh! If the righteous scarcely be saved, where shall the ungodly and the sinner appear? You may tell me 'a man must live'; I answer, 'Yes, and a man must also die.' You may tell me, 'a man cannot starve'; I answer, 'No, but neither can he burn.' You may tell me, 'a man must mind his business'; I answer, 'Yes, and the first business is that of his soul.'

Once more I affectionately set before you, through Christ Jesus, the forgiveness of sins – full and complete forgiveness – free and unconditional forgiveness – ready, present, everlasting forgiveness – your sins cast behind God's back and remembered no more.[135] I set it before you, and in my Master's name I ask you to accept it. O! turn not away from so merciful an invitation. Do not hear of the blood, the cross, and the sepulchre, and remain unmoved. Do not

[129] Genesis 19:14.
[130] Matthew 3:7.
[131] Romans 6:21.
[132] Hebrews 12:14.
[133] Psalm 9:17.
[134] Hebrews 12:29.
[135] Isaiah 38:17, 43:25.

love this passing-away world better than eternal life. Here, at the beginning of a new year, dare to be bold and decided; come out of Egypt, repent, believe, and be saved. O! taste and see that the Lord is good; blessed are all they that trust in Him.[136]

Dear Brethren, I do fear for you. I pray God that I may live to see you fearing for yourselves.

II. Secondly – *There are not a few among you about whom I stand in doubt.*

Some of you to whom I now speak have many things about you that rejoice a minister's heart. You are regular and moral in your lives; you are not stained with glaring outward sins; you keep up many decent and proper habits; you are diligent in your attendance on means of grace; you appear to love the preaching of the Gospel; you are not offended at the truth as it is in Jesus,[137] however plainly it may be spoken; you like religious company, religious books, and religious talk; you wish to be real Christians; you assent and agree to everything we say. And all this is well.

But I cannot see any movement in your souls. You are like those that stand still. Week after week, and month after month, rolls over your heads, and you are just where you were; nothing the better for all you receive – like Pharoah's [*sic*] kine[138] – if not rather worse. There is the same regularity, the same constant attendance, the same wishing and desiring, the same way of talking about religion, the same assent to all you hear – but what is there more? There is no going forward from strength to strength; no continual addition to your spiritual treasures; no increase of faith, and hope, and charity;[139] no growth in grace.[140] Your souls would seem to be at a dead lock. And all this is wrong.

[136] Psalm 34:8.
[137] Ephesians 4:21.
[138] Genesis 41:17-21.
[139] 1 Corinthians 13:13.
[140] 2 Peter 3:18.

I cannot read the secrets of your hearts. Perhaps there is some pet bosom sin which you are holding fast, and will not give up. This is a worm that checks the growth of many a professing Christian. Perhaps you are kept back by the fear of man; you are afraid of the blame or laughter of your fellow creatures. This is an iron chain that fetters many a soul. Perhaps you are careless about private prayer and communion with God. This is the cause why multitudes are weak and sickly in spirit. But, whatever your reason be, I warn you in all affection to take care. Your state is neither satisfactory nor safe. O! escape for your life. Strive to enter in.[141]

Brethren, what can I say to move you? I scarcely know on which side you ought to be placed. The bat is thought to be a creature of a doubtful nature – some call it a bird, and some a beast – judge ye whether this ought not to be the account of your state. I dare not call you careless about religion, but I cannot call you decided. I shrink from numbering you among the ungodly, but I may not place you among the Lord's children. You have some light, but is it saving knowledge? You have some feeling, but is it grace? You are not profane, but are you men of God? You dwell so near the borders, that I cannot discern to what people you belong. You may not be dead, but like old worn out trees, I hardly know whether you are alive. Are you not, then, halting between two opinions?[142] Yes! this is your case, and you have got no rest. Like the Gibeonites, you are found in the train of Israel, but like them you have neither Israel's portion, Israel's consolation, nor Israel's reward.[143] I cannot help doubting about you. Surely there is a cause.

Now let me tell you plainly there must be an alteration in you; there must be a move. There is no real standing still in religion. If God's work is not going forward, the devil's is, and if we are not moving forward, we are going back. It is not enough to wear

[141] Luke 13:24.
[142] 1 Kings 18:21.
[143] Joshua 9.

Christ's livery; we must also fight Christ's battles. It is a small thing to cease to do evil; we must also learn to do well. It will not suffice to do no harm; we must also labour to do good. Let us tremble lest we be found unprofitable buriers of talents,[144] and barren cumberers of the ground.[145] He that is not with Christ is against Him.[146]

Have you grace in your heart or not? Wishes and convictions and desires, are all excellent in their way, but they alone will never save you. I like to see buds and blossoms on a tree, but I like better to see ripe fruit. You are almost persuaded; so was king Agrippa, but he was not saved.[147] You tremble at the Word; so did Felix, but he was not saved.[148] The way side hearers listened, but they took *no root* – they were not saved. The stony ground hearers listened with joy, but the Word had *no depth* in them – they were not saved. The thorny ground hearers brought forth something like fruit, but the Word had *no room* in them – they were not saved.[149] The five foolish virgins carried lamps, but they were not saved.[150] Herod did many things and heard John the Baptist gladly, but he was not saved.[151] Baalam wished to die the death of the righteous, but he died in sin.[152] And shall you be saved as you are? Remember Lot's wife.[153] Take care!

Brethren, I call upon you to be more in earnest. I ask you to put on the whole armour of God;[154] to fight and to overcome. Surely you cannot know Jesus Christ aright, if you are content to slumber

[144] Matthew 25:18.
[145] Luke 13:7.
[146] Matthew 12:30.
[147] Acts 26:28.
[148] Acts 24:25.
[149] Matthew 13:18-22.
[150] Matthew 25:1-13.
[151] Mark 6:20.
[152] Numbers 23:10.
[153] Luke 17:32.
[154] Ephesians 6:11.

on and sit still. Surely the thought of Gethsemane and Calvary should awaken and put you to shame. You may tell me of difficulties. I answer, 'the slothful never fail to see them.' 'A lion is in the way.'[155] 'Their path is like a hedge of thorns.'[156] 'They desire and have nothing.'[157] They mean everything that is good, but they get no further; their resolutions are all excellent, but, unhappily, all unfilled. Brethren, is this your case? Once more I say, 'take care.' If you will not stir up yourselves to 'go forward',[158] how should I feel anything but doubt about your souls?

But there are others among you of whom I stand in doubt, who are in worse case even than this. You are those who have fallen away from your first profession, and walk no more in the ways you once seemed to choose. Oh! may the Lord in mercy bring you back!

There was a time when all the saints of God who saw you rejoiced at the sight. You seemed then to love the Lord Jesus in sincerity,[159] and to be willing to give up the broad way for ever,[160] and forsake all for the Gospel's sake. The Word of God appeared sweet and precious to you;[161] the voice of Christ's ministers a most pleasant sound; the assembly of the Lord's people the place you loved best; the company of true believers your chief delight. You were never missing at the weekly meeting; your place was never empty at Church; your Bible was never long out of your hands; and there were no days in your life without prayer. Your zeal was indeed fervent; your religious affections were truly warm. You did run well for a season. But where are you now?

[155] Proverbs 26:13.
[156] Proverbs 15:19.
[157] Proverbs 13:4.
[158] Exodus 14:15.
[159] Ephesians 6:24.
[160] Matthew 7:13.
[161] Psalm 19:10.

You have gone back to the world. You lingered; you looked back;[162] you returned; I fear you had left your heart behind you. You have taken up the old man's deeds once more.[163] You have left your first love.[164] Your goodness has proved like the morning clouds, and as the early dew it has gone away.[165] Your serious impressions are fast dying off; they are getting weaker and fainter every day. Your convictions are fast withering up; they are changing colour like leaves in autumn – they will soon drop off and disappear. And the gray hairs, which tell of decline, are coming here and there upon you. The preaching you once hung upon, now wearies you; the books you delighted in give pleasure no more; the progress of Christ's Gospel is no longer interesting; the company of God's children no longer sought. They or you must be changed. You are becoming shy of holy people, impatient of rebuke and advice, uncertain in your tempers, careless about little sins, not afraid of mixing with the world. Once it was not so. You may keep up some form of religion perhaps, but as to vital godliness you are fast cooling down. Already you are lukewarm; bye and bye you will be cold; and before long you will be icy, religion-frozen, and more dead than you were before. You are grieving the Spirit, and He will soon leave you; you are tempting the devil, and he will soon come to you. Oh! strengthen the things which remain which are ready to die.[166] How can I possibly help feeling doubt about your souls?

But I will not let you go without trying to do you good. I do pity you indeed, because you are so unhappy. I know it; I am sure of it; it is useless to deny it. You have been unhappy ever since you fell away. Unhappy at home, and unhappy abroad; unhappy

---

[162] Genesis 19:26.
[163] Colossians 3:9.
[164] Revelation 2:4.
[165] Hosea 6:4.
[166] Revelation 3:2.

in company, and unhappy alone; unhappy when you lie down, and unhappy when you rise up. You may have got riches, honour, love, obedience, friends; but yet *the sting* remains. There is a famine of consolation about you; there is an utter dearth of inward peace. You are sick at heart; you are ill at ease; you are discontented with every body, because you are discontented with yourself. You are like a bird that has wandered from her nest – you never feel in your right place. You have too much religion to enjoy the world, and too little religion to enjoy God. You are weary of life, and yet afraid to die. Truly the words of Solomon are made good, 'You are filled with your own ways.'[167]

But mark now, there is hope even for you. There is a remedy – humbling, pride-lowering, I know – but a sure remedy; and I earnestly beseech you to take it. That remedy is the free mercy of God in Christ Jesus. Hear what comfortable words your Lord and Saviour sends to you; 'Come unto me all ye that labour and are heavy laden, and I will give you rest.'[168] 'Thou hast played the harlot with many lovers, yet return again to me.'[169] 'Though your sins be as scarlet, they shall be as white as snow; though they be red like crimson, they shall be as wool.'[170] 'Return ye backsliding children, and I will heal your backslidings.' I do pray God you may reply 'We come unto thee, for thou art the Lord our God',[171] and that I may yet see you doing your first works.

Brethren, till I see this I cannot help doubting about your souls.

III. Lastly – *There are some among you about whom I feel a good hope.*

You are those whom the Spirit has convinced of sin, and led to Christ for salvation. In yourselves you find nothing but weakness

[167] Proverbs 14:14.
[168] Matthew 11:28.
[169] Jeremiah 3:1.
[170] Isaiah 1:18.
[171] Jeremiah 3:22.

and corruption, but in the Lord Jesus you find the very things your soul requires – pardon, consolation, light, health, strength, and peace. The life that you now live, you live by the faith of the Son of God:[172] His cross, His blood, His righteousness, His intercession – these are the things on which your minds love to dwell. You worship God in the Spirit; you rejoice in Christ Jesus; you have no confidence in the flesh.[173] Brethren, I must feel a lively hope about your souls.

I know well that the world is full of trials: you have fightings without, and fears within;[174] you are yet in the wilderness; you are not at home. I know well that pride and unbelief, and sloth, are continually struggling for the mastery within you. I doubt not your hearts are so treacherous and deceitful that many a day you are sick of yourselves, and say, 'Never was heart like mine.' But notwithstanding all this, I must hope well for your souls.

Have you not got an everlasting covenant – a covenant ordered in all things, and sure?[175] Father, Son, and Holy Ghost, have all engaged for your soul's salvation. Here is a threefold cord that never shall be broken.[176] Surely here is hope.

Have you not got a Saviour whose blood can cleanse from all sin;[177] a Saviour who invites all, and casts out none that come to Him;[178] a Saviour who will not break the bruised reed nor quench the smoking flax;[179] a Saviour who can be touched with the feeling

---

[172] Galatians 2:20.
[173] Philippians 3:3.
[174] 2 Corinthians 7:5.
[175] 2 Samuel 23:5.
[176] Ecclesiastes 4:12.
[177] 1 John 1:7.
[178] John 6:37.
[179] Matthew 12:20.

of your infirmities,[180] and is not ashamed to call you brethren;[181] a Saviour who never alters, the same yesterday, today, and for ever,[182] always able to save to the uttermost,[183] always mighty to save?[184] Surely here is hope.

Is not His love a love that passeth knowledge?[185] So free and undeserved; so costly, even unto death; so powerful and all-conquering; so unchanging and enduring; so patient and forbearing; so tender and sympathizing. Truly our sins pass knowledge, and this is the very love our souls need. Surely here is hope.

Have you not got exceeding great and precious promises?[186] Promises of being kept unto the end; promises of grace for every time of need,[187] and strength according to your day;[188] promises that never yet were broken, all yea and amen in Christ Jesus.[189] Surely here is hope.

Brethren believers, these things are a strong foundation. If God be for us who shall be against us? There is no condemnation to them that are in Christ Jesus; nothing shall ever separate them from the love of God which is in Christ Jesus our Lord.[190]

Come now and let me counsel you.[191] Let me try to quicken you in the things of God. Let me persuade you all to strive this year to grow in grace.

---

[180] Hebrews 4:15.
[181] Hebrews 2:11.
[182] Hebrews 13:8.
[183] Hebrews 7:25.
[184] Isaiah 63:1.
[185] Ephesians 3:19.
[186] 2 Peter 1:4.
[187] Hebrews 4:16.
[188] Deuteronomy 33:25.
[189] 2 Corinthians 1:20.
[190] Romans 8:1, 31, 38-39.
[191] 1 Kings 1:12.

I speak as a fellow traveller in the narrow way. I know that this is for our peace. I charge you solemnly as ever you would have few days of darkness – as ever you would feel God's face smiling on your soul – as ever you would have joy and peace in believing[192] – by all your recollections of past sad short-comings – by all your hopes of comfort yet to come – I exhort you, I beseech you, to grow in grace, and go forward this year.

Here, at the beginning of another twelvemonth, I urge this matter on your attention. Standing at the head of an avenue of fifty-two weeks, I call upon all to press forward. Some days in spring the grass will grow more in a few hours, than it did before in as many weeks. Let us see to it that 1846 is a year among years – a growing year with our souls.

Brethren believers, we are but children in the Lord's service, at our very best. There is room for improvement in us all. Listen then while I remind you of a few things which we need to know better, and shall do well to learn.

We all need more knowledge of our Lord Jesus Christ. How little do we know Him! Our cold affections towards Him are a witness against ourselves. Our eyes can never be open to what He is and does for us, or we should love Him more. There are many Christians whose minds seem ever running on the doctrine of sanctification. They can argue warmly about little points of practice; yet they are cold about Christ. They live by rule, they walk strictly, they do many things, they fancy in a short time they shall be very strong. But all this time they lose sight of this grand truth; that nothing is so sanctifying as knowledge of the Lord Jesus, and communion with Him. 'Abide in me', He says himself, 'and I in you. As the branch cannot bear fruit, except it abide in the vine; no more can ye, except ye abide in me.'[193] He must be the spring of our holiness,

[192] Romans 15:13.
[193] John 15:4.

as well as the rock of our faith. Christ must be all in all.[194] I doubt not He is precious to you that believe.[195] Precious because of His offices, and precious because of His work. Precious for what He has done already – He has called us, quickened us, washed us, justified us. Precious for what He is doing even now – Strengthening us, interceding for us, sympathizing with us. Precious for what He will do yet – He will keep us to the end, raise us, gather us at His coming, present us faultless before God's throne,[196] give us rest with Him in His kingdom. But surely He ought to be far more precious to us than He ever has been yet. I take you to record, if it were the last word of my life, I believe that nothing but the knowledge of Christ will ever feed a man's spirit. All our darkness has arisen from not keeping close to Him. The forms of religion are valuable as helps, and public ordinances are profitable to strengthen us – but it must be Christ crucified for sinners; Christ seen with the eye of faith; Christ present in the heart; Christ as the bread of life, and Christ as the water of life – this must be the doctrine we must ever cling to; nothing else will either save, satisfy, or sanctify, a sinful soul. Brethren, we all need more knowledge of Christ; let us all strive and pray for it this year.

We all need more knowledge of sin. Surely we are blind to its guilt, and ignorant of its deceitfulness, or else we should never trifle with it as we too often do. Oh! if we only saw its unutterable vileness in the eyes of God, we should be amazed at our own carelessness about going into temptation; we should marvel that we had never valued the blood of sprinkling[197] and the redemption which is in Christ Jesus,[198] more.

---

[194] Colossians 3:11.
[195] 1 Peter 2:7.
[196] Jude 24.
[197] Hebrews 12:24.
[198] Romans 3:24.

We all need more knowledge of our own hearts. We fancy we are acquainted with them, and we are not. The half of the evil that is in them has hitherto been hidden from our eyes. We have not the slightest idea how much they might deceive us, if tried, or into what depths of Satan the very best of us might fall. The tongue is said to be 'a world of iniquity';[199] think then, brethren believers, what the heart must be. Oh let us anoint our eyes with eye-salve, that we may see.[200]

We all need more holiness of heart and life. Truly the vessels in the Lord's house are many of them very dull and dim. I see things missing among us that Jesus loves. I miss the meekness and gentleness of our Master: many of us are harsh, rough tempered, and censorious, and we call it being faithful. I miss real boldness in confessing Christ before men: we think much more of the time to be silent than the time to speak.[201] I miss real humility: not many of us like to take the lowest place and esteem every one better than ourselves,[202] and our own strength perfect weakness. I miss real charity: few of us have that unselfish spirit which seeketh not its own,[203] there are few who are not more taken up with their own feelings and their own happiness than that of others. I miss real thankfulness of spirit: we complain, and murmur, and fret, and brood over the things we have not, and forget the things we have: we are seldom content; there is generally a Mordecai at our gate.[204] I miss decided separation from the world: the line of distinction is often rubbed out; many of us, like the chameleon, are always taking the colour of our company; we become so like the ungodly that it strains a man's eyes to see the

---

[199] James 3:6.
[200] Revelation 3:18.
[201] Ecclesiastes 3:7.
[202] Philippians 2:3.
[203] 1 Corinthians 13:5.
[204] Esther 2:19.

difference. Brethren, these things ought not so to be. Let us be zealous and repent.[205]

We all need more watchfulness in time of prosperity. We like the course of life to run smoothly and perhaps we pray for it: but how few there are who do not find it a perilous state to their souls. The seeds of sickness are generally sown in health. It is the holiday time when lessons are forgotten. Hunger is often good for us for it keeps us awake. Remember, David committed no adultery while fleeing before the face of Saul – it was when Saul was dead, and he was king in his stead, and there was peace in Israel.[206] Let us watch and be sober.[207]

We all need more faith in times of trial. Trial is the hand of a Father chastening us for our profit, but we are very slow to believe it. He touches us, and we cry and murmur and say 'take the rod away'. Yet the rod may have been sent in answer to a prayer for holiness: it may be God's way of carrying on that work of sanctification which we profess to desire. Be sure the school of affliction is the school for learning deep things: Jacob found it so. Manasseh found it so. Blessed are they who take patiently the Lord's bitter medicines, who bear the cross in silence and say, 'It is well, for my Father gives it to me.'

We all need more preparedness for our Lord's second coming. We profess to love His appearing, to be like servants who wait for their master's return; but who that observes the ways of some of us would ever think it? There are many hearts not quite prepared to receive Jesus; He would find the windows barred, the doors shut, the fires almost out; it would be a cold and comfortless reception. Brethren, it ought not to be so. We want more of a pilgrim spirit; we should be ever looking for and hastening towards our home. That day is

---

[205] Revelation 3:19.
[206] 2 Samuel 11.
[207] 1 Thessalonians 5:6.

the day of rest and gathering together of the saints. It is the day when we shall see the King in His beauty.[208] It ought not to startle and take us by surprise: we ought to be longing for it, and saying, 'Come Lord Jesus.'[209]

Lastly, *We all need more diligence about the means of grace.* I tell you plainly I suspect many believers are very lazy in their manner of using them; they scarcely know what hungering and thirsting means.[210] I doubt whether there is much private prayer before and after sermons. Yet remember, hearing alone is not everything: when all is said in the pulpit, only half the work is done. I doubt whether the Bible is as much read as it should be. Nothing in my own short experience has surprised me so much as the contented ignorance of Scripture which prevails among believers. I doubt whether private prayer is often made a business of as it should be. We are often satisfied to get up from our knees without having really seen or heard anything of God and His Christ. And all this is wrong. It is the diligent soul that becomes fat.[211] But we often put ourselves off with excuses little better than lies.

Brethren believers, let us lay to heart the things that I have mentioned. Let us resolve, by God's help, to set them before us this year, to pray for them, strive after them, and endeavour to attain them.

This is the way to be *useful Christians.* The world knows little of Christ beyond what is seen of Him in His people. Oh! what plain, clearly written epistles they ought to be! A growing believer is a walking sermon. He preaches far more than I do, for he preaches all the week round, shaming the unconverted, sharpening the converted, showing to all what grace can do. Such an one does good indeed by his life, and after death what great broad evidences he leaves behind

---

[208] Isaiah 33:17.
[209] Revelation 22:20.
[210] Matthew 5:6.
[211] Proverbs 13:4.

him. We carry him to the grave without one unpleasant doubt. Oh! the value and the power of a growing Christian! The Lord make you all such.

This is the way to be *happy Christians*. Happiness is the gift of God, but that there is the closest connexion between full following of God and full happiness let no man for an instant doubt. A growing believer has the witness within himself. He walks in the full light of the sun, and therefore he generally feels bright and warm. He does not quench the Spirit by continual inconsistencies, and so the fire within him seldom burns low. He has great peace because he really loves God's law,[212] and all that see him are obliged to allow that it is a privilege and not a bondage to be a Christian. Oh! the comfort of a tender conscience, a godly jealousy, a close walk with God; a heavenly frame of mind! The Lord make us all of such a spirit.

Brethren believers, I want you all to be useful and happy Christians, to have full assurance of your election of God. Once more then I say, let us pray and strive this year that we may all *grow*.

And now dear Brethren, of every class, to whom I have spoken, I heartily pray that the Lord may bless and keep you all this year.[213]

We live in strange times. The world seems getting old and shaking. The shadows are long drawn, the evening appears to be coming on. Oh! that we may all turn in upon ourselves, while it is called today, and consider well our own ways, each man by himself – What am I? Where am I going? What will be the end of my present way? What is my hope? Is it a Bible hope? Is it a hope ready for use? Is it a hope that will bear up my soul? Let none of us shrink and get from under these questions.

[212] Psalm 119:165.
[213] Numbers 6:24.

I know not what a year may bring forth – but this I dare to say, some one of us will want a solid hope beneath his feet before twelve months are past. I pray God that that one of us may have a hope in which Christ is all; Christ the beginning, and Christ the end; the Alpha and the Omega; the first and the last;[214] the foundation,[215] the corner-stone,[216] the strength, and the stay. If it be not so, alas! for his soul. But he that builds on Jesus shall never be confounded.[217]

I commend you all to God and to the Word of His grace, which is able to build you up, and give you an inheritance among them which are sanctified.[218]

Pray much for yourselves. 'Ask and ye shall receive.'[219] We have not grace because we do not ask it. Pray then without ceasing.[220]

Pray much for the congregation to which you belong, that the Lord may pour His Spirit on it; that there may be no unread Bibles, and prayerless tongues amongst us.

Pray much for your minister. It is the greatest kindness you can show him. He needs much grace, and he believes the effectual fervent prayers of his people avail much to draw it down.

Now may mercy and truth, grace and peace, be with you all this year, and till the Lord comes.

I remain my dear people,

Your affectionate Minister and Friend,

J. C. RYLE
Helmingham Rectory,
1st Jan., 1846.

---

[214] Revelation 22:13.
[215] 1 Corinthians 3:11.
[216] Ephesians 2:20.
[217] 1 Peter 2:6.
[218] Acts 20:32.
[219] John 16:24.
[220] 1 Thessalonians 5:17.

(5) A Pastor's Address to His Flock at the Beginning of a New Year (December 1846)

'God is my record how greatly I long after you all.' – Philippians i. 8.

Beloved Friends and Brethren,

The third year of my ministry among you is coming to an end. Suffer me to use the occasion as I have done before – suffer me to write to you in all affection about your souls.

The end of a year is a solemn season. It ought to remind us all of eternal things. The day of grace is slipping away – the day of judgment is drawing near – the thread of life is winding up – a few more short years and every soul of us will have gone to his own place – we shall each of us be in heaven or hell. Surely it is a time for ministers to warn, and for congregations to think – it is a time for all people to commune with their own hearts and be still.[221] May the Holy Spirit enable me to speak a word in season, and may the same Spirit incline you to receive it.

I cannot reach your hearts, I know well. It is not in me – it needs the finger of God. But I can set before you my earnest wishes for every class among you, and I will do it, the Lord being my helper. Bear with me if I say things that sound sharp and hard. Set it down to my anxiety for your salvation – I mean it all for your good. I write none other things but what I have gathered from the Bible, and as such I commend them to your consciences. Consider what I say, and the Lord give you understanding in all things.[222]

I. First of all let me say, *there are very many among you whom I long to see awakened.*

You are those who have the name of Christians, but not the

[221] Psalm 4:4.
[222] 2 Timothy 2:7.

character which should go with the name. God is not King of your hearts. You mind earthly things.[223]

I grant you may be quick and clever about the affairs of this life: you are, many of you, good men of business, good at your daily work, good masters, good servants, good neighbours, good subjects of the Queen: all this I fully allow. But it is the eternal part of you that I speak of; it is your never-dying soul. And about that, if a man may judge by the little you do for it, you are careless, thoughtless, reckless, and unconcerned.

I do not say that God and salvation are subjects that never come across your minds, but this I say, they have not the uppermost place there. Neither do I say that you are all alike in your lives – some of you doubtless go further in sin than others – but this I say, you have all turned every one to his own way,[224] and that way is not God's. Brethren, when I look at the Bible I can come to only one conclusion about you – you are asleep about your souls.

You do not see the sinfulness of sin, and your own lost condition by nature. You appear to make light of breaking God's commandments, and to care little whether you live according to His law or not. Yet God says that sin is the transgression of the law[225] – that His commandment is exceeding broad[226] – that every imagination of your natural heart is evil[227] – that sin is the thing He cannot bear, He hates it – that the wages of sin is death,[228] and the soul that sinneth shall die.[229] Surely you are asleep!

You do not see your need of a Saviour. You appear to think it an easy matter to get to heaven, and that God will of course be

---

[223] Philippians 3:19.
[224] Isaiah 53:6.
[225] 1 John 3:4.
[226] Psalm 119:96.
[227] Genesis 8:21.
[228] Romans 6:23.
[229] Ezekiel 18:4, 20.

merciful to you at last some way or other, though you do not exactly know how. Yet God says that He is just, and never changes – that Christ is the only way, and none can come unto the Father but by Him[230] – that without His blood there can be no forgiveness of sin[231] – that a man without Christ is a man without hope – that those who would be saved must believe on Jesus[232] and come to Him, and that he who believeth not shall be damned.[233] Surely you are asleep!

You do not see the necessity of holiness. You appear to think it quite enough to go on as others do, and live like your neighbours. And as for praying and Bible-reading, making conscience of words and actions, studying truthfulness and gentleness, humility and charity, and keeping separate from the world, they are things you do not seem to value at all. Yet God says, that without holiness no man shall see the Lord[234] – that there shall enter into heaven nothing that defileth[235] – that His people must be a peculiar people, zealous of good works.[236] Surely you are asleep!

And, worst of all, *you do not appear to feel your danger.* You walk on with your eyes shut, and seem not to know that the end of your path is hell. Some dreamers fancy they are rich when they are poor, or full when they are hungry, or well when they are sick, and awake to find it all a mistake. And this is the way that many of you dream about your souls; you flatter yourselves you will have peace, and there will be no peace; you fancy that you are all right, and in truth you will find that you are all wrong. Surely you are asleep!

[230] John 14:6.
[231] Hebrews 9:22.
[232] Acts 16:31.
[233] Mark 16:16.
[234] Hebrews 12:14.
[235] Revelation 21:27.
[236] Titus 2:14.

Dear brethren, what can I say to arouse you? Your souls are in awful peril: without a mighty change they will be lost. When shall that change once be?

You are dying, and not ready to depart – you are going to be judged, and not prepared to meet God – your sins are not forgiven, your persons are not justified, your hearts are not renewed. Heaven itself would be no happiness to you if you got there, for the Lord of heaven is not your friend. What pleases Him does not please you. What He dislikes gives you no pain. His word is not your counsellor. His day is not your delight. His law is not your guide. You care little for hearing of Him. You know nothing of speaking with Him. To be for ever in His company would be a thing you could not endure; and the society of saints and angels would be a weariness, and not a joy. At the rate you live at, the Bible might never have been written, and Christ might never have died, the Apostles were foolish, the New Testament Christians madmen, and the salvation of the Gospel a needless thing. Oh! awake, and sleep no more!

Think not to say, You cannot believe your case is so bad, or the danger so great, or God so particular. I answer, The devil has been putting this lying delusion into people's hearts for nearly six thousand years. It has been his grand snare ever since the day he said to Eve, 'Ye shall not surely die.'[237] Do not be so weak as to be taken in by it. God never failed yet to punish sin, and He never will. He never failed to make His word good, and you will find this to your cost, one day, except you repent.

And think not to say, You are a member of Christ's church, and therefore feel no doubt you are as good a Christian as others. I answer, This will only make your case worse, if you have nothing else to plead. You may be written down and registered among God's people; you may be reckoned in the number of the saints; you may sit for years under the sound of the Gospel; you may use holy forms,

[237] Genesis 3:4.

and even come to the Lord's table at regular seasons – and still, with all this, unless sin be hateful, and Christ precious, and your heart a temple of the Holy Ghost, you will prove in the end no better than a lost soul. A holy calling will never save an unholy man.

And think not to say, You have been baptized, and so feel confident you are born of God, and have His grace within you. I answer, You have none of the marks which St John has told me in his first Epistle, distinguish such a person. I do not see you confessing that Jesus is the Christ – overcoming the world – not committing sin – loving your brother – doing righteousness – keeping yourself from the wicked one.[238] How then can I believe that you are born of God? If God were your Father you would love Christ: if you were God's son you would be led by His Spirit. I want stronger evidences. Show me some repentance and faith; show me a life hid with Christ in God;[239] show me a spiritual and sanctified conversation – these are the fruits I want to see, if I am to believe you have the root of the matter in you, and are a living branch of the true vine.[240] But without these your baptism will only add to your condemnation.

Beloved brethren, I speak strongly, because I feel deeply. Time is too short, life is too uncertain, to allow of standing on ceremony. At the risk of offending, I use great plainness of speech. I cannot bear the thought of hearing any of you condemned in the great day of assize – of seeing any of your faces in the crowd on God's left hand, among those who are helpless, hopeless, and beyond the reach of mercy. I cannot bear such thoughts – they grieve me to the heart. Before the day of grace is past, and the day of vengeance begins, I call upon you to open your eyes and repent. Oh! consider your ways and be wise.[241] Turn ye, turn ye, why will ye die?[242]

[238] 1 John 2:10, 29; 3:9; 5:1, 5, 18.
[239] Colossians 3:3.
[240] John 15:1-5.
[241] Proverbs 6:6.
[242] Ezekiel 33:11.

Here, at the beginning of a new year, I pray you to be reconciled to God. The Lord Jesus who came into the world to save sinners[243] – Jesus, the appointed mediator between God and man – Jesus, who loved us and gave Himself for us[244] – Jesus sends you all a message of peace. He says, 'Come unto me.'[245]

'Come' is a precious word indeed, and ought to draw you. You have sinned against heaven[246] – heaven has not sinned against you: yet, see how the first step towards peace is on heaven's side – it is the Lord's message, 'Come unto me.'

'Come' is a word of *merciful invitation*. Does it not seem to say, 'Sinner, I am waiting for you, I am not willing that any should perish, but that all should come to repentance.[247] As I live, I have no pleasure in the death of him that dieth.[248] I would have all men saved and come to the knowledge of the truth.[249] Judgment is my strange work[250] – I delight in mercy.[251] I offer the water of life to every one who will take it.[252] I stand at the door of your heart and knock.[253] For [a] long time I have spread out my hands to you.[254] I wait to be gracious.[255] There is yet room in my Father's house.[256] My long-suffering waits for more of the children of men to come to the mercy-seat before the last trumpet is blown – for more

[243] 1 Timothy 1:15.
[244] Galatians 2:20.
[245] Matthew 11:28.
[246] Luke 15:18, 21.
[247] 2 Peter 3:9.
[248] Ezekiel 18:32.
[249] 1 Timothy 2:4.
[250] Isaiah 28:21.
[251] Micah 7:18.
[252] Revelation 21:6.
[253] Revelation 3:20.
[254] Isaiah 65:2.
[255] Isaiah 30:18.
[256] John 14:2.

wanderers to return before the door is closed for ever. Oh! sinner, come to me.'

'Come' is a word of *promise and encouragement*. Does it not seem to say, 'Sinner, I have gifts ready for you; I have something of everlasting importance to bestow upon your soul; I have received gifts for men, even for the rebellious;[257] I have a free pardon for the most ungodly; a full fountain for the most unclean; a white garment for the most defiled; a new heart for the most hardened; healing for the broken-hearted;[258] rest for the heavy-laden;[259] joy for those that mourn. Oh! sinner, it is not for nothing that I invite you! All things are ready[260] – come, come unto me.'

Beloved brethren, hear the voice of the Son of God. See that ye refuse not Him that speaketh.[261] Come away from sin, which can never give you real pleasure, and will be bitter at the last. Come out from a world which will never satisfy you. Come unto Christ. Come with all your sins, however many and however great – however far you may have gone from God, and however provoking your conduct may have been. Come as you are – unfit, unmeet, unprepared as you may think yourself – you will gain no fitness by delay. Come at once, come to the Lord Jesus Christ.

How indeed shall you escape, if you neglect so great salvation?[262] Where will you appear if you make light of the blood of Christ, and do despite to the Spirit of grace?[263] It is a fearful thing to fall into the hands of the living God,[264] but never so fearful as when men fall from under the Gospel. The saddest road to hell is that which runs

257 Psalm 68:18.
258 Psalm 147:3.
259 Matthew 11:28.
260 Matthew 22:4.
261 Hebrews 12:25.
262 Hebrews 2:3.
263 Hebrews 10:29.
264 Hebrews 10:31.

under the pulpit, past the Bible, and through the midst of warnings and invitations. Oh! beware, lest like Israel at Kadesh, you mourn over your mistake when it is too late;[265] or like Judas Iscariot, find out your sin when there is no space for repentance.

Arise, beloved brethren, and call upon the Lord. Be not like Esau: sell not eternal blessings for the things of today.[266] Surely the time past may suffice you to have been careless and prayerless, God-less and Christless, worldly and earthly-minded; surely the time to come may be given to your soul.

Pray, I beseech you, that with the old year you may put off the old ways and the old habits, and that with the new year you may become new men, new creatures in Christ Jesus.[267] I yield to none in wishes for your happiness, and my best wish is that the year 1847 may see the birth day of your soul. This is a better thing than riches or health, or honour or learning. A man may get to heaven without these, but he cannot get there without conversion. Verily if you die without having been born again, you had far better never have been born at all. No man really lives till he lives unto God.

II. The second thing I have to say is this, *there are many among you whom I long to see decided followers of Christ.*

You are those who are wavering and halting between two opin-ions.[268] You seem not to have made up your minds. You appear to stand in doubt which is the true way of serving God, and which the false. One day a man might think you loved Christ – another he might suppose you did not care for Him at all. You are like the twilight – I cannot call you darkness – and yet you are not light in the Lord.[269] There is so much right about you, that I cannot speak

[265] Numbers 14.
[266] Genesis 27.
[267] 2 Corinthians 5:17.
[268] 1 Kings 18:21.
[269] Ephesians 5:8.

to you among the openly ungodly; and yet there is so much wrong about you, that without a change you will never be saved. Oh! that this change might begin at once! Oh! that this year might be a year of decision in your hearts.

Wavering brethren, of all classes in a congregation, you are the most difficult to address: no state is so dangerous as yours.

You see something of the evil of sin, and its awful consequences, but not all. You have thoughts about judgment and hell, and you would like to avoid them; but you never really try.

You see something of the blessedness of heaven, but not all. Its peace, and rest, and joy, and happiness, are things that come across your mind, but you never really seek to obtain them.

There have been times when you have appeared convinced; there seemed to be much melting and softening going on in your heart. You have been at Sinai, and been alarmed. You have been at Bochim, and wept.[270] You have been at Calvary, and had prickings of conscience. And yet those times have passed away, and your old things still remain.

You have often looked like men going on pilgrimage: you seemed ready to come out from the world; and then you have suddenly stopped, and gone no further.

You have done many things that are good, but, unhappily like Herod, you leave many undone. You give up many habits that are bad, and yet you keep sufficient to make it plain you have no true grace in your hearts.

Oh! wavering brethren, what can be done for your souls? I am distressed for you.

Many of you are so like true christians [*sic*], that the difference can hardly be seen. You are no opposers of true religion. You have no objection to the preaching of the Gospel, and often take pains

---

[270] Judges 2:4-5.

to hear it. You can enjoy the company of believers, and appear to take pleasure in their conversation and experience. You can even talk yourself of the things of God as if you valued them. All this you can do.

And yet there is nothing real about your religion – no real witnessing against sin – no real separation from the world – no peculiarity – no warfare. You can wear Christ's uniform in the time of peace, but, like the tribe of Reuben, you are wanting in the day of battle.[271] Times of trouble prove that you were never really on the Rock. Times of sickness and danger bring out the rottenness of your foundations. Times of temptation and persecution discover the emptiness of your professions. There is no dependance [sic] to be placed upon you. Christians in the company of christians [sic], you are worldly in the company of the worldly. One week I shall find you reading spiritual books, as if you were all for eternity – another I shall hear of your mixing in some earthly folly, as if you only thought of time. And so you go on, beating about in sight of land, but never seeming to make up your mind to come into harbour; showing plainly that you have an idea of the way of life, but not decided enough to act upon your knowledge.

Oh! wavering brethren, what can be done for you? I tell you solemnly, I tremble for your souls. In your present course you will never taste peace – you will go on without comfort, and go off without hope.

Truly you are a wonder in creation. You stand alone. The devil wonders at you, how you can see so much of the way to heaven, and not walk in it. The angels wonder at you, how you can know so much of the Gospel, and yet stand still. Ministers wonder at you, how you can march up to the borders of the promised land, and yet not strive to enter in. Believers wonder at you, how you can taste so

---

[271] Numbers 32.

much of the good word of God,[272] and yet not determine to eat and live for ever. Take heed, lest at last you prove a wonder to yourselves.

Wavering brethren, let me ask you a simple question. How long do you mean to continue as you are? When do you intend to cease from being almost christians [*sic*], and become decided? When do you leave Agrippa, and join Paul?[273] You know in your heart and conscience you are not yet saved – you have no oil in your lamps[274] – you have not the marks of Christ's people – you are not true saints. You dare not deny what I say.

When then do you propose to alter? What is the thing that you are waiting for? Oh! turn not away from my question: sit down and answer it if you can.

Are you waiting *till you are sick and unwell?* Surely you will not tell me that is a convenient season. When your body is racked with pain – when your mind is distracted with all kinds of anxious thoughts – when calm reflection is almost impossible – is this a time for beginning the mighty work of acquaintance with God? Do not talk so.

Are you waiting *till you are old?* Surely you have not considered what you say. You will serve Christ when your members are worn out and decayed, and your hands unfit to work. You will go to Him when your mind is weak, and your memory failing. You will give up the world when you cannot keep it. You will set your affections on things above, when you find nothing to set them on in things below.[275] Is this your plan? Beware, lest you insult God.

Are you waiting *till you have leisure?* And when do you expect to have more time than you have now? Every year you live seems shorter than the last: you find more to think of, or to do, and

[272] Hebrews 6:5.
[273] Acts 26.
[274] Matthew 25:3.
[275] Colossians 3:2.

less power and opportunity to do it. And, after all, you know not whether you may live to see another year. Boast not yourself of tomorrow[276] – now is the time.

Are you waiting *till your heart is perfectly fit and ready?* That will never be. It will always be corrupt and sinful – a bubbling fountain, full of evil. You will never make it like a pure white sheet of paper, that you can take to Jesus, and say, 'Here I am, Lord, ready to have thy law written on my heart.' Delay not. Better begin as you are.

Are you waiting *till the devil will let you come to Christ without trouble?* That will never be. Satan never gives up a single soul without a struggle. If you would be saved you must fight for it. Stand not another day. Arise and go forward at once.

Are you waiting *till there is no cross to be borne?* That will never be. So long as sin is our enemy, and our own bodies weak and clogged by it, so long we must endure hardness, if we would be good soldiers of Jesus Christ.[277] Go in the strength of the Lord God,[278] and you shall overcome. If there is no cross there will be no crown.[279]

Are you waiting *till all around you become decided?* That will never be. Heaven only is the place where all are saints. Earth is the place where sin reigns, and God's people are a little flock.[280] You must be content to journey alone, and swim against the stream. 'Narrow is the way that leadeth unto life, and few there be that find it.'[281] Tarry not for friends and neighbours – see that you are among the few.

Are you waiting *till the gate is wide?* That will never be. It will not alter – it is not elastic – it will not stretch. It is wide enough

---

[276] Proverbs 27:1.

[277] 2 Timothy 2:3.

[278] Psalm 71:16.

[279] *No cross, no crown* (London, 1669) was a popular work by the Quaker leader, William Penn (1644-1718).

[280] Luke 12:32.

[281] Matthew 7:14.

for the chief of sinners,[282] if he comes in a humble and self-abased spirit. But if there is anything you are resolved not to give up, you will never, with all your struggling, get in. Lay aside every weight[283] – enter before the door is shut for ever.

And are you waiting *because some few Christians are inconsistent, and some professors fall away?* Their folly is no excuse for you. Their sin will not justify your delay. Hear the word of the Lord Jesus, 'What is that to thee, follow thou me.'[284]

Oh! wavering brethren, are not your excuses broken reeds – webs that will not cover you – wood, hay, and stubble, that will not abide the fire?[285] Are not your reasonings and defences unprofitable and vain? Be honest – confess the truth.

Turn not away from good advice. I fear lest the time should come when you will seek to enter in, and not be able.[286] Here, at the beginning of a new year, I charge you throw away indecision – wait no longer – become decided for Christ.

No man is *wise* till he is decided. What can be more foolish, than to live on in uncertainty? What can be more childish than to appear not to know what is truth? – to have two ways set before us, and not be able to decide which is right? Christ is on one side, and the world on the other – the Bible is on the right hand, and man's opinion on the left – is it not a wonderful and horrible thing that you can think on these things, and yet for a moment doubt? Whether you believe the Gospel true or false, your present position is manifestly wrong. If it be true, you do not go far enough – if it be false you go too far. Oh! be decided, and be wise.

[282] 1 Timothy 1:15.
[283] Hebrews 12:1.
[284] John 21:22.
[285] 1 Corinthians 3:12-13.
[286] Luke 13:24.

No man is *safe* till he is decided. All are in peril of ruin who are not real followers of Christ – who are not converted and made children of God.

Wavering brethren, you fancy there is a middle path between conversion [*sic*]. You are mistaken. There seems to be – the devil tells you there is – but in reality there is no such thing. There are but two kingdoms, Christ's kingdom, and Satan's, there is no neutral ground between – two parties, believers and unbelievers, there is no third. Consider to which you belong.

Some people, I know, will say you are in a hopeful state. I dare not say so, while you stand still. It would be flattery, and not charity. I tell you rather your state is dangerous in the extreme. You have enough religion to satisfy you in a way – you are not as other men, careless, profligate, and the like – but still you have not enough religion to do you good. You have not the Spirit of Christ, and are none of His.[287]

It is small comfort to my mind to hear that you are not far from the kingdom of God, if you stop there. It wants another step to make you safe, and without that, all the rest is useless. I doubt not many were close to the door of the ark, when the flood came, but all alike were drowned who were not inside. Many, I dare say, came up to the gates of the cities of refuge, but none escaped the destroyer except those who really entered in. Be decided. This is the only way to be safe.

And no man is quite *happy* in his religion till he is decided. There is little peace so long as you are halting and irresolute. You please no one altogether. Jesus has no consolations for you: He will have all your heart or none. The world is not satisfied with you, they cannot understand your behaviour. True christians [*sic*] dare not comfort you: they can only look on you with suspicion and

[287] Romans 8:9.

mistrust. You are like the Samaritans of old, who served the Lord and their own idols at the same time; they formed a middle class between the Jews and Gentiles, and yet were friends with neither – they were too much Gentiles for the Jews, and too much Jews for the Gentiles. This is just your case. You are trying that which cannot be done; you are trying to serve two masters,[288] and no wonder you are ill at ease.

Wavering brethren, here at the beginning of a new year, I invite you to choose the better part.[289] Gird up the loins of your minds.[290] Quit you like men. Be strong.[291] God's conduct in punishing sin has ever been decided. Satan's conduct in tempting sinners has ever been decided – why then are you not decided too?

Cry mightily unto the Lord,[292] that with the old year you may leave behind your wavering ways. Resolve that, by His grace, you will be true soldiers, real servants, men of God indeed – that you will never rest until you know in whom you believe. Cease to halt between two opinions. Let your eyes look right on.[293] Cast loose your hold on the world. Lay hold on Christ, and commit yourselves to Him. No man ever came back from the narrow way, and reported that he was sorry for his choice. Thousands have lingered away life, as you are doing now, and have found, too late, that the fruit of indecision is eternal sorrow.

III. The last thing I have to say is this, *there are some true christians* [sic] *among you whom I long to see more holy and more bright.*

You are those who have found out your own sinfulness and lost estate, and really believe on Jesus for the saving of your souls. The

[288] Matthew 6:24.
[289] Luke 10:42.
[290] 1 Peter 1:13.
[291] 1 Corinthians 16:13.
[292] Jonah 3:8.
[293] Proverbs 4:25.

eyes of your understanding have been opened by the Spirit[294] – He has led you to Christ, and you are new men. You have peace with God. Sin is no longer pleasant to you – the world has no longer the first place in your heart – all things are become new. You have ceased from trusting in your own works. You are willing to stand before the bar of God, and rest your soul on the finished work of Him who died for the ungodly.[295] This is all your confidence, that you have washed your robes and made them white in the blood of the Lamb.[296] I thank God heartily for what He hath wrought in your souls.

Believing brethren, I write to you *about your sanctification.* There are those who think you are a class in our congregations that require little writing to: you are within the pale of salvation – you may be almost let alone. I cannot see it. I believe you need your minister's care and exhortation as much as any, if not more. I believe that on your growth in grace and holiness, not merely your own comfort, but the salvation of many souls, under God, depends. I believe that the converted members of a church should be preached to, spoken to, warned, counselled, far more than they are. You need many words of direction. You are still in the wilderness. You have not crossed Jordan. You are not yet at home.

I see Paul beseeching the Thessalonians that as they have received of Him, how they ought to walk and please God, so they would abound more and more.[297] I see him warning them not to sleep, as others do, but to watch and be sober.[298] I see Peter telling believers to give diligence to make their calling and election sure;[299]

[294] Ephesians 1:18.
[295] Romans 5:6.
[296] Revelation 7:14.
[297] 1 Thessalonians 4:1.
[298] 1 Thessalonians 5:6.
[299] 2 Peter 1:10.

to go on adding one grace to another; to grow in grace, and in the knowledge of Christ.[300] I wish to follow in their steps. I would remind you 'that this is the will of God, even your sanctification',[301] and I ask you to make it plain it is your will too. You were not chosen out of the world to go to sleep, but that you might be holy: you were not called of God that you might sit still, but that you might walk worthy of your calling.[302] Recollect those solemn words, 'He that lacketh these things is blind and cannot see afar off, and hath forgotten that he was purged from his old sins.'[303]

Why do I say these things? Is it because I think you do not know them? No: but I want to stir you up by putting you in remembrance.[304] Is it because I wish to discourage the poor in spirit,[305] and make the heart of the righteous sad?[306] No: indeed I would not willingly do this. Is it because I think true Christians can ever fall away? God forbid you should suppose I mean such a thing.

But I say what I say because *I am jealous for my Lord's honour.* I wish the elect of God to be indeed a holy nation,[307] and the sons of adoption to live as becomes the children of a King. I want those who are light in the Lord to walk as children of light,[308] shining more and more every day.

And I say it *for the good of the world.* You are almost the only book that worldly people read. Surely your lives should be epistles of Christ,[309] so plain that he who runs may read them. The world

[300] 2 Peter 3:18.
[301] 1 Thessalonians 4:3.
[302] Ephesians 4:1.
[303] 2 Peter 1:9.
[304] 2 Peter 1:13.
[305] Matthew 5:3.
[306] Ezekiel 13:22.
[307] 1 Peter 2:9.
[308] Ephesians 5:8.
[309] 2 Corinthians 3:3.

cares little for doctrine – the world knows nothing of experience – but the world can understand a close walk with God.

And not least I say it *because of the times you live in*. I write it down deliberately, I believe there never were so many lukewarm saints as there are now – there never was a time in which a low and carnal standard of christian [*sic*] behaviour so much prevailed – there never were so many babes in grace in the family of God – so many who seem to sit still, and live on old experience – so many who appear to have need of nothing, and to be neither hungering nor thirsting after righteousness,[310] as at the present time. I write this with all sorrow. It may be too painful to please some; but I ask you, as in God's sight, is it not true?

There is a generation of Christians in this age who grieve me to the heart. They make my blood run cold. I cannot understand them. For anything that man's eye can see, they make no progress. They never seem to get on. Years roll on, and they are just the same – the same besetting sins, the same infirmities of disposition, the same weakness in trial, the same chilliness of heart, the same apathy, the same faint resemblance to Christ – but no new knowledge, no increased interest in the kingdom, no freshness, no new strength, no new fruits, as if they grew. Are they not forgetting that growth is the proof of life, that even the yew tree grows and the snail and the sloth move? Are they not forgetting how awfully far a man may go and yet not be a true Christian? He may be like a waxwork figure, the very image of a believer, and yet not have within him the breath of God: he may have a name to live and be dead after all.

Believing brethren, these are the reasons why I write so strongly. I want your Christianity to be unmistakable. I want you all to grow really, and to do more than others. Here, at the beginning of a new

[310] Matthew 5:6.

year, let us remember Sardis and Laodicea[311] – let us all resolve to be more holy and more bright. Let us bury our idols. Let us put away all strange gods.[312] Let us cast out the old leaven.[313] Let us lay aside every weight and besetting sin.[314] Let us cleanse ourselves from all filthiness of flesh and spirit, and perfect holiness in the fear of God.[315] Let us renew our covenant with our beloved Lord. Let us aim at the highest and best things. Let us resolve by God's blessing this year to be more holy, and then I know and am persuaded, we shall be more happy, and shall have great peace.

I name some things, for prayerful consideration:

1. Let us then, for one thing, begin with *a humble confession of past unprofitableness and shortcomings*.

Let us acknowledge with shame and contrition that we have not hitherto lived up to our light. We ought to have been the salt of the earth[316] – but there has been little savour of Christ about us. We ought to have been the light of the world[317] – but we have most of us been little glimmering sparks that could scarcely be seen. We ought to have been a peculiar people[318] – but the difference between us and the world has been small and faint. We ought to have been like Levites among professing Christians – but we have too often behaved as if we belonged to some other tribe. We ought to have looked on this world as an inn, and we have settled down in it as if it were our home – it ought to have been counted our school of training for eternity, and we have been at ease in it as if it were our

---

[311] Revelation 3:1-6, 14-22.
[312] Genesis 35:2-4.
[313] 1 Corinthians 5:7.
[314] Hebrews 12:1.
[315] 2 Corinthians 7:1.
[316] Matthew 5:13.
[317] Matthew 5:14.
[318] Titus 2:14; 1 Peter 2:9.

continuing city,[319] or trifled away time in it as if we were meant to play and not to learn. We ought to have been careful for nothing, and we have been careful and troubled about many things – we have allowed the affairs of this life to eat out the heart of our spirituality and have been cumbered with much serving.[320] How rarely we have heard the gospel like men in earnest – and read the Bible as if we were feeding on it – and prayed as if we wanted an answer! How poor and feeble has been our witness against sin! How seldom have we looked like men about our Father's business![321] How little we have known of singleness of eye,[322] and wholeness of heart, and walking in the Spirit![323] How weak has been our faith, how feeble our hope, how cold our charity! How few of us have lived as if we believed all that is written in the Word, and moved through life like pilgrims travelling to a better land!

Oh! brethren believers, have we not good reason to be ashamed when we think on these things? Very grievous are they and we ought to feel it. Let us begin the year with self-abasement – let us cry, 'God be merciful to us sinners[324] – take away our iniquity for we have done very foolishly.'[325]

2. In the next place, *let us all seek to 'abide in Christ' more thoroughly than we have hitherto.*

Christ is the true spring of life in every believer's soul, the head on which every member depends, the corner stone of all real sanctification. Whenever I see a child of God becoming less holy than he

[319] Hebrews 13:14.
[320] Luke 10:40.
[321] Luke 2:49.
[322] Matthew 6:22.
[323] Galatians 5:16.
[324] Luke 18:13.
[325] 2 Samuel 24:10.

was, I know the secret of it, he is clinging less firmly to Christ than he did. Our root must be right, if our fruit is to abound.[326]

Brethren, let us strive after close union and communion with Christ. Let us go to Him oftener, speak with Him more frequently, trust Him more wholly, look to Him more constantly, lean upon Him more entirely. This is the way to go through the wilderness without fainting, and to run the race set before us with patience.[327] Let us live the life of faith in the Son of God. He is the vine and we are the branches – let all our strength be drawn from Him: separate from Him we can do nothing.[328] He is the sun of righteousness[329] – let us seek our comfort in Him and not in our own frames and feelings. He is the bread of life[330] – let us feed on Him day by day, as Israel on the manna, and not on our own experiences. Let Christ become more and more all things to us: His blood our peace – His intercession our comfort – His word our warrant – His grace our strength – His sympathy our support – His speedy coming our hope. Let others spend their time on new books if they will, let us rather study to learn Christ.

We know a little of Christ as our Saviour, but Oh! how small a portion have we seen of the fulness that is in Him. Like the Indians, when America was first discovered, we are not aware of the amazing value of the gold and treasure in our hands. Believe me, if we did but realize the blessedness of free and full forgiveness in Him, we should be men of a different stamp. The man who *feels* the blood of atonement sprinkled on his conscience – the man who enjoys assurance that he is washed, and justified, and accepted in the Beloved,[331]

---

[326] Philippians 4:17.
[327] Hebrews 12:1.
[328] John 15:5.
[329] Malachi 4:2.
[330] John 6:35, 48.
[331] Ephesians 1:6.

this is the man who will be holy indeed, this is the man who will bear much fruit. He will labour cheerfully – he will suffer patiently – he will witness confidently – he will press on unflinchingly – he will love warmly. Redemption is ever fresh upon his mind, and his thought is, 'what shall I render unto the Lord for all His benefits?'[332]

Brethren, let us cleave to Christ more closely. Let us draw nearer to the cross. Let us sit at the feet of Jesus. Let us drink into the spirit of the apostle when he said 'to me to live is Christ'.[333] Let us do this, and we shall grow.

3. And let us *beware of excuses.*

Reasons will never be wanting in our minds why we cannot be bright and eminent Christians *just now.* It is very possible to admire a high standard of spirituality in others, while we are content with very low practice ourselves. We persuade ourselves there is something peculiar in our particular case which makes it almost impossible to shine. But let all excuses be received, like Babylonian ambassadors, with great suspicion. They are generally the devil's coinage. Let us settle it firmly in our hearts, that there are few of us indeed who cannot glorify God just where we are without any change. All our excuses are as dust in the balance when placed against that promise 'my grace is sufficient for thee.'[334] Let us not deceive ourselves. By the grace of God we may be bright saints even now.

Let us not say, '*We have bad health.*' Remember the apostle Paul – he had a thorn in the flesh[335] – some never-ceasing ailment, probably – and yet it seemed a spur rather than a hindrance to his soul.

Let us not say, '*We have many trials.*' Remember Job. Wave upon wave came rolling over him, and yet his faith did not give way; and the record of his patience is on high.

[332] Psalm 116:12.
[333] Philippians 1:21.
[334] 2 Corinthians 12:9.
[335] 2 Corinthians 12:7.

Let us not say, '*We have families and children to make us anxious and keep us back.*' Remember David – none was ever so tried at home as he was, yet he was a man after God's own heart.[336]

Let us not say, '*We have press of distracting business to attend on.*' Remember Daniel – he had far more affairs on his hands probably than any of us, yet he found time to pray three times a day[337] and was a proverb for godliness.

Let us not say, '*I stand alone, the times are evil, and none around me serve God.*' Remember Noah. The whole world was against him, yet he did not give way. By faith he held fast.

Let us not say, '*We live in families where God is not thought of.*' Remember Obadiah in Ahab's house,[338] and Nero's servants at Rome.[339] What are our difficulties compared with theirs.

Let us not say, '*We are poor and unlearned.*' Remember Peter and John. They were as poor and unlearned as any of us, yet they were pillars of the early church,[340] they were of the number of those who turned the world upside down.[341]

No! believing brethren, such excuses for not being more holy will never do while grace may be had. Let us say rather, 'We are slothful and take no trouble – we are unbelieving and make no bold attempt – we are worldly and our eyes are too dim to see the beauty of holiness – we are proud and we cannot humble ourselves to take pains.' Let us say this and we shall more likely speak the truth. There are always ways in which we may glorify God: there are passive graces as well as active. But the way of the slothful is always a hedge of thorns.[342] The wall of Jerusalem was soon built when the Jews had

---

[336] 1 Samuel 13:14.
[337] Daniel 6:10.
[338] 1 Kings 18:3.
[339] Philippians 4:22.
[340] Galatians 2:9.
[341] Acts 17:6.
[342] Proverbs 15:19.

'a mind to work'.[343] We complain of the devil, but there is no devil after all like our own hearts. We have not grace because we do not ask it. The fault is all our own.

4. Let us *be on our guard against false doctrine.*

Unsound faith will never be the mother of really sound practice, and in these latter days departures from the faith abound. See then that your loins be girt about with truth,[344] and be very jealous of receiving anything which cannot be proved by the word. Think not for a moment that false doctrine will meet you face to face, saying 'I am false doctrine and I want to come into your heart.' Satan does not go to work in that way. He dresses up false doctrine like Jezebel – he paints her face and tires her head,[345] and tries to make her like truth. Think not that those who preach error will never preach anything that is true. Error would do little harm if that was the case. No! error will come before you mingled with much that is sound and scriptural. The sermon will be all right excepting a few sentences. The book will be all good excepting a few pages. And this is the chief danger of religious error in these times – it is like the subtle poisons of days gone by – it works so deceitfully that it throws men off their guard. Brethren, take care. Remember that even Satan himself is transformed into an angel of light.[346]

Keep clear of any system of religion which confounds the world and true believers, and makes no broad distinction between those who are true children of God in a congregation, and those who are not. Be not carried away by an appearance of great self-denial and humility. It is far easier to fast and wear sackcloth and be of a sad countenance, than to receive thoroughly the doctrine of justification by faith without the deeds of the law.[347]

[343] Nehemiah 4:6.
[344] Ephesians 6:14.
[345] 2 Kings 9:30.
[346] 2 Corinthians 11:14.
[347] Romans 3:28.

Call no man father upon earth.[348] Build not your faith on any minister or set of ministers. Let no man become your Pope. Make no Christian living your standard of what is right in faith or practice, however high his name, his rank, or his learning. Let your creed be the Bible and nothing but the Bible, and your example Christ and nothing short of Him.

Take heed, lest your minds be corrupted from the simplicity that is in Christ.[349] Be careful what books you read on religious subjects: many books of this day are leavened with doctrines which spoil the Gospel. Examine yourselves often whether you are standing in the old paths.[350] Our lost estate by nature – our recovery through our Saviour's kindness and love – our need of regeneration and renewal – our justification through grace – these are the grand doctrines, as Paul told Titus; and these are the points on which we must be sound, if we would maintain good works.[351]

5. Let us resolve to *make conscience of little things in our daily religion.*

Let us not neglect little duties – let us not allow ourselves in little faults. Whatever we may like to think, nothing is really of small importance that affects the soul. All diseases are small at the beginning. Many a death-bed begins with 'a little cold'. Nothing that can grow is large all at once – the greatest sin must have a beginning. Nothing that is great comes to perfection in a day – characters and habits are all the result of little actions. Little strokes made that ark which saved Noah. Little pins held firm that tabernacle which was the glory of Israel. We too are travelling through a wilderness – let us be like the family of Merari, and be careful not to leave *the pins* behind.[352]

[348] Matthew 23:9.
[349] 2 Corinthians 11:3.
[350] Jeremiah 6:16.
[351] Titus 3:8.
[352] Numbers 3:36-37.

Believers, do not forget how full the Epistles are of instruction about the particulars of Christian life. The apostles seem to take nothing for granted. They do not think it sufficient to say, 'be holy' – they take care to specify and name the things in which holiness is shown. See how they dwell on the duties of husbands and wives, masters and servants, parents and children, rulers and subjects, old people and young. See how they single out and urge upon us industry in business, kindness in temper, forgivingness in disposition, honesty, truthfulness, temperance, meekness, gentleness, humility, charity, patience, courtesy. See how they exhort us to honour all men,[353] to govern our tongues, to season our speech with grace,[354] to abstain from foolish talking and jesting,[355] not to please ourselves only,[356] to redeem the time,[357] to be content with such things as we have,[358] and whether we eat or drink, to do all in the name of the Lord Jesus.[359]

Brethren, some people think that to dwell on such things is bondage; but I believe it good to remind you of them – I am sure it is safe. If the Spirit of God thought it wise to dwell so much on them in the Word, I cannot doubt it must be wise for us to attend to them in our walk. It is much more easy to profess holiness in a general way, than to carry it out in particulars; and I fear that many talk familiarly of sanctification in the lump, who know but little of it in the piece.

I firmly believe that looseness about these little things in our daily behaviour, is a special means of grieving the Spirit of God,

[353] 1 Peter 2:17.
[354] Colossians 4:6.
[355] Ephesians 5:4.
[356] Romans 15:1.
[357] Ephesians 5:16.
[358] Hebrews 13:5.
[359] 1 Corinthians 10:31; Colossians 3:17.

and of bringing upon us, in consequence, barrenness and leanness of soul.

6. Let us be *more active in endeavours to do good to the world*.

Surely we may all do far more for unconverted souls than we have ever done yet. Many of us, alas! take things so quietly, that a man might suppose every one about us was converted, and the kingdom of Christ fully set up. I pray you let us lay aside these lazy habits.

Are all our friends and relations in Christ? Are all our neighbours and acquaintances inside the ark? Have all within our reach received the truth in the love of it? Have we asked them all to come in? Have we told them all the way of salvation, and our own experience that the way is good? Have we done all that we can? Have we tried every means? Is there no one left to whom we can show Christian kindness, and offer the Gospel? Can we lift up our hands to God as, one by one, souls around us are taken away, and say, 'Our eyes, O Lord, have not seen this blood, and its loss cannot in any wise be laid at our door!' Surely, my brethren, grace ought to be as active a principle in trying to spread godliness as sin is in trying to spread evil. Surely if we had a tenth part of the zeal which Satan shows to enlarge his kingdom, we should be far more full of care for other men's souls. Where is our mercy and compassion, if we can see disease of soul about us and not desire to make it less?

Let us awake to a right understanding of our responsibility in this matter. We complain of the world being full of wickedness. It is so. But do we each do our own part in trying to make it better? Do we act upon the old saying, 'The city is soon clean when every man sweeps before his own door?' Let us try more to do good to all. Let us reckon it a painful thing to go to heaven alone – let us endeavour, as far as we can, to take companions with us. Let us no longer be silent witnesses and muffled bells. Let us warn, and beseech, and invite, and rebuke, and advise, and testify of Christ, on the right hand and on the left, according as we have opportunity; saying to men, 'Come with us, and we will do you good;[360] the light is sweet,[361] come and walk in the light of the Lord.'[362] Let us not suppose no good is done in this way, because our eyes do not see it: we must walk by faith, and not by sight.[363] Let us not be weary in well-doing, because we appear to labour in vain; we may rest assured we are in the hands of a good master, in due time we shall reap if we faint not.[364]

Activity in doing good is one receipt for being cheerful Christians: it is like exercise to the body, it keeps the soul in health.

It is one great proof of love towards the Lord Jesus, and a proof that can only be given while we are alive. *Now* is the time for doing good to others, and not hereafter. In heaven there will be no missionary societies, no Bible societies, no visiting societies, no careless to warn, no ignorant to instruct, no sick to minister to, no mourners to comfort, no fainting saints to cheer. In heaven there will be love, joy, peace, thankfulness; but in heaven there will be no place for faith, zeal, courage, labour, patience – their occupation will be over – if ever we mean to show these graces it must be *now*. Oh! let us make haste, for the time is short. Let us be like Christian, in Pilgrim's Progress – when his burden fell off at the sepulchre, his first act was to try to awaken sleeping souls.[365]

---

[360] Numbers 10:29.
[361] Ecclesiastes 11:7.
[362] Isaiah 2:5.
[363] 2 Corinthians 5:7.
[364] Galatians 6:9.
[365] In John Bunyan's *The pilgrim's progress* (1678), soon after Christian's burden fell away at the cross and the empty tomb, he tried to rouse three sleeping men, Simple, Sloth, and Presumption. They each made an excuse and lay down to sleep again.

7. Lastly let us *take more pains to edify other believers.*

It is wonderful and sad to see how Scripture speaks on this matter, and then to observe the conduct of many of Christ's people. Paul tells the Corinthians, 'That the members of Christ should have the same care one for another.'[366] He says to the Thessalonians, 'Edify one another, even as also ye do.'[367] He says to the Hebrews, 'Exhort one another daily, lest any be hardened through the deceitfulness of sin',[368] and again, 'Consider one another to provoke unto love and good works – exhorting one another, and so much the more as ye see the day approaching.'[369]

Brethren, I fear we fall very short of the New Testament Christians in this respect. We are sadly apt to lose sight of this edifying one another, when we are in the company of believing friends. Prayer, and the Word, and godly conversation, are not put in the foremost place, and so we separate, nothing better, but rather worse. Far too often there is so much coldness, and restraint, and reserve, and backwardness, that a man might fancy we were ashamed of Christ, and that we thought it proper to hold our tongues, and not make mention of the name of the Lord.

These things ought not so to be. We profess that we are all fighting the same fight – contending with the same enemies – plagued with the same evil hearts – trusting in the same Lord – led by the same Spirit – eating the same bread – journeying towards the same home. Then why should we not show it? Why should we not be always ready to commune with each other? Why should we not try to help each other forward – to profit by each other's experience – to bear each other's burdens[370] – to strengthen each other's hands – to

---

[366] 1 Corinthians 12:25.
[367] 1 Thessalonians 5:11.
[368] Hebrews 3:13.
[369] Hebrews 10:24-25.
[370] Galatians 6:2.

quicken each other's hearts – to speak with each other, like Moses and Jethro, of the things pertaining to our King?[371] There is a fault among us here, and one that ought to be amended.

Let us bring out the Bible more when we get together. We none of us know it all yet; our brother may have found some pearl in it which has escaped our eyes, and we perhaps may show him something in return. It is the common map by which we all journey; let us not behave as if we had each a private map to be studied in a corner, and kept to ourselves. Oh! that the Word were like a burning fire shut up in our bones, so that we could not forbear speaking of it![372]

Let us speak oftener about the eternal home towards which we travel. Children, before their holidays, love to talk of home – their hearts are full, they cannot help it – why should not we? Surely it ill becomes the citizens of heaven to say nothing of heaven to those with whom they expect to dwell for ever. The men of this world are not shy about mentioning their plans for the future; why then should we hold our peace?

Let us then aim this year at closer communion with all true believers. This will go far to procure Christ's presence with us on our journey. The two disciples who went to Emmaus were talking of holy things when they were joined by the Lord.[373] Let us too speak often one to another and the Lord will hearken and remember it. This too will mightily promote the growth and comfort of our souls. The fire within us needs constant stirring as well as feeding to keep it bright. Many can testify that they find communion a special means of grace. As iron sharpeneth iron so doth the countenance of a man his friend[374] – and the weakest too may sharpen

[371] Exodus 18.
[372] Jeremiah 20:9.
[373] Luke 24:13-15.
[374] Proverbs 27:17.

the strongest, even as the whetstone does the scythe. He that tries to promote holiness in others shall reap a blessed reward in his own soul, he waters others and he shall be watered himself.[375]

Brethren believers, I have thought it good to name these things in writing to you about sanctification. I desire to do it in all humility. I need reminding of them as much as any. Let us all resolve to set them before us, and I am sure we shall not repent it.

And now, beloved brethren, I have done. I have told you one and all the longings and desires of my heart. Conversion for the unconverted, decision for the wavering, growth in grace for the believer – this seals up the sum of my wishes for you in the coming year.

I *can* wish you nothing better, for this is the way to true happiness. I *will* wish you nothing less, for without these things I am sure there is no peace.

Whether or not this may be the last address you may read from me, God only knoweth. I may not live to write another – you may not live to read another – all before us is uncertain – no man can tell what will be on the morrow.[376]

Death *may* be busy among us this year – let us all be found in Christ and prepared. Satan *will* be busy among us no doubt – let us all watch and pray. Let us beware of a spirit of slumber and formality, and especially in private reading and praying. Let our path to the fountain be worn with daily journeys, let our key to the treasury of grace be bright with constant use. Let the year 1847 be a year of many prayers. Let us pray more, and let us pray more earnestly. Let those who never prayed begin to pray. Let those who have prayed pray better.

[375] Proverbs 11:25.
[376] James 4:14.

Pray for *yourselves* – that you may know the Lord Jesus and cleave to Him – that you may be kept from falling – that you may serve your generation – that you may be sober in prosperity, patient in trial, and humble at all times.

Pray for *our congregation* – that the word of the Lord may have free course in it, and be glorified, that the household of faith may become stronger and stronger, and the household of unbelief weaker and weaker.

Pray for *your country* – that her ministers may preach the Gospel, and be sound in the faith[377] – that her rulers may value the Bible and govern according to it – and that so her candlestick may not be taken away.[378]

And pray not least for *your minister* – that he may be strong to work, and willing to labour for your good – that all his sickness may be sanctified, and all his health given to the Lord – that he may be ever taught of the Spirit, and thus be able to teach others – that he may be kept faithful unto death,[379] and so be ready to depart when he is called.

Let us all pray, one for the other – I for you, and you for me – and we shall be blessed in our deed.

I remain,

Beloved Friends and Brethren

Your affectionate Minister

J. C. RYLE

Helmingham Rectory, Stoneham [sic],[380]

December, 1846.

---

[377] Titus 2:2.
[378] Revelation 2:5.
[379] Revelation 2:10.
[380] That is, Stonham Aspal.

APPENDIX 6

RYLE'S FUNERAL TRIBUTE TO GEORGINA TOLLEMACHE

Georgina Tollemache of Helmingham Hall is a major figure in Ryle's autobiography. He recorded that she 'really delighted in my ministry' and was 'the brightest example of a Christian woman I ever saw'. Her unexpected death at Leamington on 18 July 1846, aged 37, was 'an enormous loss' to Ryle because it removed not only a friend but a key supporter.[1] Her body was returned to Helmingham for interment in the family vault, and Ryle exclaimed in Latin in the margins of the burial register '*eheu! quam dependa!*'[2] ('alas! oh how depended upon!').

Tollemache's burial service, on 25 July, demonstrated her significance not only for Christian life in the local village but also for wider Anglican evangelical networks in Suffolk. Her coffin was carried by twelve members of Ryle's weekly parish prayer meeting, and the pall by twelve local evangelical clergy. The roll call of these ministers included some of Ryle's closest friends, associates and mentors. They numbered senior men like Edward Barlee (rector of Worling-

---

[1] See above, p. 124.
[2] Helmingham burial register (1813-1992), Suffolk Record Office (Ipswich), FB46/D1/8. In the margin Ryle also gave two Bible texts: 1 Thessalonians 4:13-14 and Revelation 14:13.

worth), Charles Bridges (rector of Old Newton), and John Brewster Wilkinson (rector of Holbrook); clergy from Ipswich – Thomas Davidson, Charles Holland, Henry Lumsden, John William Reeve, and Walter Webb Woodhouse; and from other nearby parishes – Charles Shorting (rector of Stonham Aspal), Francis Storr (rector of Otley), John Kinsman Tucker (rector of Pettaugh), and Thomas Dennett West (perpetual curate of Rushmere St Andrew and Playford).[3]

The day after Tollemache's burial, Ryle preached her funeral sermon to large crowds, published as *Be not slothful, but followers*.[4] He expounded her Christian virtues at length, focusing especially upon her evangelical commitment, godly character and pastoral zeal. Tollemache's monument in Helmingham church recalls 'a life devoted to the service of her God and Saviour, and to the promotion of the temporal and spiritual welfare of those around her'. When her widower remarried in 1850, he wore a black band around his hat at his wedding, in memory of his first wife.[5] For Ryle, however, his ministry in Helmingham never fully recovered from the removal of his chief ally.

In this edition footnotes have been added to Ryle's text, to demonstrate the range of his biblical quotations and allusions.

[3] J. C. Ryle, *'Be not slothful, but followers': a sermon, preached in Helmingham Church, on Sunday, July 26, 1846; being the day following the funeral of Georgina Louisa Tollemache, the beloved wife of John Tollemache, Esq., M.P.* (Ipswich, 1846), p. iv.

[4] Ryle's only other published funeral tributes were to Charles Shorting, 'Comfort one another' (1864); and to Thomas Pownall Boultbee (1818-84), first principal of the London College of Divinity, Highbury 1863-84, published as J. C. Ryle, 'Our friend Lazarus sleepeth', in Gordon Calthrop, *Quiet strength: a memorial sketch of the life and works of the late Rev. T. P. Boultbee* (London, 1884), pp. 127-48.

[5] E. D. H. Tollemache, *The Tollemaches of Helmingham and Ham* (Ipswich, 1949), p. 167.

The Text

Ryle's Preface

This sermon is published at the request of some who heard it preached, and with my own hearty consent. I feel a melancholy pleasure in bearing my feeble testimony to the grace that was in her who is mentioned in it; and I only wish I could have done it with more power and effect. I have done what I could on short notice, and if any ask why I have said so much, I reply in the words of Solomon, 'Favour is deceitful, and beauty is vain: but a woman that feareth the Lord SHE SHALL BE PRAISED' – Proverbs xxxi. 30.

The 25th of July was indeed a sad day in Helmingham, and a day, I trust, that will not soon be forgotten. We had to accompany the remains of one whom we all loved, from the home where she had adorned the doctrine of her Lord, to the house appointed for all living. It was a solemn and a trying scene.

The coffin was borne by twelve of the most regular attendants at the weekly prayer meeting held in my parish.

The pall was supported by twelve of my brethren in the ministry, residing in the neighbourhood.

We carried her over the path that she had so often loved to walk in on the Sabbath while living. We bore her into the little church where she had so often delighted to worship, and join in prayer and praise. We followed her to the silent vault where she was to rest, and there thanked God that she had been kept faithful unto death.[6] And then we returned home, to sorrow – but not as others without a hope of a joyful resurrection, and to feel how true is the saying, 'Blessed are the dead which die in the Lord.'[7]

---

[6] Revelation 2:10.
[7] Revelation 14:13.

It only remains to say that this sermon has been written out from notes, and may not contain the exact words I used in delivering it from the pulpit. It contains however the outline and the substance, and some few things besides, which I had not time to introduce when it was preached. If it should be the instrument of quickening any believer, or awakening any soul whatever to become a follower of her, who 'through faith and patience inherits the promises',[8] I shall indeed thank God and rejoice.

J. C. RYLE
Helmingham, August, 1846

Hebrews vi. 12.
'Be not slothful, but followers of them who through faith and patience inherit the promises.'

Brethren,

It is a difficult thing at any time to preach to immortal souls. Never did I feel it more difficult than I do this night. You know the subject which is uppermost in all our minds. I have to speak of one whom God has taken to Himself out of our little congregation – one whom Jesus loved – and one whom we had every reason to love and honour too. I would fain make the occasion profitable to you all, and the Lord being my helper I must try to do so – but I feel it very hard.

One thing encourages me to make the attempt, and that is this. I know that she who is departed would have rejoiced if her death might be sanctified, and made useful to all who heard of it. I know her wish would have been to do good when she died, if possible, even, as we all know, she did good while she lived.

---

[8] Hebrews 6:12.

And more than this – I feel it a solemn duty myself, as her minister, to turn to good account this day of visitation. Such opportunities are seldom given to a minister. Seldom, very seldom, can we speak so confidently about the character of members of our flocks, as I can of hers. Seldom, very seldom, can we follow those to whom we have preached, to their long home, with such real consolation, or use with such unwavering hope those beautiful words, 'We give thee hearty thanks, for that it hath pleased thee to deliver this our sister out of the miseries of this sinful world.'[9]

Brethren, I wish tonight to make the character of her whom we have lost the illustration of our text. I wish to bear my testimony to the grace that was in her. I would try to show you the blessedness of living to the Lord. I would fain set before you the comfort of dying to the Lord, and leaving good evidences behind you. God forbid that the righteous should perish by our side, and we not lay it to heart! Oh! let us rather set up each of us this day a stone of remembrance; let us think, and learn wisdom.

Lift up your hearts, all ye that pray, and ask that the Holy Ghost may be amongst us with power. Pray that I may be enabled to speak the truth as it is in Jesus, and that this truth may be fastened in your hearts like a nail in a sure place.[10] Pray that we may all find it good to have come here tonight; that the death of her who is gone may be the life of many a soul, and her end the beginning of godliness in many a heart.

The text I have chosen contains five things.

I. *Warning* words, 'Be not slothful'.

II. *Encouraging* words, 'The promises'.

III. *Quickening* words, 'They who inherit'.

IV. Words of *Instruction*, 'Through faith and patience'.

---

[9] *Book of Common Prayer* (1662): order for the burial of the dead.
[10] Isaiah 22:23.

V. Words of *Duty*, 'Be followers'.

Upon each of these I desire to make a few remarks.

I. *First then there are solemn words of warning, 'Be not slothful'.*

Brethren, the apostle has here in view that indolent, lazy, idle frame of mind about religion, which is so natural to us all. Against this he bids you be on your guard.

There are four great weeds which grow naturally in the heart of every man alive – and they are these, pride, sloth, worldliness, and unbelief. All of us are plagued with these enemies, more or less, and shall be to the end. The roots of them are within us, however much, by grace, we may mortify and keep them under; and until the walls of the old house are clean taken down, they and we shall not be divided.

I stand not now to say which is the worst of the four. All are dangerous. But this I will say, that sloth needs as much watching as any, and unless watched will do as much harm.

The unconverted man is worse than slothful. He sleeps soundly, and we cannot awaken him. He has eyes but sees not – he has ears but hears not[11] – he has mind but thinks not – he heeds not our sermons, and our counsels – on him they are all thrown away. And he dreams too. He fancies often that he is spiritually rich, when in reality he is poor – that he is doing well, when in fact he is doing ill – that he is all right, when in truth he is all wrong – that he is at peace, when the Spirit says 'there is no peace'.[12] To all such we can only keep on crying 'Awake! awake!!' But they do not seem to hearken. A few stray convictions – a little fitful starting – an occasional turning from one side to the other – but nothing more can we see. Such men far too often sleep on till they are dead. 'A little more

---

[11] Jeremiah 5:21; Mark 8:18.
[12] Jeremiah 6:14, 8:11; Ezekiel 13:10.

sleep and a little more slumber',[13] they go on crying, and bye and bye we have to meet them in their coffins at the churchyard gate; and where is their hope? Oh! ye that pray, pray for the sleeping, pray for the living dead.

But even God's believing children have only too much need to be warned against spiritual sloth. They too are fearfully heavy, carnal, earthly-minded, compared to what they should be. They too are always inclining to become drowsy, and close their eyes, and need continual reminding to keep awake. Sad is it to see how soon their hands hang down, and their knees wax faint – how soon their love becomes cold, their repentance dull, their zeal blunt, and their faith weak. Oh! what a palsy, what a worm at the root is the spirit of slumber!

Sloth is the reason why so many believers in the Lord Jesus continue only babes in grace. They ask little, and they obtain little. They take little pains, and so make little progress. Sloth causes little prayer – little prayer causes little grace – little grace causes little brightness.

Sloth is too often the reason why false doctrines are so readily received. Some men will not take the trouble to examine whether new opinions are true. They embrace them when put forth with any show of truth, without enquiring, 'What saith the Scripture?'[14] They will often catch at any teaching which seems to save them the labour of personal communion with Christ, personal growth in grace, personal sanctification, personal faith. Sloth has been the strength and support of many a heresy.

Brethren believers, if you would see good days, take the apostle's advice, and 'Be not slothful'. Guard against spiritual drowsiness. Watch against the beginnings of it. It is a sin that grows upon a

---

[13] Proverbs 6:10, 24:33.
[14] Romans 4:3; Galatians 4:30.

man very quickly. 'I cannot' today will soon lead on to 'I will not' tomorrow. Jesus was not slothful in working the work of your salvation. The devil is not slothful in labouring to work your ruin. And why will you sleep? Oh! there will be sleeping enough in the grave – there will be rest enough in the new Jerusalem – but for the time present let us cast aside our slumber, let us all watch.

Anything, anything to be kept awake in a sleepy world! Count that the best preaching which keeps your soul most awake. Reckon those the best books which keep your soul most awake. Value those friends most highly who will not let your soul alone. Bless God for those conditions of life which keep your eyes most open and fixed upon eternal things. Anything, anything, I say once more, to be kept awake!

Brethren believers, all things around you cry loudly, 'Be not slothful.' Everything says, 'Sleep not, do not stand still.'

Mornings and evenings come and go in quick succession; years roll on one after another; harvests grow and ripen, and are cut and carried; congregations change and alter by degrees, and face after face disappears. Friends and relations go forth, and are scattered far and wide. Gray hairs come here and there upon us, and remind us that we are getting nearer to our end. Grave after grave is opened in our sight for those we know. And all these things are meant to teach the same lesson, 'Sleep not! sleep not! do not stand still!'

Men and brethren, Jesus stands at the door of every heart among you and knocks.[15] In every afflicting providence – in every cross and trying visitation – in every startling circumstance he brings before you, Jesus is calling to your soul, 'Awake, arise, and come away.' A voice from the tomb is crying to you all tonight, 'Be not slothful, awake, and sleep no more.' Oh! let not that voice speak in vain!

[15] Revelation 3:20.

II. *I pass on to speak of the second thing my text contains – a word of encouragement, 'the promises'.*

The promises are God's gracious offers to sinful man of everything that man's soul requires. The word of God is full of them. It is a storehouse and treasury of promises, and whosoever will may take of them freely. Who is there among you that doubts God's love to sinners? Let him open his Bible and behold the promises. Come every one that is labouring and heavy laden, come and see.[16]

Here you will find *comfortable* promises for the life that now is. Grace for every man, woman, and child, that will have it. Pardon for the most guilty – cleansing for the most corrupt – forgiveness for the most ungodly – bread for the hungry, water for the thirsty, milk for the weak, wine for the heavy in heart, healing for the sick, rest for the heavy laden, heart's-ease for the sorrowful, balm for the wounded, peace for the rebellious, life for the dead, riches for the poor, strength for the feeble, power for them that have no might – and all yea and amen in Christ Jesus.[17] 'Oh! taste and see that the Lord is good'[18] – 'Eat O friends, drink, yea drink abundantly, O beloved.'[19]

Here too you will find *glorious* promises for the life which is to come. Glory for every man, woman, and child, that will have it. A sure victory over the world, the flesh, and the devil, in the end; a better resurrection at the coming of the Lord; a full acquittal in the day of judgment; a place at the right hand, and a robe of white; a rest from labour and weariness; a freedom from indwelling sin; deliverance from care and tears; an abode in heaven, which can never be taken down; the fellowship of angels; the never-ending companionship of just men made perfect[20] – and above all, the presence of the

---

[16] Matthew 11:28.
[17] 2 Corinthians 1:20.
[18] Psalm 34:8.
[19] Song of Songs 5:1.
[20] Hebrews 12:23.

Lamb of God himself – and all yea and amen in Christ Jesus. Surely there is encouragement here.

Here too you will find *broad* promises. God's promises are high as heaven, and wide as the sea. All are invited in them, and none shut out. They are for the poor as well as for the rich, for the unlearned as well as for the learned – they are for all. No man shall be able to say, 'Jesus held out no promise to me, Jesus never asked me to come to Him and be saved.' The length, and breadth, and depth, and height,[21] of the promises will make that man speechless in the day of judgment. Think not, any one of you, to shake off your own responsibility, and say, 'God never called me.' The promises alone will be your condemnation. The broader they are the more hopeless will be your case. The wider the door, the more without excuse your soul, if you do not enter in.

Here too you will find *sure* promises. God's promises were never broken – they are all yea and amen in Christ Jesus; written in Christ's blood, and sealed by Christ's Spirit. They are the word of Him who cannot lie.[22] They are not like the world's promises, vain, deceitful, treacherous, and disappointing. They are not like the devil's promises, smooth and plausible, but, as Eve found to her sorrow, foundationless and false. Our God is the God of truth. He never failed yet to keep His word, and He never will. If He hath said a thing he will do it, and if He hath spoken He will make it good.[23] His word is better than man's deed. When He promises man has no need to doubt.

Brethren, this day I set before you the exceeding great and precious promises,[24] comfortable, glorious, broad, and sure. I ask you to receive them, to come to Christ and live.

[21] Ephesians 3:18.
[22] Titus 1:2.
[23] Numbers 23:19.
[24] 2 Peter 1:4.

Promises have been the food of God's children in every age of the world. Enoch, Abraham, Moses, all lived upon them, and did well. Why should not you? Promises are the lights set up to guide us into the harbour of eternal life – no man ever steered by them yet, who did not find himself at last in the haven where he would be. Why should they not guide you? Promises are the current money which supports God's people – we have not our King Himself yet, but we have, in the promises, His image and superscription. And all this treasure of promises is laid open to you. Oh! see that you refuse not Him that speaketh.[25] Reject not the strong consolation[26] that is set before you. Here is encouragement for all who want it. The kingdom of God is very nigh you. Jesus holds out the golden sceptre to you all, and invites you to make your petition.[27] Come then, and lay hold upon the promises this night – ask, seek, believe, and live.

III. *Our text contains a quickening word; it speaks of those who 'inherit' the promises.*

Brethren, there have been millions of professing Christians of whom we could only say with weeping, they have no portion in the inheritance here spoken of. They have gone to their own place. They have inherited the lot of their own choosing. They have reaped according as they have sown. Weeping and wailing, and gnashing of teeth;[28] the worm; the fire;[29] blackness, darkness, hopelessness, despair! This is the miserable cup they now drink.

Not so the redeemed of the Lord,[30] who have heard Christ's voice, and followed Him. They sleep in Jesus, and are at peace. Of them the text says, 'They inherit the promises.' They have in hand

[25] Hebrews 12:25.
[26] Hebrews 6:18.
[27] Esther 5:2-3.
[28] Matthew 8:12, 13:42, 50.
[29] Mark 9:46.
[30] Isaiah 62:12.

what they had long looked for. They grasp what they had only seen through a glass darkly.[31] They possess something substantial in place of hope. They obtain a reality instead of a thing known only by the hearing of the ear. And compared to this life all this is *inheritance* indeed.

I know well they do not yet receive their full reward. I know well their happiness will not be perfect until they are clothed in their heavenly bodies, at the coming of Jesus, and the resurrection of the just.[32] But still I do believe they inherit a joy of which you and I can form but little conception; they reap already a degree of blessedness, of which at best we have but a faint idea.

They are *with Christ*, saith the Spirit. 'Today', said Jesus to the dying thief, 'today shalt thou be *with me* in paradise.'[33] 'To depart', said Paul to the Philippians, 'to depart and be *with Christ* is far better.'[34] Brethren, I may not be able to explain the state of those who sleep in Jesus, between the time of death and resurrection, but when I read they are with Christ, I feel it is enough. Where He is there must be peace; where He is there must be comfort; where He is there must be joy. Their souls are with Christ, and I ask no more.

And then *they rest from their labour*, saith the Spirit.[35] They have gone home. They are no longer tossed about on the restless sea of this never quiet world. They are no longer wearied with the daily conflict against indwelling sin. At length they may lay aside their armour, and say to the sword, 'rest, and be still'.[36] Fighting and struggling, watching and fearing, wrestling and praying – all this

---

[31] 1 Corinthians 13:12.
[32] Luke 14:14.
[33] Luke 23:43.
[34] Philippians 1:23.
[35] Revelation 14:13.
[36] Jeremiah 47:6.

is over. They are safe at length, and the former things are passed away.[37]

Comfort ye, comfort ye,[38] with these words, all ye that mourn over departed believers. Comfort ye, comfort ye, refrain your voice from weeping, and your eyes from tears[39] – they 'inherit the promises'. Their warfare is accomplished; their battle is fought; their course is run. They have crossed Jordan; they have begun to enter the promised land; they are for ever beyond the reach of sin, the world, and the devil; they are gone to that place where the wicked cease from troubling, and the weary are at rest. Oh! let us not sorrow over them, as those who have no hope.[40]

Let us mourn, if you will, for ourselves – but not for them. We have still to labour, but they are at rest. We are still at sea, but they are safe in harbour. We are still in the wilderness, but they are at home. We are still carrying about a body of death[41] and corruption, but as for them, their old house is at length taken down. Let us rather bless God that at last they inherit the promises. Let us give all diligence that we may go to them, and not allow ourselves to wish it possible that they might return to us.

IV. *The fourth thing our text contains, is a word of instruction. You are told the way in which men have inherited the promises. It is 'through faith and patience'.*

This is the path that all the saints of God have walked in to this hour. There never has been, and there never will be, any other. From righteous Abel[42] down to the last soul brought in by the election of

---

[37] Revelation 21:4.
[38] Isaiah 40:1.
[39] Jeremiah 31:16.
[40] 1 Thessalonians 4:13.
[41] Romans 7:24.
[42] Hebrews 11:4.

grace[43] – all the heirs of promise[44] will prove to have travelled by the same road: all will reach heaven by the same way.

Faith was the *strength* of all who inherit the promises. They believed on an unseen Saviour; they looked not to themselves but to Jesus, and this made them all what they were. They lived by faith[45] – they stood by faith[46] – they walked by faith[47] – they kept the faith;[48] and so entered into rest. Being justified by faith they had peace with God.[49] This was the victory that overcame the world, even their faith.[50]

This kept them from *despair* when they thought of their own countless iniquities; they saw by faith the blood of Jesus, cleansing them from all sin.[51] This kept them from *fainting* when they groaned under their own indwelling corruption – they saw by faith Jesus interceding for them at God's right hand[52] – bearing their names upon his breast and shoulders before the Father's throne.[53] This kept them from *fear* when they looked forward to the day of judgment; they saw by faith the white robe of Christ's righteousness around them, and the Lamb of God appearing as their advocate, and pleading their cause. This made them hold on through all the narrow way; they saw before them Him that is invisible; they came up out of the wilderness leaning on the Beloved one;[54] they looked not at

---

[43] Romans 11:5.
[44] Hebrews 6:17.
[45] Romans 1:17; Galatians 3:11; Hebrews 10:38.
[46] Romans 11:20; 2 Corinthians 1:24.
[47] 2 Corinthians 5:7.
[48] 2 Timothy 4:7.
[49] Romans 5:1.
[50] 1 John 5:4.
[51] 1 John 1:7.
[52] Romans 8:34.
[53] Exodus 28.
[54] Song of Songs 8:5.

the things seen, which are temporal, but at the things unseen, which are eternal.[55] Oh! brethren, well may the apostle Peter speak of faith as 'precious faith'.[56]

And patience was the *character* of all who inherit the promises. They endured and were not weary of the Lord's service. They continued patiently in well doing.[57] They possessed their souls in patience,[58] being assured that bye and bye they would reap if they fainted not.[59] They were content to wait on the Lord, and have their good things hereafter.

The rushing current of the fashion of this world, which set so strongly against them, could not prevail to turn them aside. They did not wait lazily for all around to join them; they travelled patiently alone, rather than not travel towards heaven at all.

The vain pleasures of the world, which allure so many hearts, had no power to draw them out of the way. They had tasted the honey of the promises, and this made what the children of the world call happiness appear sweet no more. Like Moses, they chose rather to suffer affliction with the people of God, than to enjoy the pleasures of sin for a season. They esteemed the reproach of Christ no disgrace. They bore the cross – they thought lightly of the shame, for they had respect unto the recompence of the reward.[60]

Brethren, would you inherit the promises? This is the old path. This is the good way. If you love life see that the faith and patience of the saints be yours.

---

[55] 2 Corinthians 4:18.
[56] 2 Peter 1:1.
[57] Romans 2:7.
[58] Luke 21:19.
[59] Galatians 6:9.
[60] Hebrews 11:25-26.

V. *The last word I would have you remember in the text is a word of duty. The apostle says to us 'be followers' of them who inherit the promises.*

Doing ought to be the fruit of hearing. Coming to church and attending, listening to sermons and admiring – all this is a barren and unprofitable religion, so long as there is nothing done. Doing is the reality of religion – action is the only real sign of life. We preach in order that you may practice [*sic*] – we speak in order that you may do – we counsel in order that you may act. We cry 'awake thou that sleepest',[61] that we may see you arise and repent – we lift up Christ that we may see you arise and flee to the cross – we urge you to grow in grace, that we may see you arise and press on. We want doing to be the result of all our sermons. Alas! that every week so much breath should be spent to so little purpose – so much said and so little done.

Brethren, those who inherit the promises were all *doing* men – not men of words only, but men of deeds. I want you all to be like them – I call upon you to be followers of their faith and patience. Walk in the footsteps of the flock of Christ, if ever you would be found in the true fold. Live after the example they have left behind them, if ever you would die their death. Imitate the conduct of the saints who have gone before you in this your day of grace, if ever you mean to be numbered with them in the day of glory.

They inherit. *Take comfort.* These words are written for your encouragement. Others, you see, have gone before you on the way that leads to everlasting life, and got safe home – why should not you? They had no helps or advantages which are not freely offered to you. Their strength, their comforts, their provisions, the weapons of their warfare – all are within your reach, and all may be your own.

[61] Ephesians 5:14.

They inherit. *Take care.* These words may prove your condemnation. They were men of like passions with yourselves, but they overcame the world, the flesh, and the devil, by the blood of the Lamb. Surely their victory will leave you without excuse, if you are not saved also. Surely if their sins were forgiven, and their hearts were renewed, the same can be done for you. The Lord's hand is not shortened[62] – the Lord's grace is still sufficient[63] – the Lord's ear is still open.[64] The things that were possible for them are still possible for you. Oh! if you would not be found speechless and defenceless in the great and dreadful day, walk in the tried path of faith and patience – 'be followers of them who inherit the promises'.

And now let me wind up all by speaking to you about her whom yesterday we carried to the grave; whose honoured remains are now waiting beneath our feet for the resurrection of the just. And let the things I have to say of her be taken home by each of you, as the application of my text.

It has pleased God to remove from amongst us one of the brightest members of our little congregation. One whom we all knew and honoured has been added to the great cloud of witnesses,[65] and now inherits the promises. I feel I should be neglecting a solemn duty if I did not try to impress the event upon you all. Suffer me then before the bustle of this selfish world has deadened your better feelings, before the impression that this awful blow has made becomes worn and indistinct – suffer me to bear my feeble testimony to the grace that was in our departed sister, and to say to all, 'Follow her, even as she followed Christ.'[66]

[62] Isaiah 59:1.
[63] 2 Corinthians 12:9.
[64] Psalm 34:15; 1 Peter 3:12.
[65] Hebrews 12:1.
[66] 1 Corinthians 11:1.

Brethren, I shall speak of her who is gone without hesitation or reserve. Bear with me a little while I do it. Believe me I do it not to raise her reputation as a Christian – she needs no praise of mine – I do it for your own benefit – for the profit and edification of your souls.

There are many of you here, you know well, without Christ. Alas! that it should be so. How am I straitened till I see you coming to Him by faith, and Christ be formed in you.[67] There are many of you here, you know well, lingering, undecided, halting between two opinions.[68] Alas! that it should be so. Oh! that I could hear of you coming out boldly from the world, and saying to Jesus, 'there is none upon earth I desire beside thee'.[69] There are not a few believers here, you know well, lukewarm and barren, compared to what they might be. Alas! that it should be so. Oh! that I may soon hear of you bearing much fruit. Brethren, whatever be your state in God's sight, this night let me try to quicken one and all by the example I have to set before you.

This night I would fain show you that Christ's service is indeed pleasant, and that a person may be truly happy, and yet live unto God. This night I would have you all take notice that a Christian may live in this world of sin, and yet, by grace, not be of the world – that you may be encompassed by temptation, and yet keep yourself pure. This night, I would have you learn the lesson that a soul may have every draw-back and yet, by grace, be eminently holy – that it is possible to be surrounded by all that can make life attractive, or gild earth, or obscure heaven, and yet for all that, to set your affection on things above, give your heart to Jesus, and be unspotted by the world. She that is gone is an example of the truth of what I say. 'Follow her as she followed Christ.'

[67] Galatians 4:19.
[68] 1 Kings 18:21.
[69] Psalm 73:25.

Brethren, it is a hard thing to be rich, and at the same time a disciple of Christ. You that are poor do not think so. But you are mistaken: the Lord Jesus himself shall answer you. 'It is easier for a camel to go through the eye of a needle than for a rich man to enter into the kingdom of God.'[70] Cease then to desire riches. Gold and silver are heavy weights to carry, if a man would so run as to obtain.[71] It is far more difficult to follow Jesus and be rich than to follow Jesus and be poor. It is hard to walk in high places and not become giddy. Happy the man who is there and does not fall. It is hard to carry a full cup and not to spill it – to live amongst comforts and luxuries and not to be insensibly taken up with them – to dwell in the midst of sweet and pleasant things, and yet keep your soul in the right tone, in vigour, and in health. But the things which are impossible with men, are possible with God.[72] She that is gone did all this. Oh! let us bless God for giving us such a signal proof of what His grace can do.

Come now and listen to me while I single out some especial features in her character, as a Christian, and call your attention to them. I wish to dwell on some particular graces which shone most brightly in her. Time would not let me speak of those general things which she had in common with all the family of God. I must of necessity confine myself to particulars; and I do it the more willingly because they are particulars in which believers are too often sadly deficient – and because I shall thus give you a more real and living picture of what she was herself.

But while you listen do not, do not misunderstand me. Do not go away and say that I told you about an angel and a perfect being – such as none can hope to be on earth. I do not say that she was such – I do not want you to look at her in that light. I am going to speak

[70] Matthew 19:24.
[71] 1 Corinthians 9:24.
[72] Luke 18:27.

of a sinner, not of an angel – a sinner saved by grace, and grace alone. I do not want to exalt her, but her Lord and master, whose Spirit made her to differ. Her gifts were not the easy-growing weeds of nature's garden, but the precious wheat which had been sown by the Holy Ghost. She was born by nature a child of wrath even as others.[73] She became by redeeming mercy a child of grace; and all that she was, and did, and attained to, she owed to Christ. Christ was the fountain from which the stream of her good words and works all flowed. Christ was the root from which the precious fruits of the Spirit which she brought forth, all took their rise. Christ was the foundation on which the fair superstructure of her character was all raised, and all her holiness sprung from union with Him. What she was, she was by the grace of God, and as such I am not ashamed to speak fully of her. Her faults were her own, but her graces were jewels lent her by the King of kings; and I feel that in speaking of her as I shall do, I am not magnifying her so much as Christ.

1. *The first point that I would name in her character as a Christian was her faith.*

I think this could not fail to strike any Christian who was long in her company. She seemed to believe, unhesitatingly, whatever God had said in the Bible. She never appeared to doubt as to what was right and duty, when once she had a plain text before her, and could see, 'thus saith the Lord, and thus it is written'. She appeared to enjoy a settled confidence and persuasion that whatever God said must be true – whatever God promised would surely be performed – and whatever God commanded ought implicitly to be obeyed; and that to act on this belief was sure to bring a blessing and success.

Who can calculate the value of a spirit of faith like this? This is the spirit that turns mountains into vallies [*sic*], and rough places

---

[73] Ephesians 2:3.

into smooth.[74] This is the spirit that expects great things, and so attempts great things[75] – that stops not for fear of failure, but goes on sure of success – that goes down into the wilderness without fear, and believes it will be carried through without harm – that halts not, saying, 'the Canaanites are before us', but rather presses on, saying, 'we must be conquerors, for God is on our side'. This is the spirit that does great exploits, and is the parent of gracious acts. It keeps a man in perfect peace[76] – it lifts him above the fear of evil tidings[77] – it makes him valiant for the truth[78] – it enables him to be patient in tribulation,[79] and to feel confident 'it is well'[80] – it gives him decision when he has to choose – firmness when he proceeds to act – confidence when he goes to pray. Such was the spirit, brethren, of her that is departed. She had an unhesitating faith.

Alas! for the scarcity of such a spirit. How many of us appear certain of nothing at all! We hardly seem to believe what we profess or to be really confident and sure of what we hold. There comes a trouble, and, like Peter, we look at the waves more than at Jesus, and begin to sink.[81] There comes a danger, and, like Ahaz, our hearts are moved as the trees of the forest before the wind.[82] Truly when the

[74] Isaiah 40:4; Luke 3:5.

[75] 'Expect great things – attempt great things', was the epigram of William Carey (1761-1834), Baptist missionary to India, as recorded, for example, in Charles Bridges, *The Christian ministry; with an inquiry into the causes of its inefficiency; with an especial reference to the ministry of the establishment* (third edition, London, 1830), p. 229.

[76] Isaiah 26:3.

[77] Psalm 112:7.

[78] Jeremiah 9:3.

[79] Romans 12:12.

[80] 2 Kings 4:26.

[81] Matthew 14:30.

[82] Isaiah 7:2.

Son of Man cometh, shall he find faith on the earth?[83] Oh! brethren believers, it is a great grace to believe all that is written in the Bible. In this simplicity of faith, I charge you, follow her that is departed, even as she followed Christ.

2. *The second thing that I will name to you, was her love to the pure doctrines of Christ's Gospel.*

I do believe she loved the simple truth as it is in Jesus above gold and precious stones. It was sweeter to her than honey and the honey-comb.[84] Not everything that is called Christianity in these days deserves the name – there is often much talking about the Gospel, and yet no glad tidings proclaimed – much preaching about Christ, and yet Christ crucified not really set forth. All this she knew well, and had an uncommon jealousy about soundness in the faith. She had none of that false charity which confounds light and darkness, bitter and sweet, truth and error, and dreams that all professing Christians mean the same in the end. Her charity was the apostolic charity, which can only 'rejoice in the truth'.[85]

No quantity of learning or intellect in a preacher or speaker – no possible amount of eloquence or reputation – could ever win her confidence, unless she heard from that man sound speech about the leading doctrines of Christ's Gospel. Justification by faith – regeneration – sanctification – Christ the only way of salvation – the indwelling of the Spirit the only sure mark of God's children – these were the truths she loved to see clearly stated, and when there was a deficiency on these points, whatever others thought, she was not satisfied. She was one that seemed determined to 'prove all things', and to hold fast nothing but what was good.[86]

[83] Luke 18:8.
[84] Psalm 19:10.
[85] 1 Corinthians 13:6.
[86] 1 Thessalonians 5:21.

The false opinions of the day we live in which have moved so many of whom we once hoped better things, never moved her. She saw the tide of fashion setting strongly in favour of new doctrines, and heard the specious reasonings of those who support them, but her own mind was never for a moment shaken. The torrent of dangerous books which has of late years overflowed our country, books containing enough religion to attract but not enough to do good – books which please the eye, but do not profit the heart – books in which the first things are put last and the last things put first – books in which Christ has not his rightful office and faith has not its rightful place – all these which have carried so many Christians off their feet had never any influence on her. She loved simple Gospel truth – and everything else she counted unprofitable and vain – unsaving, unsatisfying, and unsanctifying to man's soul.

Alas! for the scarcity of such a spirit as this! Jealousy about sound doctrine appears almost unknown. Poison seems allowable if taken in small quantities. Errors of doctrine may now be overlooked, it seems, if only mingled with a certain quantity of truth. Brethren, take heed what you are doing. The absence of *one* single ingredient may neutralize your medicine and make it even hurtful. The presence of *one* single portion of arsenic may turn your whole loaf of bread into a deadly poison. Oh! in this godly jealousy for Bible truth, follow, I charge you, her that is departed, even as she followed Christ.

3. *The third particular point that I will mention in her character, was her love to all true Christians.*

She had a hand and a heart for almost all, and many of you have reason to know this – but those who held the highest place in her regard, were the household of faith.[87] Her delight was in the saints

---

[87] Galatians 6:10.

and the excellent of the earth;[88] she honoured them that feared the Lord.[89] To be in the company of bright and eminent Christians seemed her chief enjoyment. She loved all who love the Lord Jesus Christ in sincerity,[90] whatever might be their rank or calling. She really seemed to feel that believers are all one family in Christ Jesus – and like the early Church at Jerusalem, ought to have one heart and one soul[91] – and like members of one body to take a deep and lively interest in each other. You might say of her, as was said of an old Reformer, she 'loved all in whom she saw *something of Christ*'.[92]

And, brethren, ought not grace to be the chief thing in our esteem? Is not that the one thing which God regards? When the eyes of the Lord behold the earth, this is the only thing that he can see with unmixed satisfaction, for it is a part of Himself. The Lord seeth not as man seeth. Man looketh at the outward appearance, but the Lord looketh at the heart.[93] He cares not for rank and title and wealth and greatness; He values men according to their grace. A cottage where the fruits of the Spirit are brought forth is a more honourable place in his sight, than the most splendid palace where Christ is not magnified, and his name above every name.[94] Surely we ought to be of the same judgment too.

And, brethren, is not this the frame of mind which will best fit us for an abode in heaven? Grace will be everything in heaven, for it is the only door by which any one can pass to glory. Surely grace should be everything also with you and me on earth. We should love all men, but especially the brethren.

[88] Psalm 16:3.
[89] Psalm 15:4.
[90] Ephesians 6:24.
[91] Acts 4:32.
[92] The ecumenically-minded German reformer, Martin Bucer (1491-1551), welcomed all those in whom he saw '*aliquid Christi*' (something of Christ).
[93] 1 Samuel 16:7.
[94] Philippians 2:9.

This was the mind of her I speak of. She was a lover of grace. Nothing, I think, gave her more real pleasure than to hear of a work of grace having begun in any soul; and if that work went back she truly sorrowed, and if it went forward she truly rejoiced.

You who belong to my own congregation have little idea how well she was acquainted with you all by character, as well as by name. She took a deep interest in your spiritual condition. If there was at any time a soul among you in which there appeared to be some good thing beginning – if any man or woman among you became unusually diligent about means of grace, or shewed [*sic*] by your manner of life symptoms of some inward change – no one, I really think, felt a more sincere interest about that person than she did. She would inquire about him constantly. She would often ask how he was going on – whether he was making progress – whether he had any peculiar difficulties – whether he was really growing in grace and the knowledge of our Lord Jesus Christ[95] – whether he was indeed coming out from the world.

You little know how she took notice of all among you who were true Christians. Your names, your history, your trials, your circumstances, your character, all were familiar to her. She seemed to have in her mind a book of remembrance for all who feared the Lord, and thought upon his name. The joy of the angels over one sinner that repenteth is a kind of joy, I believe, to which she was no stranger.[96]

Alas! for the scarcity of this habit of mind in these days! How few even of true Christians appear to realize it at all. How many believers hedge themselves in with suspicions and jealousies, and seemingly believe nothing, and hope nothing about others!

How little open-handedness and open-heartedness can be found! How many fasten down upon the faults of brethren, and

[95] 2 Peter 3:18.
[96] Luke 15:10.

refuse to see their good things! How few have an eye ready to see true grace in a neighbour, and a heart ready to cherish it and help forward its work! What abundance there is of reserve, and coldness, and shyness, and silence! What a dearth of communion, and confidence, and brotherly kindness and response!

Brethren, in this love to true Christians, follow, I charge you, her that is departed, even as she followed Christ.

4. *The next point I will notice in her character, was her unworldliness.*

You all know she might have had as much of what is called worldly happiness as she pleased. She did not give up the world because she could not keep it, nor turn away from it because it forsook her. Oh! no! She came out from the world by choice and not by necessity. Truly, if she had been mindful of the country from whence she came out, she might, like the patriarchs, have had opportunity to have returned. But she desired a better country, that is an heavenly.[97] She might any day have joined in the world's pleasures, walked in the world's path, lived in the world's excitement. But she cared for none of these things. Oh! let us not forget this. Separation from the world is easy work, comparatively, when you have nothing to tempt you to go into it, or your position makes it impossible – but to keep clear of the world when there are no natural barriers to check you, this is indeed hard.

Seldom did I ever see one who thought less of the world, to all appearance, than she did. The love of the world and the fear of the world – the secret liking to go along with it, the secret dread of going against it – neither of these seemed to have any effect upon her mind. She was no slave, as many are; she called not the world her master, but God. The world's ways – the world's fashions – the world's customs – the world's opinions – all these were nothing to

[97] Hebrews 11:16.

her. She was free in the highest sense of the word; for she was one of those whom the truth of Christ made free.[98]

Let no one misunderstand me on this point. She never gave unnecessary offence, or sought to carry more crosses than God called upon her to bear. She was tenderly afraid of throwing stumbling-blocks in the way of others by needless eccentricities. She was one of all others who walked in wisdom towards them that were without,[99] and tried as far as was lawful to win the world.

But this I say, she did not make the world her guide and counsellor. She did not live by its rules and standard, and wear its chains. She was not one who was ever asking that melancholy question, 'What does the world do? What is most *usual?* What will people *say?* What will be *thought* if I do such and such things?' The world's sayings and doings and thinkings were but a drop of water in the balance to her; her grand question was, 'What is the Lord's will concerning me? What is written in the word of God?'

And when she found her duty plainly marked out in Scripture, she did not stop, as many, till the world should come up and join her. She did not wait for all the world to become decided before she became decided, she would set her face steadily towards Jerusalem,[100] even though she went alone. Truly she was independent of man's opinion in religious things. The Bible was the map by which alone she steered, and she seemed to say to it as Ruth to Naomi, 'Whither thou goest, I will go.'[101]

Alas! for the scarcity of such a character as this! I fear there is far more worldliness among some of the children of God than we see upon the surface. It creeps out and bubbles up in many little things that they do. It oozes out in their entertainments and way of

[98] John 8:32.
[99] Colossians 4:5.
[100] Luke 9:51.
[101] Ruth 1:16.

living – in their apparel – in their conversation – in their employment of time – in the education and dress of their children – in the
management of their households – in the society they tolerate – in
the way they conduct their business or earthly callings. In all these
things the evidence of something rotten within may often be traced.
Oh! the deceitfulness of our hearts![102] Many really live in such a way
that the world would seem to be the first thing and to fill the best
chamber in their heart – and as for religion, it only has the vacant
places – lies on the top – occupies the spare room – is treated as a
lodger and a visitor, and no more.

'Keep in with the world, as far as you can, and *afterwards* have
as much religion as you can', that seems the rule by which many
walk. Oh! the deceitfulness of our hearts! Few, very few make the
world bend to the Bible – many, far too many make the Bible bend
to the world.

Brethren, in this freedom from a worldly spirit follow, I charge
you, her that is departed, even as she followed Christ.

5. *The next point that I will mention in her character was her zeal to
do good to others.*

It is not her carefulness in doing good to the bodies of others
that I speak of now, though many of you know I might dwell on
this – I mean her carefulness to do good to souls. Neither shall I
speak of what she was in this respect in all the varied relations of
life that she filled, as a wife, a mother, a daughter, a mistress, and
though last, not least I could testify, as a faithful friend. I might do
it, but I forbear.

Her zeal to do good to souls was indeed unceasing. It was not
merely shown in giving money to Societies or subscribing to assist
religious objects. Such zeal no doubt deserves our thanks, but we

[102] Jeremiah 17:9.

must not forget it neither requires time nor trouble from the giver. Her zeal was a far higher, nobler zeal than this. She was always trying to win *individual* souls to Christ. It seemed a constant employment with her. By word of mouth or by letter, by speaking or by writing, by warning or by encouragement, by exhortation or by advice, by one way or another she appeared always trying to lead others to heaven. The salvation of souls seemed never out of her mind. Her life was a constant endeavour to draw others to Christ, to prayer, and to the word. Verily she had the true spirit of a Missionary. She had found the Gospel precious to her own soul, and she would have liked all the world to know its value too, and taste its comforts.

It is written of our Lord Jesus Christ that 'He went about doing good';[103] so also in a measure you might say of her that is departed. She was like Dorcas – 'full of good works'.[104] Few, I believe, were ever for any period within her reach, who could not testify that what I say is true. High and low, rich and poor, old and young, masters and servants, all who have been for any time near her know what I mean – it will not be her fault if they never think of their souls. I suspect she never was long with any one without saying a word for God or showing her interest in their salvation, by the gift of a tract or book. All men could see she did not wish to go to heaven alone: the words of Moses to Hobab seemed a living principle in her mind, 'come with us and we will do thee good'.[105]

And think not her zeal was a zeal without *wisdom*. She was wonderfully taught by the Spirit how to speak a word in due season.[106] She was not one who would cast pearls before swine, or give that which is holy to the dogs;[107] she had a very quick discernment of

[103] Acts 10:38.
[104] Acts 9:36.
[105] Numbers 10:29.
[106] Proverbs 15:23.
[107] Matthew 7:6.

the time to speak, and what was best to say, and how it ought to be said – her words were indeed 'fitly spoken'.[108]

Her zeal too was a zeal always mingled with *kindness*. Some people unhappily put on such a tone and manner when speaking to others about their souls, that they raise a dislike to the truths they want to enforce, and do as much harm as good. It was not so with her. Like the wise woman in thirty-first of Proverbs, 'The law of kindness was in her lips.'[109] The persons to whom she spoke would never feel that she was a harsh reprover – whatever they might think of her opinions, they would have a deep impression, I think, that she was an affectionate well-wisher to their souls.

But her zeal was always accompanied with a holy *boldness*. She really seemed to fear the face of no man when she had God's work in hand – nothing made her afraid to speak out. I do believe she would have realized the saying of David – (Psalm cxix. 46) 'I will speak of thy testimonies before kings and not be ashamed.' I do not think she ever shrunk from confessing Christ before men, whatever her company might be – the words of David seemed engraven on her heart – (Psalm lx. 4) 'Thou hast given a banner to them that feared thee, that it may be displayed because of the truth.'

Brethren, who shall calculate the amount of good that zeal like this does even in this dark world? Who can tell what might be done, if we who believe would speak, as she who is departed did, every one to his neighbour about his soul? All men have consciences. Many are only waiting for us to begin and wondering that we hold our peace. It is a line of conduct that God loves and God will honour. I declare to you my firm persuasion that the judgment day will tell us of numberless souls that are saved by this means. Many I doubt not will meet her of whom I am speaking before the throne of God, and bless her for her faithful words.

[108] Proverbs 25:11.
[109] Proverbs 31:26.

Alas! indeed for the scarcity of this grace! Seldom indeed do we find believers who are forward to speak to others about their salvation. Surely if our hearts were more full of Christ our tongues would be more ready to speak of Him. If we felt the value of souls aright, we should not let them travel onwards towards destruction so easily. Oh! you who are silent in your own homes and before your friends, as if you had not a word to say on Christ's behalf – Oh! you who live on as if Christ had never died, and behave in society as if there was no such book as the Bible – take shame to yourselves for your half-heartedness and resolve to lay it aside. Beware of cowardice under the name of prudence: beware of laziness under the cloak of humility.

Brethren, in this burning zeal for the souls of others, follow, I charge you, her that is departed, even as she followed Christ.

6. *The next point that I will mention was her cheerfulness.*

She was a Christian, and so she had her trials, and those not few. All God's brightest children are trained in the school of suffering – they are sanctified and purified in the furnace of affliction.[110] She had the daily plague of her own heart, as you and I have. She had the constantly recurring cross of ill-health to bear. She witnessed sickness frequently and deaths oft among those she loved best. And yet for all this a stranger might almost suppose she had never known what trial was, and never had cause to shed a single tear.

Of all the Christians I ever did see, she certainly was the most bright and the most cheerful. Of all I ever saw she seemed to have the most enjoyment of her religion. Many perhaps were more advanced than she was, but none, I am sure, were more truly happy in their Master's service. She never appeared to see clouds above her, but only blue sky. She *looked* like one who really felt she was going to heaven, who really felt that she was washed, sanctified and

[110] Isaiah 48:10.

justified,[111] who really felt that there was no condemnation for her,[112] that her iniquity was all forgiven, her sin all pardoned,[113] her name written in the book of life[114] and her mansion in heaven prepared.[115] Some Christians it does one good to *hear*, but she was one of the few that it even does one good to *see*.

And, brethren, let me tell you plainly I think this rejoicing spirit is one that we are all bound to aim at. Some people may believe it very proper and scriptural to be always sad and cast down. I cannot see this in the Bible. I find that joy is a fruit of the Spirit – we should pray for it as we do for meekness and temperance.[116] I find St Paul telling the Philippians three times, to 'rejoice in the Lord' always.[117] I find St Peter speaking of heaviness as the exception, and rejoicing as the rule.[118] Surely these things cannot be gainsayed.

She that is departed appeared to understand something of this. She was a constant witness to all who saw her that it is a happiness and not a burden to serve God – that his commandments are not grievous[119] – that there is great peace for those who love God's law[120] – that the ways of Jesus are indeed ways of pleasantness, and his paths paths of peace.[121] She was like a sun-beam, bright herself and making others bright too.

Believe me, we ought to bear this in mind far more than we do. We ought to recommend our religion by our demeanour, and to make it beautiful as well as clear: we ought to show men that

---

[111] 1 Corinthians 6:11.
[112] Romans 8:1.
[113] Psalm 103:3.
[114] Revelation 13:8, 17:8, 20:15.
[115] John 14:2.
[116] Galatians 5:22-23.
[117] Philippians 3:1, 4:4.
[118] 1 Peter 1:6.
[119] 1 John 5:3.
[120] Psalm 119:165.
[121] Proverbs 3:17.

we have joy and peace in believing,[122] and that it is a comfortable thing to walk with God. It may not be fair to judge of the Gospel by the appearance of those who believe it, but so long as men do so, we should be very careful to throw no stumbling blocks in their way. Let us beware lest we give men a disagreeable impression of religion by unnecessary sadness of countenance, and so bring up an unfavourable report of the good land,[123] and cause offences to come. She that is departed has indeed left us a bright example in this respect: she was a living proof that 'a merry heart doeth good like a medicine.'[124]

Alas! indeed, for the scarcity of this grace, even among true Christians! How few seem to feel the harm that the absence of a rejoicing spirit must do to the world! Oh! you who are always nourishing a gloomy frame of mind, as if it was essential to true religion – Oh! you who live as if you were attending eternal funerals, and felt it a duty to be sad and melancholy – Oh! you who look as if you were dissatisfied with your Master, your livery, your wages, and your work, and did not mind the world knowing it – learn, I beseech you, to look on gloominess as a wrong thing, and learn of her who is departed, to rejoice in the Lord. Why should the children of a king go mourning all their days?[125] The Bible is not removed from you – Christ lives, though all else die – the love of the Father does not change, though all else fade – the Spirit is not withdrawn, though all else be taken away. Why should you help the devil? Why should you give the world occasion to say, 'the Gospel does not bring peace?'

Brethren, in this cheerfulness, follow her that is departed, I charge you, even as she followed Christ.

[122] Romans 15:13.
[123] Numbers 13:32.
[124] Proverbs 17:22.
[125] First line of a hymn by Isaac Watts (1674-1748).

7. The last particular point that I shall name in her character, was her consistency.

Brethren, when I speak of consistency, I do not mean to tell you that she was a perfect, faultless person. I never heard of a literally perfect person. I do not believe there ever was one. Abraham, the father of the faithful, was not perfect:[126] David, the man after God's own heart, was not perfect:[127] John, who leaned on the bosom of our Lord, was not perfect:[128] and if any one told me of a child of Adam who had attained perfection, I should not believe him. Doubtless she who has been taken from us was not perfect – she was a sister of Abraham, and David, and John, and she had her faults.

But this I will say, she was one of the most equable Christians I ever met with. She was one in a thousand for being nearly always the same. She was always ready for the Bible, and the things of God. Christ and the word seemed always welcome to her heart. There was a wonderful freshness about her religious feeling; it never seemed faded, and old and dry – it was ever green. You could never speak of Scripture and the things of the world to come, without finding her ready to meet you. And she would enter into it all so warmly, that a man might think she had never heard of the Gospel before that day.

Most Christians we meet with are sadly variable. They are seldom long the same. They are like the moon, sometimes waxing, sometimes waning. They are like the tide, sometimes high, and sometimes low. We cannot feel quite sure that we shall find them ready for spiritual conversation – the door of their heart open, and their minds in a religious frame. But it was not so with her. Her heart seemed never quite out of tune. The cold damp weather of this world appeared to have little effect upon it. It was like a well-tuned instrument of music, generally in harmony with divine

[126] Romans 4:11; Galatians 3:7.
[127] 1 Samuel 13:14.
[128] John 13:23.

324

things: and seldom indeed would you fail in finding some string, at any rate, which would respond to the touch of religion. She was one that you could meet after a long absence with confidence, and feel sure that she had not altered – that she was still the same.

Alas! indeed, for the scarcity of this grace! How many Christians are uncertain in their frames. We have no assurance that we shall find them ready for communion about eternal things. One day we knock at the door of their hearts, and are at once admitted. Another day we stand knocking in vain, until we are tired. There is no voice nor answer to our call, and we find to our sorrow, that to spiritual things our brother is *not at home*.

Brethren, in this consistency and equableness of spirit, follow her that is departed, I charge you, even as she followed Christ.

Such then were the leading points in the Christian character of her whom God has taken from us. I have purposely avoided those general features of character which she had in common with other children of God. Time would not allow me to touch on them, and even now, though I have said much, I could easily say far more.

But what were the roots from which the fair fruits I have been dwelling on, took their origin? What was the hidden underwork – the unseen foundation – on which the building of her character all rested? The things I have spoken of were the things seen – the face and hands of the clock – what was the machinery out of sight, which influenced and moved the whole? Suffer me, brethren, to dwell for a moment on this matter. Believe me, these unseen things are of first importance. Write them upon the table[129] of your memory – lay them to heart if you would really follow her – mark them down, for they are indeed worthy to be had in remembrance.

Know then, *for one thing*, she had a very deep sense of the sinfulness of sin generally, and of her own sinfulness in particular. She

---

[129] That is, the tablet.

was truly remarkable for real humility and self-abasement. And this was not put on like a cloak for walking abroad, and merely talked of without being felt – it was an every-day garment, it was sincere.

With all her good works she never appeared to have any high thoughts of her own usefulness. With all her spiritual attainments, she never gave one the idea of being proud. She seemed to have an abiding sense of her own unworthiness, and to feel that at best she was an unprofitable servant.[130] Nothing, I think, annoyed her more than to hear herself flattered and praised. Like Moses, her face shone, and she did not know it.[131] I really believe, if asked who was the chief of sinners[132] she would at once have written down her own name. Often have I heard her say that no man knew his own heart, if he would not willingly confess that he saw more evil in himself, than in any one else in all the world.

Oh! mark this, all you that are spiritually rich and increased with goods and think that you have need of nothing.[133] He that humbleth himself is the man that shall be exalted.[134] You must begin low, if you would build high. Humble yourselves if ever you would enter in at the strait gate.[135]

Know *for another thing*, that she was one who was ever looking to the Lord Jesus Christ. Faith in Christ and communion with Christ, these were the main-springs of her life and made her what she was. She lived by faith in the Son of God[136] – Christ and his finished work her confidence against the guilt of sin – Christ and his grace her strength against the power of sin – Christ and his second coming her hope of deliverance from the presence of sin – Christ

---

[130] Luke 17:10.
[131] Exodus 34:29.
[132] 1 Timothy 1:15.
[133] Revelation 3:17.
[134] Luke 14:11, 18:14.
[135] Matthew 7:13.
[136] Galatians 2:20.

was indeed all things to her. His blood, his atonement, his death, his resurrection, his mediation, his intercession, his love that passeth knowledge,[137] his willingness to receive, his power to save, his second advent, these were the things which were her soul's delight.

Verily she did realize the mighty doctrine of the fifteenth of John, that 'Christ is the vine and we are the branches' – that to abide in Him is the way to grow, to go forward, to bear much fruit.[138] She did seem to feel that looking to Jesus is the way to become like Him, and be filled with the Spirit – that union with Him is the way to be strong, that without Him we can do nothing[139] – that through Him we can do all things[140] – that in ourselves we have nothing but weakness and sin – but that believing on Jesus all things are ours.

Christ was the bread of her soul – the bread on which she daily fed and became strong.

Christ was the light of her soul – the light after which she walked and was not in darkness.

Christ was the fountain of her soul – the fountain in which her conscience was daily washed and made clean.

Christ was the sun of her soul – the sun in whose beams she walked and was made bright.

Christ was the shepherd of her soul[141] – she came up out of the wilderness leaning on Him[142] – and so was more than conqueror.[143]

The preaching she delighted in was the preaching which contained most of Christ. The ministers she valued most were those who spoke fully and freely of Christ. The texts she loved were those that said most of Christ. The books she liked best were those that

---

[137] Ephesians 3:19.
[138] John 15:5.
[139] John 15:5.
[140] Philippians 4:13.
[141] 1 Peter 2:25.
[142] Song of Songs 8:5.
[143] Romans 8:37.

exalted Christ. The friends she thought most highly of, were those who had most communion with Christ. Christ was the criterion by which every thing was valued – the standard according to which every thing took its place in her mind – the measure to which every thing was referred. Brethren, Christ is all in Scripture, and Christ will be all in heaven – and she seemed to think He ought to be all in her heart.

Oh! mark this, all you that are content to give Christ a little honour and no more – who think to use Him as a makeweight to supply your deficiencies, but not as the corner-stone of your souls. Believe me, Christ must be every thing in your life, if ever death is to be your gain.

Know *lastly*, brethren, that she who is departed was one of unwearied diligence in using private means of grace. Think not, I beseech you, for one moment that spiritual eminence was ever attained by any soul without spiritual diligence. Such a notion is a delusion of the devil. 'There are no gains without pains', is the proverb of the world, and it holds good too about the soul. There never will be growth in grace without private labour and toil.

She of whom I speak was most diligent in the study of the Bible. She was such a one as David describes in the first Psalm, 'Her delight was in the law of the Lord and in his law did she meditate day and night.'[144] She loved the Bible, and she searched it like one digging for hid treasure. Her reading was not a mere formal reading of a certain portion a day, as it often is, and then the book is put out of sight and out of mind. Her Bible seemed the meat and drink of her soul, more precious than her necessary food, sweeter also than honey and the honey-comb.[145] And the word of Christ did 'dwell in her richly'.[146] It dwelled in her – not merely as a visitor or a lodger,

---

[144] Psalm 1:2.
[145] Psalm 19:10.
[146] Colossians 3:16.

but as an inhabitant; and it dwelled in her richly too: it shone out in all the windows of her conversation. Like David 'she hid the word in her heart', and this was one great means of keeping her from sin[147] and making her 'thoroughly furnished unto all good works'.[148]

And besides this she was most diligent, I believe, in private prayer. I suspect we little know how much she prayed, and this I am inclined to think was one great secret of her Christianity. Our public life will generally bear the impress of what we are upon our knees. I believe that prayer was the key that obtained her such abundant access to the treasury of grace that is laid up for the saints in Jesus. Prayer gave her power to walk straight forward through the world, not turning to the right hand or the left.[149] Prayer enabled her to be, as she was, 'steadfast, unmoveable, always abounding in the work of the Lord'.[150]

I believe she knew what it was to pray without ceasing[151] – to watch unto prayer[152] – to continue instant in prayer[153] – to pray always and not to faint.[154] I believe she realized something of the Spirit of adoption, and that just as a little child will go to its earthly parent, so did she go to her Father in heaven and cast all her cares from the greatest to the least upon Him,[155] saying, 'Abba Father, this or that thing disturbs me; Father, give me help, strength, grace sufficient for my need.' Brethren, the praying people, the men of desires, these are the people that obtain the best gifts, these are the Christians that are strong.

---

[147] Psalm 119:11.
[148] 2 Timothy 3:17.
[149] Proverbs 4:27.
[150] 1 Corinthians 15:58.
[151] 1 Thessalonians 5:17.
[152] 1 Peter 4:7.
[153] Romans 12:12.
[154] Luke 18:1.
[155] 1 Peter 5:7.

Oh! mark this you that are lazy and careless about means of grace, and yet wonder that you do not get on. Remember the word I give you this day, 'The soul of the *sluggard* desireth and hath nothing, but the soul of the *diligent* shall be made fat' – Prov. xiii. 4.

And now, beloved brethren, in conclusion let us all give God hearty thanks that He hath delivered our sister out of the miseries of this sinful world,[156] and taken her home. Let us thank Him unfeignedly for the grace bestowed upon her, and for having mercifully lent her to us so long, that we might see what His grace can do. Truly we have had amongst us an epistle of Christ[157] – we have seen a bright and shining light[158] – we have beheld a real Christian. Let us bless God for such a privilege. The Lord grant that we may all follow her – that we may all go to our homes tonight better for what we have seen and heard.

Oh! unconverted people in this congregation! Oh! worldly men and worldly women, who mind earthly things and have not yet thought of turning to God! Oh! lingering souls who once did promise well, but now are hanging back and giving no sign of life! Oh! undecided souls who are halting between two opinions, having too much religion to be happy in the world, and keeping too much of the world to be happy in your religion! Listen I pray you, every one, to the appeal I make to your consciences this night – listen if ever you mean to listen to counsel in your lives.

See what a blessed thing it is to live and die a decided Christian! See what a blessed thing it is to leave behind you great broad evidences; to have made it plain whose you were, and whom you served, so that your friends can bury you without doubts, and speak and think of you with joy! See what a crushing answer you have tonight to all your excuses and pretences! It *is* possible to have many

---

[156] *Book of Common Prayer* (1662): order for the burial of the dead.
[157] 2 Corinthians 3:3.
[158] John 5:35.

temptations and yet to be a bright Christian. It *is* possible to be happy – yea far happier than you are – and yet walk closely with God. She that has gone has left you all an example. Have you difficulties? So had she. Have you an evil heart? So had she. Have you the world to conquer? She had she. But she overcame by the blood of the Lamb and so may you.[159] Grace was sufficient for her, and it is also sufficient for you.[160]

Oh! that this day might be a turning point in your lives! Oh! that it might be a time of awakening from spiritual sloth, a time of beginning a new life and a walk with God. Oh! that the events of the last few days might convince you that this world is but a shadow and the world to come the reality – that the things seen are all passing away, and Christ and the word the only portion which will never change! Oh! that you may each go to your own chambers when you leave this house, and there pray as you never prayed before.

And you too, believing brethren, learn a lesson this night. See what the grace of God can do for flesh and blood like yourselves, and learn to be ashamed of your shortcoming, and your negligence, your unprofitableness and your little fruit. Oh! let the time past suffice you to have been cold and selfish! Oh! let the time to come prove to the world that you really have the mind of Christ![161] Why should not each one of you be an epistle of Christ, an epistle so plain that he who runs may read it? Why should you not be bold? Why should you not be zealous? Why should you not be useful? Why should you not be light and salt in the middle of this dark corrupt world?[162] The Lord's arm is not straitened. The free grace which made our departed sister what she was is still the same – and Jesus says to you, 'Ask and ye shall receive.'[163]

---

[159] Revelation 12:11.
[160] 2 Corinthians 12:9.
[161] 1 Corinthians 2:16.
[162] Matthew 5:13-14.
[163] John 16:24.

Awake then to a sense of your responsibilities – awake to a sense of the happiness you are missing and the good you are leaving undone – awake and sleep no more. Shake yourselves from the chains that Satan would fain cast round you. 'Lift up the hands that hang down and the feeble knees, and make straight paths for your feet.'[164] Think not what others are doing, think of Christ and heaven and souls and sin – let the dead bury their dead,[165] let others slumber if they will – do you seek first the kingdom of God[166] – go forward, go up, go on, and sleep no more.

Brethren, if you loved her that is departed, walk in her ways; if you loved her, follow in her steps. This is the true way to honour her, to follow her even as she followed Christ.

[164] Hebrews 12:12-13.
[165] Matthew 8:22.
[166] Matthew 6:33.

RYLE'S LAST WILL AND TESTAMENT

Although Ryle's last will and testament, written in 1897, belongs to the end of his life, not to his 'early years', it is included in this volume because of what it reveals about the provenance of the Ryle family heirlooms. Amongst his four youngest children he distributed precious artefacts such as the Ryle Family Bible, his mother's jewellery, a marble bust of his father, and numerous family portraits. Some of these items are still held by their descendants.

There are some surprises in the will. In particular, Ryle's eldest child, Georgina, is conspicuously absent. She was incapacitated through long-term mental illness and presumably provision had already been made for her care. Ryle records in his autobiography that Georgina's mother suffered from puerperal mania following childbirth, so mental illness ran in the family.[1] Georgina spent most of her adult life confined to lunatic asylums. At the time of the 1881 census, aged 33, she was a patient at The Shrubbery, a very small private asylum in Southall, west of London, where there was just

---

[1] See above, p. 125.

one other patient.² Next she moved to Ashbrooke Hall, 'a licensed house for insane ladies' at Hollington near Hastings, where there were five patients.³ There she was diagnosed with 'mania' from which she suffered for more than a quarter of a century, to the end of her life.⁴ Georgina Ryle's last home, for fifteen years or more, was The Priory, Roehampton, a much larger asylum of approximately eighty patients, catering especially for those from wealthy families. She died there in February 1915, aged 67, and was buried alongside her mother and her other Plumptre relatives at Nonington.⁵ She did not attend her father's funeral, and his will makes no mention of her.

Another surprise is that despite Ryle's personal wealth (valued at his death at £25,000) he left no bequests to evangelical societies, apart from donating his books to the Liverpool diocese. Nor did his testament double as a testimony to his Christian faith, in contrast to the wills of some other Victorian and Edwardian evangelicals. For example, Ryle's friend Richard Hobson (1831-1914), minister from 1869 to 1901 of St Nathaniel's, Windsor, in the Liverpool slums, began his will with a Trinitarian formula ('In the name of the Father and of the Son and of the Holy Ghost. Amen') and ended as follows:

² In the census returns, asylum patients were usually recorded by their initials, to disguise their identities – see 'G. M. R.' [Georgina Matilda Ryle], 1881 census, The National Archives [TNA], RG11/1335, fo. 45. Close to The Shrubbery was Southall Park, a larger asylum which burned down in 1883, killing five people, including the proprietor.

³ Georgina Ryle's will (dated 4 July 1888, proved at London on 23 April 1915) was written at Ashbrooke Hall and witnessed by Letitia Hitch, the proprietor of the asylum. Georgina was still resident there at the 1891 census (TNA, RG12/768, fo. 18).

⁴ Georgina Ryle's death certificate records that she suffered from 'mania' for 26 years and three months – that is, from late 1888 to February 1915.

⁵ 'G. M. R.' was a patient at The Priory in the 1901 census (TNA, RG13/491, fo. 146) and the 1911 census (TNA, RG14/2450).

Finally in this my last Will and Testament I place on record to the Glory of God that as I have learnt in Holy Scripture, God's most Blessed Word, and by the inspiration of the Holy Ghost, I die as I have ever lived in the full belief of a saving interest in the covenant of love between the Father, the Son and the Holy Ghost from all eternity, which is all my salvation and all my desire; that is, I know God the Father hath loved me with an everlasting love, I know God the Son loved me and gave himself for me on Calvary, and I know God the Holy Ghost begat me when yet a child unto a lively Hope, under whose Blessed and sanctifying influence I have ever lived, though not without sin alas. I am fully convinced that the moment my loved, ransomed and saved soul leaves the body it will at once be with Christ for ever having been through faith alone washed in His most precious Blood, clothed in His spotless righteousness, and sanctified by his spirit. As to my whole life of service to God, I only pray, Lord accept what is thine own and pardon what is mine for Jesus Christ['s] sake. Amen.[6]

Ryle's will was far more prosaic, a simple distribution of his possessions amongst the four surviving children of his second marriage: Isabelle Ryle (1851-1921), who lived with her father until his death, latterly as his private secretary;[7] Reginald Ryle (1854-1922), a medical doctor; Herbert Ryle (1856-1925), president of Queens' College, Cambridge, and later bishop of Winchester and dean of Westminster; and Arthur Ryle (1857-1915), an artist.

A third surprise is that although Reginald was the eldest son, his bequest was listed last of the four children. Perhaps this signifies an emotional distance in their relationship. Reginald rejected the Christianity of his youth in favour of rationalism. He was an

---

[6] Will of Richard Hobson, 12 December 1913, proved at Liverpool on 26 January 1915.

[7] Sarah A. Tooley, 'Ladies of Liverpool', *The Woman at Home* vol. 4 (April 1895), pp. 6-8.

J. C. Ryle's three sons, as young men.

J. C. Ryle's eldest son, Reginald Ryle, whose descendants included Professor Gilbert Ryle (1900-76), philosopher, and Sir Martin Ryle (1918-84), astronomer royal and winner of the Nobel prize for physics.

advocate of Darwinian evolution, a friend of the Huxley family, and a member of the Aristotelian Society for the Systematic Study of Philosophy.[8] Herbert, the middle son, was more intimately involved with his father, despite drifting towards liberal evangelicalism, and was entrusted with Ryle's Bibles and sermon manuscripts, as well as most of the family portraits.

Ryle resigned his ministry as bishop of Liverpool on 1 March 1900, and retired to Lowestoft on the Suffolk coast, where he died on 10 June, aged 84. In accordance with his wishes, his body was returned to Liverpool for burial at Childwall churchyard, next to his third wife. His will was proved at the Principal Probate Registry in London on 18 October 1900. The text in this edition is from the official typescript, but punctuation and paragraph breaks are added to aid readability.

[8] Dorothy Porter, 'Changing disciplines: John Ryle and the making of social medicine in Britain in the 1940s', *History of Science* vol. 30 (June 1992), p. 140. This information is based on Porter's interviews in November 1991 with Reginald Ryle's grandsons, John Creagh Ryle and Anthony Ryle.

The Text

This is the last will and testament of me, John Charles, by Divine permission Bishop of Liverpool. I hereby revoke all former wills and testamentary dispositions made by me. I appoint my sons, Herbert Edward Ryle and Arthur Johnston Ryle, and John Gamon, Registrar of the Diocese of Liverpool,[9] (hereinafter called 'my Trustees') to be the Executors and Trustees of this my Will.

I bequeath the following legacies free of legacy duty. To my brother [*sic*], John Rowdon, the sum of one hundred pounds.[10] To my housekeeper, Mary Debenham, the sum of one hundred pounds.[11] To each of my servants who shall be living with me at my decease a sum equal to six months' wages in addition to the wages due to him or her.[12] To the said John Gamon the sum of fifty pounds for his trouble in acting as an Executor and Trustee of this my Will; and, To Richard Farmer, my secretary, ten pounds.[13]

I bequeath to my daughter, Jessie Isabelle Ryle, the diamond cross and bracelet with hair of my mother's six children in them.[14]

[9] John Gamon (1838-1908), solicitor, registrar of the Chester diocese and simultaneously (from 1880) registrar of the Liverpool diocese, which was carved out of Chester.

[10] John Rowdon, one of the bishop's servants. Presumably 'brother' is a copyist's error for 'butler'.

[11] Mary Elizabeth Debenham (1842-1926) served the Ryle family for over forty years, first at Helmingham and Stradbroke in the 1860s and 1870s, and then in Liverpool. She rose from being the youngest housemaid, to housekeeper and cook.

[12] Ryle's household at No. 19 Abercromby Square, Liverpool, was a sizeable establishment, employing also a lady's maid, four housemaids, two kitchen maids, and two footmen (see 1891 census, TNA, RG12/2914, fo. 35). However, by the time of his death he had retired to a much smaller house in Lowestoft.

[13] Richard Farmer (*c.* 1854-1948), solicitor, partner with John Gamon in 'Gamon, Farmer and Co.', deputy registrar of Liverpool diocese.

[14] The will of Jessie Isabelle Ryle (27 December 1916, proved at Lewes on 13 January 1922) bequeathed this diamond cross and gold bracelet to her brother and sister-in-law, Herbert and Nea Ryle. Amongst female members of the family she

Also one silver teapot, one silver coffee pot, one silver tea urn, one silver cream jug, and as much of the rest of my plate not herein otherwise specifically bequeathed and plated articles and of my household linen and furniture as she shall require and shall select for her own use for the purpose of setting up housekeeping or otherwise, together with one hundred volumes of my books.

I bequeath to my son, Herbert Edward Ryle, my marble bust of my father[15] and all my family pictures; and I desire that he will exercise his discretion in deciding whether the large picture of myself in Convocation robes which I include amongst the said family pictures be offered to the City of Liverpool to be added to the permanent collection in the Walker Art Gallery at Liverpool,[16] and as to giving to either of his brothers, Reginald John Ryle and Arthur Johnston Ryle, any of the said family pictures which either of them may desire to possess.[17] I also bequeath to my said son, Herbert Edward Ryle, the large photographs of myself and of my third wife in the gallery[18]

---

also distributed items of jewellery she had inherited in 1860 from her mother – a diamond ring and onyx clasp bracelet, a gold watch and chain, a pink topaz cross, and a pearl cross.

[15] This marble bust of John Ryle was one of the early commissions for the sculptor Thomas Thornycroft (1816-85) and was exhibited at the Royal Academy in 1839; see Algernon Graves, *The Royal Academy of Arts: a complete dictionary of contributors and their works from its foundation in 1769 to 1904* (8 vols, London, 1905-6), vol. 7, p. 383. In the 1920s the bust was on display in Herbert Ryle's Westminster deanery, but is now lost.

[16] The Walker Art Gallery, opened in 1877, was named after its chief benefactor, Sir Andrew Barclay Walker (1824-93), brewer, mayor of Liverpool. The large portrait of Ryle in convocation robes hung in the dining room of his palace at Abercromby Square, alongside those of Ryle's grandfather and of Ryle as a young man; see 'The bishop of Liverpool and his work: an interview', *The Quiver* vol. 23 (November 1887), p. 31.

[17] The will of Reginald John Ryle (28 June 1922, proved at London on 23 January 1923) bequeathed three of these family portraits to his children: of his great-grandfather, John Ryle senior; his grandfather, John Ryle junior; and his uncle, Frederic Ryle. These portraits are still with his descendants.

[18] The upper landing of the bishop's house.

Thomas Thornycroft's marble bust of John Ryle (now lost),
one of the items bequeathed in J. C. Ryle's will.

of my residence, my large thick old quarto family Bible containing family names at the beginning of the book,[19] my Omerod's [*sic*] History of Cheshire, my many marked Bibles which I wish on no account to be sold,[20] and all my manuscript sermons and notes of sermons as to which he will use his discretion whether they or any of them be burnt or kept.[21] I also bequeath to my said son, Herbert Edward Ryle, my old family clock in the gallery of my residence, the large silver cup given to me by the parishioners of Stradbroke when I became Bishop of Liverpool, one chimney piece clock to be selected by him, and two hundred and fifty volumes of my books.

I bequeath to my son, Arthur Johnston Ryle, my small silver teapot with J. R. on it, my very old silver cup for sugar, one chimney piece clock to be selected by him, and two hundred and fifty volumes of my books.

I bequeath to my son, Reginald John Ryle, the silver inkstand given to me as Captain of the Cheshire Yeomanry, one chimney piece clock to be selected by him, my large writing table with drawers, and two hundred and fifty volumes of my books.

I direct that all the rest of my silver plate be not sold but be divided among my children, the said Herbert Edward Ryle, Reginald John Ryle and Arthur Johnston Ryle, to whom I bequeath the same. And I direct that if my said four children herein named do not agree as to the selection and distribution of any of the books or other

---

[19] For the Ryle Family Bible, see Appendix 1.

[20] The last time they met, in January 1900, Ryle gave to Richard Hobson the Bible he had used in his study for over fifty years, as a memento of their friendship. Ryle's Bible used for preaching was buried with him, 'clasped to his breast', placed in his coffin by Herbert Ryle. See Richard Hobson, *What hath God wrought: an autobiography* (London, 1903), p. 293, republished by the Banner of Truth Trust as *Richard Hobson of Liverpool: the autobiography of a faithful pastor* (Edinburgh, 2003); 'Funeral of Bishop Ryle', *Liverpool Daily Post*, 15 June 1900, p. 3; 'The dean of Westminster in Macclesfield: centenary commemoration at the parish church', *Macclesfield Courier and Herald*, 21 October 1916, p. 3.

[21] These sermon manuscripts do not survive.

articles hereby bequeathed, my trustees shall have the fullest power to give directions as to the order and mode of choice and selection and distribution thereof, and such directions shall be conclusively binding upon all persons interested. And also to decide what article or articles pass under any specific bequest herein contained.

I bequeath all the rest of my books for the use and benefit of the Victoria Church House for the Diocese of Liverpool at South John Street in Liverpool in aid of the foundation of a library at the said Church House, and I direct that any legacy duty payable in respect of this bequest shall be paid out of my estate and that the receipt of the Trustees or Managers for the time being of the said Church House shall be a good discharge to my Executors for the books comprised in this bequest.[22]

I devise and bequeath all my real and personal estate not hereby otherwise disposed of unto my Trustees. Upon trust that my Trustees shall sell, call in, and convert into money, the same or such part thereof as shall not consist of money and shall with and out of the moneys produced by such sale, calling in, and conversion, and with and out of my ready money, pay my funeral and testamentary expenses and debts and the legacies bequeathed by this my Will or any Codicil hereto. And shall stand possessed of the residue of

---

[22] Victoria Church House, Liverpool, was intended as a thank-offering for the Diamond Jubilee of Queen Victoria in 1897, but Ryle never lived to cross the threshold. The foundation stone was laid in August 1899 and Bishop Francis Chavasse appealed in September 1900 for another £20,000 to complete the building as a fitting memorial to Ryle (see 'The Ryle Memorial', *The Record*, 14 September 1900, p. 859). It housed the Ryle Library as a resource for the diocese, created by the bequest of his books, augmented by many other donations, such as 970 volumes from the Liverpool Clerical Society in July 1901, and a valuable collection of 17th and 18th century volumes previously housed at St Peter's Church (see George Harford (ed.), *Liverpool diocesan church house: classified catalogue of the library with full author and subject indexes* (Liverpool, 1903)). Frederick Pomeroy was commissioned to sculpt a marble bust of Ryle for the library. Church House was gutted in the Luftwaffe's Blitz of Liverpool in May 1941, with the loss of the entire Ryle Library and many precious diocesan records.

the said moneys, In trust for my said four children, Jessie Isabelle Ryle, Reginald John Ryle, Herbert Edward Ryle, and Arthur Johnston Ryle, in equal shares. Whereas I have advanced to my said son, Reginald John Ryle, the sum of one thousand pounds (in two amounts of five hundred pounds each) and to my said son, Herbert Edward Ryle, the sum of five hundred pounds, Now I direct and declare that the said sums of one thousand pounds and five hundred pounds so advanced to the said Reginald John Ryle and Herbert Edward Ryle respectively shall be deemed part of my residuary estate and be taken in part satisfaction of the share of the same residuary estate herein bequeathed to each of them, the said Reginald John Ryle and Herbert Edward Ryle. And I declare that the said John Gamon shall be entitled to charge my estate for all business done by him in relation to my estate or the trusts of this my Will, including acts which an executor or trustee could do personally in the same manner as he would have been entitled to charge my executors and trustees for the same if he had not been himself an executor or trustee but had been employed by my Executors and Trustees to do such business as their solicitor.

In Witness whereof I the said John Charles, Bishop of Liverpool, the Testator, have to this my last Will and Testament, written on this and the two preceding sheets of paper, set my hand this twelfth day of October one thousand eight hundred and ninety seven:

J. C. LIVERPOOL

Signed and acknowledged by the said Testator, John Charles, Bishop of Liverpool, as and for his last Will and Testament in the presence of us, present at the same time, who in his presence at his request and in the presence of each other have hereunto subscribed our names as witnesses:

THOS. J. MADDEN, 108 Bedford St, Liverpool, Archdeacon of Warrington[23]

T. HOLLINS ARDEN, 53 Lord Street, Liverpool, Solicitor.[24]

This is a Codicil to the last Will and testament of me, John Charles, by Divine permission Bishop of Liverpool, which Will bears date the twelfth day of October one thousand eight hundred and ninety seven. Whereas I have lately advanced to my son, Arthur Johnston Ryle, named in my said Will, the sum of four hundred pounds, Now I direct and declare that the sum of four hundred pounds so advanced shall be deemed part of my residuary estate and be taken in part satisfaction of the share of the same residuary estate bequeathed to my said son, Arthur Johnston Ryle, by my said Will. And in all other respects I confirm my said Will.

In Witness whereof I the said John Charles, Bishop of Liverpool, the Testator, have to this Codicil to my last Will and Testament set my hand this first day of March in the year of our Lord one thousand eight hundred and ninety eight:

J. C. LIVERPOOL

Signed and acknowledged by the said Testator, John Charles, Bishop of Liverpool, as and for a Codicil to his last Will and Testament in the presence of us, present at the same time, who in his presence at his request and in the presence of each other have hereunto subscribed our names as witnesses:

JOHN GAMON, Sol[icito]r, Liverpool

T. HOLLINS ARDEN, 53 Lord Street, Liverpool, Solicitor.

[23] Thomas John Madden (1853-1915), archdeacon of Warrington 1895-1906, of Liverpool 1906-15, one of Ryle's honorary chaplains from 1891, editor of Ryle's final volume, *The Christian race and other sermons* (London, 1900).

[24] Thomas Hollins Arden (1868-1942), solicitor from 1889 with Gamon, Farmer and Co., Liverpool.

INDEX

About the Publisher

The Banner of Truth Trust originated in 1957 in London. The founders believed that much of the best literature of historic Christianity had been allowed to fall into oblivion and that, under God, its recovery could well lead not only to a strengthening of the church, but to true revival.

Inter-denominational in vision, this publishing work is now international, and our lists include a number of contemporary authors along with classics from the past. The translation of these books into many languages is encouraged.

A monthly magazine, *The Banner of Truth*, is also published and further information will be gladly supplied by either of the offices below or from our website.

THE BANNER OF TRUTH TRUST

3 Murrayfield Road
Edinburgh, EH12 6EL
UK

PO Box 621, Carlisle
Pennsylvania, 17013
USA

www.banneroftruth.org